THE DECORATIVE
DESIGNS OF
FRANK
LLOYD
WRIGHT

(overleaf) Signature of Frank Lloyd Wright used during his Oak Park years.

DAVID A. HANKS was born in St. Louis, Missouri. He received an A.B. in English literature and an A.M. in education from Washington University in St. Louis. His museum career began at The St. Louis Art Museum where he worked in the Department of Education.

Mr. Hanks has been Associate Curator of American Decorative Arts at The Art Institute of Chicago and Curator in the Department of American Art at the Philadelphia Museum of Art. He is currently working on a decorative arts survey for the Smithsonian Institution. While at The Art Institute of Chicago he organized the major exhibitions, "American Art of the Colonies and Early Republic"; and "The Arts and Crafts Movement in America, 1876–1916," and the departmental exhibition, "Louis Sullivan: Drawings and Architectural Fragments from the Permanent Collection."

Among Mr. Hanks's publications are articles on Robert Jarvie, the Chicago silversmith, and Gothic Revival furniture in Philadelphia for The Magazine *Antiques*.

THE DECORATIVE

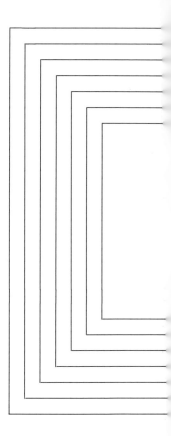

DESIGNS OF FRANK LLOYD WRIGHT

David A. Hanks

E. P. DUTTON • NEW YORK

TO MY FATHER

For information contact: E. P. Dutton, 2 Park Avenue, New York, N.Y. 10016

Library of Congress Catalog Card Number: 78-55777
ISBN: 0-525-08958-6 (cloth) 0-525-47477-3 (DP)

Published simultaneously in Canada by Clarke, Irwin & Company Limited, Toronto and Vancouver

Designed by Barbara Huntley

10 9 8 7 6 5 4 3 2 1

First Edition

CONTENTS

Published in association with an exhibition originated by Renwick Gallery of the National Collection of Fine Arts, Smithsonian Institution, Washington, D.C., and cosponsored by the Grey Art Gallery and Study Center, New York University, for presentation at:

RENWICK GALLERY OF THE
NATIONAL COLLECTION OF FINE ARTS
Washington, D.C.
December 16, 1977–July 30, 1978

GREY ART GALLERY AND STUDY CENTER
New York University, New York
September 26–November 4, 1978

THE DAVID AND ALFRED SMART GALLERY
The University of Chicago, Illinois
January 10–February 25, 1979

Grants in support of the author's research leading to the exhibition and to its presentation at the Grey Art Gallery and Study Center and The David and Alfred Smart Gallery were provided by the National Endowment for the Arts, Washington, D.C.; The Graham Foundation for Advanced Studies in the Fine Arts, Chicago, Illinois; the Illinois Arts Council, Chicago; the Woods Charitable Fund, Chicago, Illinois; and the Joe and Emily Lowe Foundation, New York.

LENDERS TO THE EXHIBITION:

Albright-Knox Art Gallery, Buffalo, New York
Curtis Besinger, Lawrence, Kansas
Carolyn Mann Brackett, Silver Spring, Maryland
The Burnham Library, The Art Institute of Chicago, Illinois
Mr. and Mrs. John J. Celuch, Edwardsville, Illinois
Chicago Historical Society, Illinois

Cooper–Hewitt Museum, The Smithsonian Institution's National Museum of Design, New York, New York

Mr. and Mrs. Robert R. Elsner, Jr., Milwaukee, Wisconsin

Mr. and Mrs. Waldron Faulkner, Washington, D.C.

Ellis and Jeanette Fields, River Forest, Illinois

Greenville College, Illinois; The Richard W. Bock Sculpture Collection

Grey Art Gallery and Study Center, New York University Art Collection, New York

Mr. and Mrs. Wilbert R. Hasbrouck, Palos Park, Illinois

Mr. and Mrs. Robert L. Jacobson, Milwaukee, Wisconsin

The Johnson Foundation, Racine, Wisconsin

Donald Kalec, Oak Park, Illinois

Mr. and Mrs. Roger Kennedy, New York, New York

Mrs. Robert A. Leighey, Mount Vernon, Virginia

The Library of Congress, Washington, D.C.

Los Angeles Municipal Art Gallery, California

Randell C. Makinson, Pasadena, California

The Metropolitan Museum of Art, New York, New York

Municipal Arts Department, City of Los Angeles, California

The Museum of Modern Art, New York, New York

Mrs. Nora Natof, Lovettsville, Virginia

The Newberry Library, Chicago, Illinois

Mr. and Mrs. Jon S. Pohl, Evanston, Illinois

Pope–Leighey House, Mount Vernon, Virginia; A property of the National Trust for Historic Preservation

H. C. Price Company, Bartlesville, Oklahoma

Mr. and Mrs. Harold C. Price, Bartlesville, Oklahoma

Mr. and Mrs. John D. Randall, Williamsville, New York

Mr. and Mrs. Tim Samuelson, Chicago, Illinois

Dr. and Mrs. Elias Sedlin, New York, New York

The David and Alfred Smart Gallery, The University of Chicago, Illinois

Southern California Chapter, American Institute of Architects, Los Angeles

Stanford University, California

State University of New York at Buffalo

Steelcase Inc., Grand Rapids, Michigan

University Archives, State University of New York at Buffalo

Mr. and Mrs. David Wright, Phoenix, Arizona

Mrs. Frank Lloyd Wright, Taliesin West, Scottsdale, Arizona

Mrs. John Lloyd Wright, Del Mar, California

Mr. and Mrs. Robert Llewellyn Wright, Bethesda, Maryland

Yesteryear, Inc., Kankakee, Illinois

Frank Lloyd Wright in Spring Green, Wisconsin, 1924.

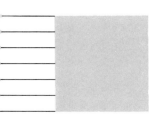

INTRODUCTORY NOTE

Looking today at an exhibition of Frank Lloyd Wright's decorative designs—his vases, chairs, or leaded windows—one can become painfully aware of qualities missing in our present surroundings and, if indeed Wright is a founder of what is fondly called modern design, one wonders why such qualities did not survive. For example, there is the matter of scale. Although sometimes monumental in concept, his designs bear a comforting relationship to the human viewer and look as if they were made solely for his inspection and delight. Although the principle of the design may be schematic, capable of infinite reproduction, the individual object, nicely attuned to the eye, seems very much itself. Its primary virtue is not that it can be mass-produced—and looks it—but that it can be individually seen. Wherever one happens to be in a Wright house seems to be the center because the spaces give the uncanny impression of adjusting themselves to the viewer, somehow appearing to be custom-made for the moment. Yet nothing could be more impersonal than the constituent parts. A similar effect is created by his furnishings. They focus attention on a particular play of forms which at the moment seems unique, rather than on a general class of experience we might call modern.

A part of this seeming miracle by which the general becomes the specific is dependent on the trapping of attention. Nothing is to be assumed in a Wright design; the object demands a careful scrutiny. Although in his earliest designs he caught the mind by an intricate formal complexity, he quickly learned that the subtle variation of a simple organizational premise was even more engaging. So the viewer is made party to a witty formulation and is allowed to regard it as his very own.

Possibly this close attention, the concentration on the specific, is what seems so foreign to our present perception. Many of the principles for which Wright stood— clarity of materials and structure, machine manufacture, geometric precision of design—have taught the modern eye to see the individual object as an example of its class and to pass over the specific aspects of the thing in admiring what it stands for. It is difficult to regard a manufactured product as a unique object; we expect it to deny its uniqueness and draw its quality from an emphasis on its possible repetition. We are thus freed from the object as such. But in this freedom, something is lost; possibly it is the nice adjustment between sense and thought.

A collection of objects designed by Wright calls one's senses again to account.

There is nothing individually capricious or bizarre to suggest uniqueness; just a carefully tuned ordering of parts that will not be hurried.

—JOSHUA C. TAYLOR
Director, National Collection of Fine Arts

FOREWORD

This exhibition of Wright's furniture and decoration is especially welcome at the present time, when there are signs that a new swell of interest in Wright's work is beginning to rise, because it brings into focus an aspect of Wright's architecture that was not only essential to it but toward which modern scholarship has hitherto directed insufficient attention. It is the aspect which can be only roughly described by the word *decoration*, and which has to do with every detail and surface of Wright's buildings and their physical appurtenances—from wall stripping and moldings to window glass, curtains, furniture, rugs, tableware, lighting fixtures, and appliances. What becomes clear is that Wright was determined to create a new style of architecture, aimed toward the physical organization of a new, complete, and wholly integrated environment. That style was to encompass everything; so Wright had to "design" everything. (And that was the word he used about the making of forms—not *represent*, as he would have put it, but *design:* conceive, plot out, make new.) Despite the more or less supportive presence of contemporary architects and sculptors during Wright's early years in Chicago, he essentially had to do it all alone, to make the whole style up, as Louis Sullivan had said about Frank Furness, out of his own head. Like Furness, of course, Wright had a good deal of the past to go on, in his case the whole extraordinarily rich nineteenth-century architectural tradition, where "ornament" had normally been held in high respect as an intrinsic element of architectural form. Hence Wright inherited a lot, and his work should indeed be regarded as one of the nineteenth century's ultimate achievements. But he reworked it all.

The wooden strippings that shape the interiors of his Prairie houses are perhaps the best and most cogent example of that. They came to Wright from Japan as modified in American Shingle–Style practice. Wright rigorously restudied and clarified their profiles into industrially viable components (as described by Wright in his famous talk "The Art and Craft of the Machine" of 1901). In his hands they became the final and most precise element through which the space and scale of individual interiors were defined and modulated. They were handled differently in every building and were apparently varied to suit, among other things, the height of the client. Wright might pull their horizontal elements down to just above head height or push them up, manipulating them in plan and section, thickening and thinning, and so suggesting a potentially infinite number of frames for space, where classic architecture, for example, although developed over thousands of years, had proposed only a few. The lighting fixtures were intricately woven into the whole system as was, most importantly, the window glass, shaded where Wright wanted it to be by intense Froebel patterns, elsewhere left crystal clear. The space could be dark or light, at once volumetric and flowing, the scale gentle or grand. And it is touching to note that Wright did not decisively work his way back to the abstract Froebel shapes of his childhood—which were to become essential components of his mature architecture and graphics—until he designed a playroom for his own children in 1895. Before that, his decorative motifs, although derived from several nineteenth-century sources, had been primarily Sullivanian in character.

The contemporary architect reels when he recognizes the number of drawings Wright had to make for all this. He was like a painter—touching every square inch of his building, inside and out. During the International Style years from the 1920s to the 1960s, when ornament was despised, even those of us who loved Wright's and Sullivan's work and realized the importance of its "decoration" could not wholly grasp what an enormous achievement this was, what it meant in terms of architectural integrity, to say nothing of man-hours. Only now, when architects are attempting rather feebly to fill out architecture's range of possibilities by employing ornament once more, do we begin to grasp the depth and scope of Wright's achievement, not only in its formal virtuosity but in the completeness of its intellectual structure and in its astounding particularity. Again, we are reminded of Friedrich Froebel and of how important that kindergarten play with abstract forms must have been for Wright's development. It is probable that no architect who had not had that experience could have brought such love and confidence, such unremitting care and so much hard-bought time, to the interminable detailing that the utter totality of Wright's overall architectural conception required. And the effects were surely circular. Preoccupation with the detail must often have led back to a reconsideration of the scheme as a whole; the growth was integral, rich, and three-dimensionally rewarding.

Now, because of this renewed realization, all of Wright's work must be studied again, starting, as David Hanks does here, with the very beginning, when Wright began to redesign every inch of the American environment, shaping a whole new world of form entirely by himself—a world by no means computerized or purely schematic, but densely physical, intrinsically ordered, and as various as the individuals for whose living it was intended.

As time went on, it is true, there were critical changes in Wright's decorative detailing. The stripping tended to disappear by the 1920s in favor of broader, often heavier, effects based upon monumental models such as pre-Columbian Indian forms. In the 1930s a general simplification occurred, suggested in part by the International Style, whose beginnings Wright's earlier work had strongly affected. Late in life the relation of the decorative schemes to the larger aspects of Wright's design became somewhat problematical. Some confusion in scale between large and small, previously the strongest aspect of Wright's work, may be felt to have occurred. The excursion into mass-produced, commercially marketed furniture, well documented by Hanks, was not an especially happy one and perhaps not overly sympathetic to Wright. Some of the drawings for those projects are hard to credit to his hand. None of that matters very much. The principle had been laid down. One can approve it or not but can hardly help but appreciate the power with which Wright put it into practice. It surely embodied the ultimate American dream. Everything was to be made anew, and Wright set out to do it.

—Vincent Scully

PREFACE

The idea of a book on Frank Lloyd Wright's decorative designs began in 1974 when I met with Cyril Nelson, editor at E. P. Dutton, to discuss the possibility of such a publication. It was not until 1977, however, that through a grant from the National Endowment for the Arts, I was able to take five months' leave of absence to do the necessary research for the book. When Lloyd E. Herman, Director of the Renwick Gallery, heard of the plans for the publication, he expressed an interest in organizing an exhibition on the subject for which the book might serve as catalogue.

As research began in April 1977, it was discovered that loan requests were then being sent out for another exhibition on Wright's decorative designs, by the Grey Art Gallery and Study Center of New York University. Robert Littman, Director of that museum, and his associate, Cynthia Nachmani, met with Lloyd Herman and me to discuss the possibility of cooperating in organizing an exhibition of the most significant examples of Frank Lloyd Wright's decorative designs. Littman and Nachmani agreed to share information on objects that they had located for their exhibition and to collaborate on the exhibition being organized by the Renwick Gallery.

An exhibition on Frank Lloyd Wright could hardly be considered without the inclusion of a showing in the Chicago area, where many of his most important commissions were designed. Edward A. Maser, Director, and Katharine Lee Keefe, Curator, of The David and Alfred Smart Gallery at the University of Chicago were enthusiastic about showing the exhibition there, so near one of Wright's most famous houses—that of Frederick C. Robie—now owned by the university. A significant collection of objects from this house is now owned by the Smart Gallery. Support from The Graham Foundation for Advanced Studies in the Fine Arts helped to make it possible to show the exhibition there.

Planning an exhibition on the decorative designs of Frank Lloyd Wright presented many challenges. Since Wright always considered his furnishings and architecture as one, how would an exhibition of his decorative designs be organized? As Wright's houses have changed owners through the years, the furnishings that were integral to the structure were removed from their original setting, sold to museums and collectors, given away, or destroyed. Few of Wright's early houses have any of their original furnishings, and none is intact in terms of the complete unity of the decorative scheme. Even many of the later houses have been considerably altered.

By exhibiting an actual object juxtaposed with a photograph of the original interior, this exhibition attempted to re-create its appearance, so that Wright's concept of the unity of furnishings and architecture can be understood. When possible photographs of the interior and exterior architecture accompany each object in the exhibition, so that each can be seen as part of the architectural whole.

Choices of objects for the exhibition were made on the basis of the aesthetic quality, the variety of forms, and the use of materials in Wright's design vocabulary and on the basis of representation of chronological periods. The completeness of the furnishings designed for Wright's early commissions has helped to emphasize that period of his career. For the interiors of many of his later houses, he considered some of the furniture available on the market, including that of his design, acceptable. Craftsmanship, which usually depended on economic considerations, was also a criterion.

Rather than attempt to show Wright's decorative designs from the many structures incorporating them, the exhibition concentrates on a selection of major commissions notable for their decorative schemes, such as the Midway Gardens and the Imperial Hotel. The commissions chosen are represented by clusters of objects, drawings, and photographs, so that at no time is the object considered in isolation.

Some choices were made for practical reasons. For example, Wright's Usonian furniture is represented by a bench-section and a perforated board from the Pope–Leighey House, since this is one of the few Wright houses open to the public. Furniture from the Herbert Jacobs House—the first Usonian house—would otherwise have been chosen. Certain objects are considered important today because of their rarity, such as the cup and saucer and the lamp designed for the Midway Gardens; they are among very few objects to survive from that commission. As with any exhibition, certain objects requested were not lent. Hence there are some rather noticeable omissions, such as representation of the Avery Coonley House and Fallingwater by other than photographs.

■

In doing the research and writing of this book, I was fortunate to be able to return to Chicago, where research facilities and a proximity to many of Frank Lloyd Wright's houses made my task easier. Equally important has been the interest of Chicagoans in Wright's work, which has been a great encouragement. Wright himself paid tribute to "the broad free spirit of Chicago."

Many people assisted me in the preparation and writing of this book. One person who has been most helpful to me from the very concept of the exhibition and book through several drafts to the last stages of editing is Irma Strauss, a Wright enthusiast, who has pursued with diligence her research on the architect and his master, Louis Sullivan, for years. She has freely shared her findings with me, which was of invaluable help, but of more importance have been her enthusiasm and continual support. She should be acknowledged as an inspired coauthor.

I wish also to acknowledge the help of The Frank Lloyd Wright Foundation. Mrs. Frank Lloyd Wright was most generous in allowing cherished objects to be lent for the exhibition and photographs of drawings from the Taliesin archives, Taliesin

West, Scottsdale, Arizona, to be shown. Bruce Brooks Pfeiffer, Director of Archives, was also of great help and gave generously of his time. He spent days with me going through the many beautiful drawings in the Taliesin collection, identifying those that were by Wright's hand, as well as identifying objects. He and the Taliesin Fellowship gave me a warm welcome in both Wisconsin and Arizona and enhanced my appreciation of the beauties of organic architecture. I should also like to thank Wesley Peters and John de Koven Hill of Taliesin West for their generous assistance.

The beginning of the research for this catalogue and exhibition was made possible by a grant from The Graham Foundation for Advanced Studies in the Fine Arts. I am indebted to its Director, Carter H. Manny, Jr., for his interest in this study. Through a second generous grant, The Graham Foundation made it possible for the exhibition to travel to Chicago. A grant from the National Endowment for the Arts enabled me to take a leave of absence from the Philadelphia Museum of Art for five months to continue the research on which this exhibition and catalogue are based.

Donald Kalec was extremely helpful, not only as a lender and photographer but also in sharing his research, his suggestions, and his information. Tom Heinz also shared his information on Wright's art glass. To Edgar Tafel, who was enthusiastic about the exhibit from the beginning, I owe a great debt, since he not only told me of objects and collections but was willing to share his experiences as a member of the Taliesin Fellowship for sixteen years. Curtis Besinger of the University of Kansas was also of great help. Mrs. Waldron Faulkner was generous and kind in sharing information about her parents' famous house and in making a grant to the Smart Gallery toward the restoration of the Robie House dining table.

The staff at various museums, universities, and libraries were most helpful to me in doing the research: Annette Fern, Carolyn Hurt, Daniel Starr, and Debbie Ezzio of The Burnham Library, The Art Institute of Chicago; Shonnie Finnegan, the State University of New York at Buffalo; Sharon Darling, The Chicago Historical Society; Brian Spencer and Marilynn Drucker, Milwaukee Art Center; Katharine Keefe, The David and Alfred Smart Gallery, The University of Chicago; Ann Williams, University of Kansas; Stewart J. Johnson, The Museum of Modern Art, New York; Morrison H. Heckscher, Marilynn Johnson Bordes and R. Craig Miller, The Metropolitan Museum of Art; John W. Keefe, The Art Institute of Chicago; and Barbara Ballinger of the Oak Park Public Library.

I am also extremely grateful to Shakeela Saba Siddiq, not only for typing the manuscript of the catalogue through numerous drafts but also for astute preliminary editing; she also typed the voluminous correspondence that was necessary in the organizing of the exhibition.

Also the following: Joanna Barton; Rudy Bernal; Wendy Burrows Carlton; Carroll S. Clark; The Queene Ferry Coonley Foundation, Inc.; Tessa Craib-Cox; Mr. and Mrs. Albert Haas; Lloyd E. Herman; David B. Keeler; T. Royce Leach; Pamela Leaderman; Val E. Lewton; Frank Linden, Jr.; Robert Littman; Darwin R. Martin; Edith I. Martin; Edward A. Maser; Ellen M. Myette; Cynthia Nachmani; Lorraine Robie O'Connor; Mr. and Mrs. Franklin Orwin; Christian Rohlfing; Carl Snoblin; Paul Sprague; Mr. and Mrs. Helmut Strauss; Joshua C. Taylor; Leon Regan

Upshaw; John Vinci; The Women's Architectural League, Chicago Chapter; The Women's Board of The University of Chicago; the late Mrs. Philip Wrigley; and Anne Zeller.

Any book on Frank Lloyd Wright must depend upon certain basic works, and I wish to acknowledge the two monographs about Wright's work, on which my architectural remarks are based: Grant Carpenter Manson, *Frank Lloyd Wright to 1910*, New York, 1958; and Henry-Russell Hitchcock, *In the Nature of Materials: The Buildings of Frank Lloyd Wright, 1887–1941*, 1942 (reprinted by Da Capo Press, New York, 1973). I also wish to thank those people owning Wright houses: Laura and Lewis Bradford; Alice Shaddle Baum; Mr. and Mrs. William Walker; Thomas Publishing Company; Mr. and Mrs. Isador Zimmerman; Dr. and Mrs. Henry Fineberg; Mr. and Mrs. Robert R. Elsner, Jr.; Mr. and Mrs. Louis Clark; Mr. and Mrs. James W. Howlett; Mrs. Robert A. Leighey; Mr. and Mrs. David Wright; Mr. and Mrs. Robert Llewellyn Wright; Mr. and Mrs. Harold C. Price; Ellis and Jeanette Fields; Marvin Hammack. And of course special thanks go to the lenders who generously lent objects that were sometimes in daily use. For example, Mrs. John Lloyd Wright graciously lent her cup and saucer from the Midway Gardens, which serve as a daily reminder of her late husband.

DAVID A. HANKS
Chicago, Summer 1977

The following short titles for standard references have been used:

Ausgeführte Bauten, for *Ausgeführte Bauten und Entwürfe von Frank Lloyd Wright,* Berlin: Wasmuth, 1910. Introduction reprinted, New York: New American Library, 1974.

The Early Work, for *Frank Lloyd Wright: The Early Work,* New York: Horizon Press, 1968.

Hitchcock, for Henry-Russell Hitchcock, *In the Nature of Materials: The Buildings of Frank Lloyd Wright, 1887–1941,* New York: Da Capo Press, 1942 (reprinted 1973).

Manson, for Grant Carpenter Manson, *Frank Lloyd Wright to 1910,* New York: Reinhold Publishing Corporation, 1958.

An Autobiography, for Frank Lloyd Wright, *An Autobiography,* New York: Longmans, Green, and Company, 1932.

"In the Cause of Architecture," for "In the Cause of Architecture," *Architectural Record,* 1908, 1914, 1927, 1928, 1952, reprinted in *In the Cause of Architecture,* New York: McGraw-Hill Book Co., 1975.

In general the dates given to the objects in this exhibition are those of the building as given by Henry-Russell Hitchcock in *In the Nature of Materials,* since Wright usually conceived of the building as a whole from the first, and sketches for furniture were sometimes included in the plans of the house. Wright's studio would not begin the working drawings for the furniture, of course, until the drawings for the house were finished. Therefore the dates given to furniture on these drawings are sometimes one, two, or more years after the date given for the building.

Dimensions are usually given in inches. Height precedes width and depth. Measurements and medium are given only for those objects lent for the exhibition.

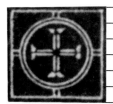

THE DECORATIVE
DESIGNS OF
FRANK
LLOYD
WRIGHT

THE DEVELOPMENT
OF ORNAMENT

Most of Frank Lloyd Wright's (1867–1956) ideas about ornament evolved from advanced design theories that began during the eighteenth-century Enlightenment and that were developed in the nineteenth century. Philosophers of the seventeenth and eighteenth centuries posited that reason would reveal nature's secrets and that the resulting knowledge would bring progress and joy to the world. Whereas medieval and Renaissance artists had represented plants and flowers for their symbolic significance, naturalists in the last quarter of the seventeenth century often used representations of plants to abstract and schematize botanical knowledge. By the 1860s certain fundamental facts had been established from the systematic analysis of the living organism: first, its whole being was dependent on the integration of its parts, and second, the form reflected its progress or growth, adapted through evolution to use and the environment. Frustrated by the lifeless architecture and decorative products derived from historic forms and produced by machine, nineteenth-century design theorists undertook a search for a style more characteristic of the age of science and knowledge. The detailed study of natural phenomena and organic forms became a nineteenth-century preoccupation.

One of the most profound impacts on the character of Wright's work were the contributions of the educator Friedrich Froebel (1782–1852). Around 1800 he attended the University of Jena, which was then the focal point in Germany for the early study of scientific biology and nature philosophy, the new approach to botany that was related to the emerging discipline of aesthetics. Froebel translated his love of nature into a revolutionary educational system that was tested in 1837 when he opened his first kindergarten in Germany. In his "occupations" and "gifts"—lessons developed as play activities—children were encouraged to perform tasks, often to the accompaniment of music. One task would be to work out nature patterns with geometric shapes of smooth cardboard on four-inch grids or unit lines, in order to understand the harmonies and proportions of natural objects.

A. W. N. Pugin (1812–1852) interjected morality into the creative act (*Contrasts*, written in 1835, and *True Principles of Christian Architecture*, published in 1841), believing that the value of art was related to the ideals it engendered. He saw the architect, properly religious and truthful, as the one capable of bringing about the good life. Deriving the decorative arts from architecture, he developed principles that espoused the truthful revelation of structure—fighting against the three-dimensionality of the flat plane in decoration. To achieve the qualities of propriety, repose, and unity, he recommended that naturalized ornament be conventionalized through geometry to bring out the underlying form, thus anticipating later designers.

Owen Jones (1809–1874), whose *Grammar of Ornament* was published in 1856 (a copy of which was owned by Wright; see fig. 2), also urged "a return to Nature for fresh inspiration." Jones's book was one of the most important publications on decoration in the second half of the nineteenth century and was in its ninth printing by 1910. It was a compendium of colored plates based on the history of ornament taken from archaeological monuments. All major cultures were included, even the designs of "savage tribes." The historic drawings of ornament, which Jones considered to be conventionalized, were included to serve as an inspiration in the search for new theories or a new style. Jones believed that the ornaments of the past were beautiful only because they responded, by association, to the needs and values of the cultures and periods from which they had been derived. This was a breakthrough in thought, as the search for a more truthful representation of the new age could now reach for clues in the styles of cultures, not by imitating them but by understanding the organic and natural laws that created them. The natural drawings of leaves and flowers at the end of Jones's book, one of which is seen in figure 2, was described by the author as "representing the basic geometric form of nature and . . . best calculated to awaken a recognition of the natural laws which prevail in the distribution of form." He believed that a new style of ornament might be conceived independently from . . . and be the most likely way to . . . a new style of architecture (this achievement would come ultimately from the design contributions of Louis Sullivan and the engineering contributions of his partner, Dankmar Adler). Thirty-seven general propositions were listed in Jones's book, which included principles that Wright later advocated: "As Architecture, so all works of the Decorative Arts, should possess fitness, proportion, harmony, the result of all which is repose" (Proposition 4, *Grammar of Ornament*, p. 5). Reminiscent of Wright's own words was Jones's Proposition 13: "Flowers or other natural objects should not be used as ornaments, but conventional representations founded upon them sufficiently suggestive to convey the intended image to the mind, without destroying the unity of the object they are employed to decorate" (p. 6).

Figures 1 through 9 illustrate the process of conventionalization from the natural plant source (fig. 1) to the more abstract designs of Wright's architecture. The wild flower or weed seen in figure 1 is among the twelve photographs taken by Wright and included in his book *The House Beautiful* (1896–97; see fig. 192). The conventionalized floral designs used to ornament the pages of this book were derived from such natural plants, which Wright illustrated to show his source in nature. The architect's son, John Lloyd Wright, recalled his father's interest in the photography of native plants:

> My father had an 8 x 10 plate camera and built a dark-room off the balcony of his Oak Park Studio where he developed the plates, sensitized Japanese paper and printed from his photographs. He was fond of the soft texture of Japanese

paper such as this item and also the prints of weeds, in the book *The House Beautiful* published by Mr. Winslow and himself 1896–97. Louis Sullivan photographed roses. F. L. W. photographed native shrubs, weeds and wild flowers. This print was acquired by way of my mother [Catharine Lloyd Wright]. (Memo describing original photographic print in John Lloyd Wright Collection, Avery Architectural Library, Columbia University, December 1968)

The conventionalization of nature was not confined to England and America. In a French design book, Victore Ruprich-Robert's (1820–1887) *Flore Ornementale* of 1866 (fig. 4), the title page combines naturalistically rendered and conventionalized plant forms. Ruprich-Robert was also interested in natural science and analyzed organic and inorganic plants, making cross sections and seeking geometric forms in order to derive a new style of ornamentation unlike that of the past. He saw nature as a growth process and analyzed plants from their budding to mature states and from the simple to the complex.

The Discourses of Eugène Emmanuel Viollet-le-Duc (1814–1879) represented "all that there is to know," to Wright. Viollet-le-Duc sought knowledge from biology and applied the criterion of functional and structural expression to style in the natural organism. He found truthful expression in the engineering structures of the day but felt that other buildings were falsely clothed in confused and vulgar ornamental forms.

One of the most influential of the English reformists was Christopher Dresser (1838–1904), whose books were known in America. Dresser, who held professorships in botany, also applied natural laws to ornament and decorative design. He analyzed geometric forms using the scientific method and considered all ornament as related to the underlying form of architecture. The word *ornament*, as used by Dresser, could imply that the entire object was an ornamental form and that ornament was not merely something applied to it. Dresser's *Principles of Decorative Design*, published in London in 1873, included concepts with which Wright would have concurred:

1. The material of which an object is formed should be used in a manner consistent with its own nature and in the particular way in which it can be most easily "worked."
2. When an object is about to be formed, the material (or materials) that is (or are) most appropriate to its formation should be sought and employed.
3. The orderly repetition of parts frequently aids in the production of ornamental effects.
4. If plants are employed as ornaments, they must not be treated imitatively but must be conventionally treated or rendered into ornaments.

Much more abstracted than Jones's drawings and more like Ruprich-Robert's are the plant and floral designs seen in the plate from Dresser's book (fig. 3). Dresser provided an important link between England and America. He visited Philadelphia on the occasion of the 1876 Centennial Exposition and was invited to lecture at the newly formed Pennsylvania Museum and School of Industrial Art.

1 (*above, left*). Wildflower photographed by Frank Lloyd Wright for photogravure in *The House Beautiful*. 1897

2 (*below, left*). Plate XCV, "Leaves from Nature," Owen Jones's *The Grammar of Ornament*. London. 1856.

3 (*above*). Figure 61, Christopher Dresser's *Principles of Decorative Design*. London. 1873.

4 (*below*). Title page, V. Ruprich-Robert's *Flore Ornementale*. Paris. 1866.

Dresser called for a national style of ornament that could compare, in symbolic content, with that of great civilizations of the past. For example, the Egyptians developed ornamental forms "expressive of national peculiarities of character, of religious faith, of wants and of feelings as well as of individual idiosyncracies" ("Art Industries," *The Penn Monthly*, January–March 1877, pp. 15–16). Wright's own writings later echoed Dresser's when he described the process that the Egyptian artist went through in transforming the natural flower into decoration in stone (Frank Lloyd Wright, "A Philosophy of Fine Art," Lecture to the Architectural League, The Art Institute of Chicago, 1900).

James O'Gorman has traced the development of the conventionalization process in the essay of his catalogue *The Architecture of Frank Furness* (Philadelphia Museum of Art, 1973). Furness's drawing of a flower in elevation revealed its geometric symmetry and pattern (fig. 5). The desk designed in carved walnut relief by Furness about 1875 for the Washington Square house of his brother demonstrates this Dresser-inspired conventionalized ornamentation. Furness provided the link of Dresser and other English reformists with Louis Sullivan (1856–1924) and Frank Lloyd Wright.

Sullivan worked briefly for Furness and Hewitt in 1873 before going to Chicago. Sullivan's early designs for ornaments (fig. 6) were thus the result of the long evolutionary process that has been outlined in this chapter. They were based on a conventionalized interpretation similar to those of Furness but marked by a greater abstraction. (Early drawings by Sullivan similar to flowers drawn by Ruprich-Robert are in The Burnham Library of The Art Institute of Chicago.) Sullivan's drawings for flowers revealed his studied interest in the basic structures of plants. In the 1890s, he developed this Dresser/Furness ornament into his own personal vision, which so strongly influenced Wright.

In "Ornamentation and the Organic Architecture of Frank Lloyd Wright" (*Art Journal*, Fall 1965), James M. Dennis and Lu B. Wenneker distinguish between Sullivan's and Wright's ornamentation. Both Sullivan and Wright employed abstractions from nature. However, Sullivan used a "synthetic" approach, beginning with simple geometric shapes and adding to them until he arrived at a form of foliation distinctly his own. Although at first Wright followed this approach, he soon started to reverse the process analytically by taking an actual flower and breaking it down into basic abstract shapes, arriving at geometric designs similar to those with which Sullivan began.

■

Wright's early Sullivanesque ornament is discussed on pages 9–16, and these illustrations show his own developing ornament from the relatively naturalistic rendering of the flowers in the design for a window of around 1900 (fig. 7) to his more highly conventionalized floral design, seen in the abstracted hollyhock as the chief motif of the Aline Barnsdall House of 1920 (fig. 8).

Despite Sullivan's monumental achievements and Wright's acknowledgment of his master's genius, Wright felt that Sullivan had not realized his true goal of an organic architecture that would express the freedom of democratic man. Wright did believe that in the "plasticity" and "living intricacy" of Sullivan's terracotta ornament the background vanished so that the material and the ornament

5 (*above*). Drawing by Frank Furness, *The Architecture of Frank Furness* by James F. O'Gorman, published by The Philadelphia Museum of Art, The Falcon Press, Philadelphia, 1973, F.S. 19, p. 36.

6 (*below, left*). Drawing by Louis Sullivan, *A System of Architectural Ornament*, reprinted by The Eakins Press, New York, 1966.

7 (*right*). Window (drawing), Frank Lloyd Wright. c. 1900–1910. (Copyright © 1977 The Frank Lloyd Wright Foundation, all rights reserved)

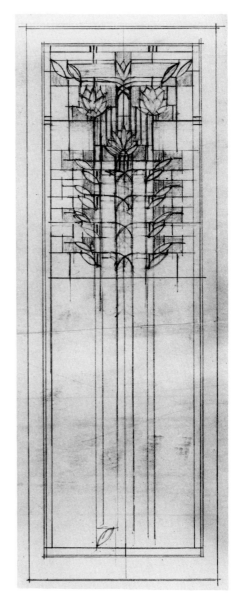

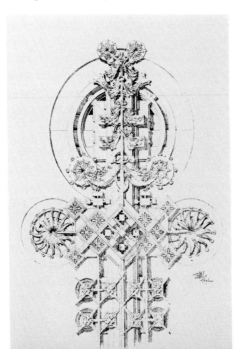

were unified causing the ornament to become organic. He did not believe, however, that organic ornament made an organic architecture. Wright felt that Sullivan's ornament had only expressed the articulation of the bony structure and had not been intrinsic to or of the building. For a true integration of ornament and building, Wright had to take up and continue Sullivan's struggle. For this he had to invent an entirely new architectural language that was based on forms that the machine could make and based on the true nature of materials. His goal would ultimately be to erase the boundaries between interior and exterior and to make "aesthetic and structure completely one" where the conventionalization of a natural form would become essentially the building ("Organic Architecture," 1935, from the *Architect's Journal*, August 1936. Reprinted in *Frank Lloyd Wright on Architecture*, edited by Frederick Gutheim, New York: Grosset & Dunlap, 1941).

Since Wright firmly believed that the reality of architecture was not in the facade of the building but was in its interior space, where human activity occurs, he extended his concept of conventionalization to refer to this belief. Conventionalization thus became to Wright "that interior harmony which penetrates the outward form or letter and is its determining character; that quality in the thing . . . that is its significance and its life for us." Wright called this "poetry" and believed that only the Japanese culture held clues for the attainment of this "determining character" of architecture so it might reflect the true ideals of the American people (Frank Lloyd Wright, *The Japanese Print*, 1917, reprint; New York: Horizon Press, 1967).

The culmination of this nineteenth-century process of conventionalization occurred in Wright's twentieth-century designs for entire buildings that were based on growing organisms, seen, for example, in Wright's S. C. Johnson Company's Research Laboratory (fig. 9). Its central core, which served as a ventilating shaft, and fourteen stories of research laboratories are based on the concept of an abstract tree, which Wright described in the 1948 *Architectural Forum*:

> The structure again is a trunk with a taproot, carrying lateral floor-slabs like branches, the glass shell hanging firm from each alternative floor slab. . . . It may be truly said in every sense in scheme and structure that here is an organic building.

Wright's theory of organic architecture, as O'Gorman and others have pointed out, was in part an outgrowth of this process of conventionalization and abstraction from nature. In *An Autobiography*, Wright stated the meaning of ornament as the "imagination giving natural pattern to structure itself" (1943 edition; p. 142). Wright's organic architecture demanded a unity of the ornament with the building, as well as with the furnishings and the site. Wright considered his buildings living organisms in which all was unified in an architectural whole.

If a building "is conceived in organic sense all ornamentation is conceived as of the very ground plan and is therefore of the very constitution of the structure itself." Wright described his buildings as "organic abstractions," which in their "severely conventionalized nature sympathize with trees and foliage around them with which they were designed to associate." He also described his use of natural foliage and flowers for decorations in the interiors, in planters at outside windows and on ledges, and often in lush exterior landscaping: "Although the buildings are complete without efflorescence, they may be said to blossom with the season." This architectural decoration serves as "a sure foil for the nature forms from which it is derived and with which it must intimately associate" ("In the Cause of Architecture," 1908).

Furnishings like ornamentation were conceived of as part of the organic whole:

In Organic Architecture then, it is quite impossible to consider the building as one thing, its furnishings another and its setting and environment still another. The Spirit in which these buildings are conceived sees all these together at work as one thing. All are to be studiously foreseen and provided for in the nature of the structure. Incorporated (or excluded) are lighting, heating and ventilation. The very chairs and tables, cabinets, and even musical instruments, where practicable, are of the building itself, never fixtures upon it. No appliances or fixtures are admitted as such where circumstances permit the full development of the organic character of the building scheme.

8 (*below, left*). Hollyhock frieze, Aline Barnsdall Hollyhock House, Los Angeles, California. 1920.

9 (*below, right*). S. C. Johnson and Son Research Tower (elevation), Racine, Wisconsin. 1944 (*Architectural Forum*)

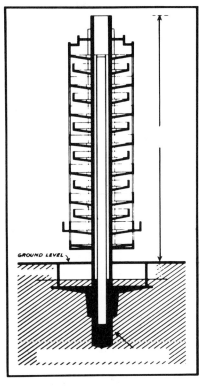

Floor coverings and hangings are at least as much a part of the house as the plaster on the walls or the tiles on the roof. (Preface to *Ausgeführte Bauten*, 1910)

Wright's early use of organic ornament was seen in his early houses. The residence that the twenty-five-year-old architect designed in July 1891 for Dr. Allison W. Harlan was one of the commissions that Wright referred to as his "bootlegged" houses, presumably undertaken without Sullivan's knowledge. Wright remembered the Harlan House in Chicago (fig. 10) as the one that caused the break with Sullivan, who discovered it being built two blocks from his own home. As was true of so many of Wright's subsequent clients, Dr. Harlan, a dentist, was an imaginative person; in a letter to a Chicago newspaper on February 16, 1882, he made the first public proposal to hold the World's Columbian Exposition in Chicago.

The regular symmetry of the facade and the wide eaves of the low hip roof gave the Harlan House a sense of order and quiet. Particularly noteworthy in terms of the early development in Wright's use of ornament was the striking balcony that extended across the house at the second-floor level. This horizontal balcony was relieved by vertical piers that framed a series of fretwork panels. These panels were also used underneath the balcony, from which the example in figure 11 was salvaged. Originally backed, the fretsaw-cut pattern may have been seen against a panel of the same wood.

10. Allison W. Harlan House, Chicago, Illinois. 1892.

Fretted decoration was then typical of the Victorian house, but its design was new here and its treatment, although similar to that of the James Charnley House (Chicago, 1891) balcony, was innovative in its adaptation of a prevalent decorative device to express architectural intent. Here Wright's purpose was to use the balcony to emphasize the horizontal aspect of the house. The panel's cutout design was derived from a plant motif—in this instance the oak leaf and its intertwining stems. Although detailed more simply than most of Sullivan's ornament, important design elements learned from Sullivan were used here so that the ornament was integral to the building. The interior entrance area embraced a monumental open stair hall. Both the stairs' tall wood newel post and its balustrade contained carved Sullivan-esque ornament that echoed the delicate fretwork of the exterior balcony.

The William Winslow House, designed in June of 1894 (fig. 12), also provided

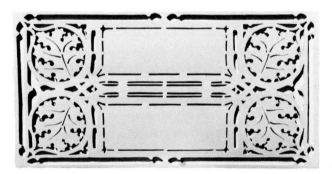

11 (*left*). Architectural fragment (panel), Allison W. Harlan House, Chicago, Illinois. 1892 (razed 1963). Wood, 28″ x 55¼″ (71 cm x 40.3 cm). (Lent by Mr. and Mrs. Tim Samuelson, Chicago, Illinois)

12 (*below*). William Winslow House, River Forest, Illinois. 1894. (*The Architectural Review*, vol. 7, no. 6, June 1900, plate XXXVI)

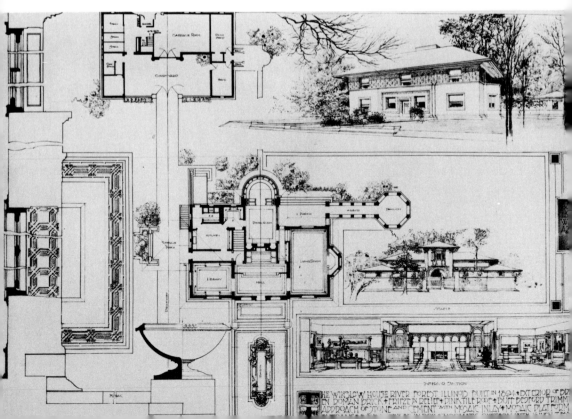

Wright with a great opportunity to display his virtuoso skills as a designer of ornament (see figs. 13–16). Areas of Sullivanesque foliage ornament contrast with plain surfaces. A porte cochere on the north side of the house allowed horse-drawn carriages to stop at the house and then proceed to the stable behind. The complex rear facade of the Winslow House, seen in part here (fig. 16), is in strong contrast to the simplicity of the front (fig. 12). The porte cochere as seen in this early photograph does not have the Sullivanesque leafage that appears in the spandrels today. One has a good view of Wright's early ironwork (probably made by Winslow Bros.), its simple verticals capped by round balls in a manner similar to the later, more complex Francis Apartments gate (fig. 20). The photograph also shows the secondary and shorter iron fence, which protected the stairs that led to the basement. (This stairway was subsequently moved to the position where the young woman, perhaps Mrs. Winslow, stands on a terrace.) The house's decorative frieze in relief at the second-story level and the Gothic decoration of the tower, reminiscent of that used for the Moore House in Oak Park, are also seen.

Some of Wright's most beautifully executed and exuberant Sullivanesque ornament is found in the Winslow woodwork—the front door (fig. 13) being a primary example. Here the stylized oak tree has a very thin, attenuated trunk, which grows into an ebullient efflorescence of foliage that is confined to the rectangular panel at the top. The interior hallway also has conventionalized ornament in the spandrels of the carved arcade (fig. 14), a detail of which is seen in figure 15.

The Francis Apartments, built in 1895 (figs. 17 and 18) at 4304 Forestville Avenue on the South Side of Chicago, had what Robert Spencer called a quiet, impressive dignity in the clean-cut facade that

> gives it an enviable air of well-bred distinction among the rabble of slatternly, dowdy and illiterate "flats" of the neighborhood. The grammar of this building is simplicity itself with the sufficient and evident preparation for structure at the base, the sheer rise of uninterrupted wall surface, completed finally and gracefully in the simple rich crown with fretted sky-line. (*The Architectural Review*, June 1900, p. 71)

Wright referred to his early buildings as "all characterized to a certain extent by the Sullivanian idiom, at least in detail" (*An Autobiography*, p. 127). For example, the design of the meandering interlocking circles used in the gray terra-cotta blocks from the exterior of the Francis Apartments (fig. 19) is seen in the grille for the side lunettes of Sullivan's Getty Tomb. Sullivanesque flowers appear where the circles meet and foliage where the circles overlap. The blocks seen here, however, are geometrically complex, with the insertion of octagonal shapes within the circles, which also interlock, forming hexagonal shapes in the spaces between—reminiscent of the design of the Waller urn (fig. 59).

These two blocks, which were among those forming the five horizontal bands around the ground story of the building, were salvaged when the Francis Apartments was demolished in 1971. The interlocking-circle design continued into the bands of the wrought-iron entrance gates, where variations of the circle motif were incorporated.

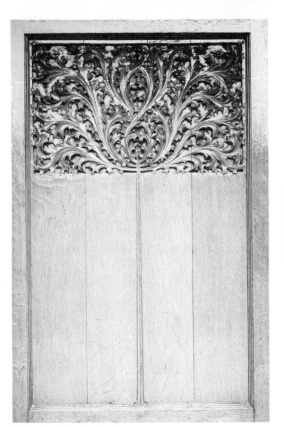

13 (*above, left*). Door (detail), entrance, William Winslow House, River Forest, Illinois. 1894. 14 (*below*). Entrance hall, William Winslow House. 15 (*above, right*). Arcade (detail), entrance hall, William Winslow House.

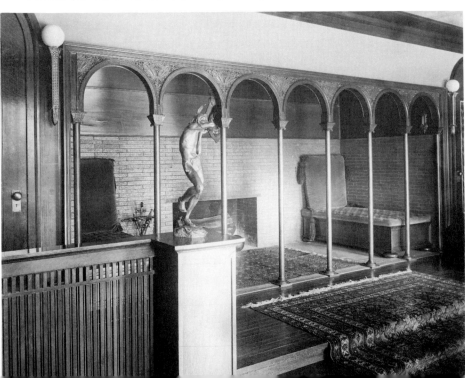

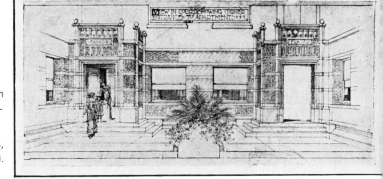

16 (*above*). Rear facade, William Winslow House, River Forest, Illinois. 1894.

17 (*below*). Francis Apartments, Chicago, Illinois. 1894. 18 (*right*). Court, Francis Apartments.

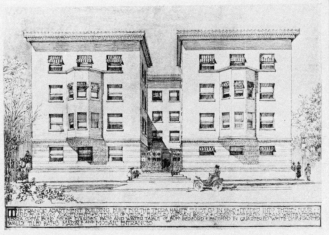

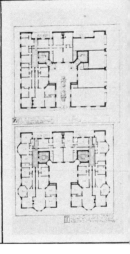

According to an article in 1901, great advances had been made in the manufacture of terra-cotta, which was so suited to "an architecture of ornament" (*House Beautiful*, vol. 9, February 1901, p. 154). Its cost depended "on the extent to which each block may be repeated, and the price of models and molds." One of the difficulties in the use of this material is that "alterations cannot be made, not only because the material cannot be cut but the pieces have to be ordered beforehand and made for the positions they are to occupy" (p. 156).

One of the few examples of Wright's designs for wrought iron to survive, the gate in figure 20, was one of four sections, the outer two of which were stationary, that spanned the entrance of the Francis Apartments. The geometric design carried the thrust of the horizontal rows of ornamental terra-cotta tiles. In the top row, Wright incorporated his own early symbolic signature, which was a cross within a circle and a square.

The ornamental band represented an advanced stage of the horizontal balcony of the Harlan House and anticipated the bands of casement windows of the Prairie houses. The Francis ornament was at eye level and of human scale. It not only gave the building a decorative base but provided the very humane amenity of a decorative pattern for the street landscape and the passerby. The interior court leading to the entrance doors of the building was also lavishly decorated with Sullivanesque ornament.

Contemporary with the Winslow House was the Chauncey Williams House designed in May 1895, also on the old Waller Estate in River Forest. Its steep, pitched roof and angular facade contrast with those of the Winslow House; however, a striking adaptation of Sullivanesque ornament was used around the top of the arched doorway and on the inner door (fig. 21).

19 (*below*). Two blocks, Francis Apartments, Chicago, Illinois. 1895 (razed 1971). Terra-cotta, 17⅞" x 17⅜" x 4" (45.4 cm x 44.1 cm x 10.1 cm) each. (Lent by Mr. and Mrs. Tim Samuelson, Chicago, Illinois)

20 (*right*). Entrance gate (section), Francis Apartments. (The Art Institute of Chicago; Gift of The Graham Foundation)

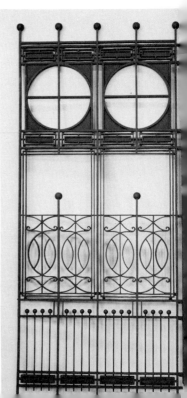

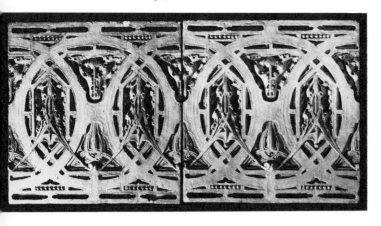

Another interesting example of Wright's early ornamentation, which was now becoming uniquely his, is seen in his designs for the prism lights and plates for the American Luxfer Prism Company. In 1894 Wright entered a design in a competition for a projected office building in Chicago for the Luxfer Prism Company, which promoted the use of their glass blocks in place of window glass for commercial buildings. Wright exhibited an example of electroglazing for the Luxfer Prism Company in the 1898 Chicago Architectural Club Annual Exhibition and three examples of "Luxfer Electro-Glazed Art Glass" in the 1899 exhibition. According to the *Official Gazette* of the U.S. Patent Office (vol. 81, pt. 3, no. 10), Wright patented a series of designs for the Luxfer Prism Patents Company. Fourteen prism lights and twenty-six prism plates were patented between October 2, and October 23, 1897. One of the prism lights (fig. 22), patented October 4, 1897, has a highly geometric design based on a flower composed of circles and squares. Another of the prism plates (fig. 23), patented October 22, 1897, is composed of four conventionalized

21 (*below*). Inner door (detail), Chauncey Williams House, River Forest, Illinois. 1895.

22 (*right*). Design for Luxfer prism, American Luxfer Prism Company, Chicago, Illinois. 1894.

23 (*below, right*). Design for Luxfer plate. 1894.

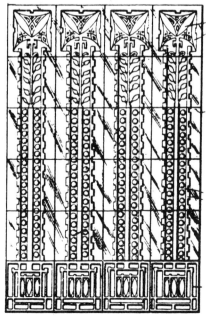

erect flowers similar to those drawn for *The House Beautiful* in the same year (fig. 192). Other Luxfer patent designs were taken out by Edward C. Waller, one of Wright's clients, an indication of the inventiveness of those for whom Wright designed houses. The contract for the Luxfer Prism Company enabled Wright to build his studio next to his Oak Park house.

■

Wright's own house provided him an opportunity to experiment with ornamentation. Of particular note is the jigsawed ceiling grille (fig. 24), installed in the dining room that was created in the 1895 remodeling. Recessed lighting, which was set into the ceiling behind the screen and became part of the architecture, was described in a contemporary account: "Great ingenuity has been used in the arrangement of the electric light. . . . There is not a bulb in sight, but let into the ceiling and actually part of it, is a screen of intricate pattern, covered with thin paper. The light is turned on above and filters through much subdued" ("Successful Homes," *House Beautiful*, vol. 1, no. 3, February 1897, p. 67). This recessed lighting was made possible by the lowering of the ceiling. John Lloyd Wright recalled the house of his childhood, where "lights filtered through fret-sawed ceiling grilles" (*My Father Who Is on Earth*, New York: G.P. Putnam's Sons, 1946, p. 15).

The design of the ceiling grille is rich and complex. It combines conventionalized oak leaves (seen also on the Harlan House panel) and geometric elements similar to those seen in *The House Beautiful*. The idea of the cutout panel was to continue throughout Wright's career—and was seen later in the perforated panels of the Usonian houses (fig. 180).

24. Ceiling grille, dining room, Frank Lloyd Wright House, Oak Park, Illinois. c. 1895.

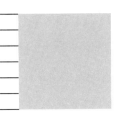

EXPERIMENTATION

Frank Lloyd Wright's interest in objects was coincidental with his tendency to experiment in rearranging them continually, much to the distraction of his family. An arrangement was only for the moment, as it no doubt was changed again soon after Wright was able to record it in a photograph. According to John Lloyd Wright, his father owned an 8″ x 10″ camera, and the photograph shown in figure 25 shows the Oak Park living room around 1890. It shows Wright's arrangement of the furniture, acquired at auction sales before he had been able to design his own furnishings. The arrangement indicates his sense of organic composition at an early date. According to members of Wright's family, he would spend entire Sunday afternoons arranging and rearranging the living room. The result here was a pyramidal, asymmetrical composition. In comparing the Oak Park living room with a later room in Taliesin II (1914) at Spring Green (fig. 26), one sees many changes, but the careful arrangement of objects in an asymmetrical organic composition that resembles Japanese prints was the same. In both rooms, a concentration of objects to the left provided a focus for the composition. Area rugs were used parallel or perpendicular to the furniture arrangement to lead from one space to another. Loose cushions were used for color, variation of composition, and comfort on the built-in seats in each room. A variety of contrasting textures was evident, and plants, cushions, rugs, and textiles softened both rooms.

An architectural background of horizontal molding, against which the arrangements were set, visually widened the room. In each room, Wright's love of beautiful objects of the past is apparent. In the earlier room, an interest in Renaissance objects is seen in the side chair and in the paintings (both of which were probably nineteenth-century copies). The room at Taliesin demonstrates Wright's growing passion for Oriental objects: the screen, statue, rug, and vases. These and furniture made to his own design create a sense of harmony and feeling of repose that the earlier room lacks. Wright later hated the Renaissance style because it was a conglomeration of previous forms and therefore lifeless—inorganic—not meeting the human needs of the time.

Olgivanna Lloyd Wright later wrote about her husband's rearranging rooms:

We have changed the furniture at Taliesin East and Taliesin West so many times that no one here can remember how it was from year to year. And when-

25 (below). Living room, Frank Lloyd Wright House, Oak Park, Illinois. c. 1890.

26 (left). Living room, Taliesin II, Spring Green, Wisconsin. 1914.

ever Mr. Wright and I traveled and stopped at a hotel the first thing we did was to change the furniture around in our rooms. Even if we stayed just two or three days we changed everything. Then we would go and buy flowers, branches or fruit to make the short stay as beautiful as it could be made in an impersonal hotel room. (*The Shining Brow: Frank Lloyd Wright*, New York: Horizon Press, 1960, p. 46)

The rearrangement of objects in a room could transform the interior more easily than could the architecture. Wright's own studio provided a means of continual experimentation with three-dimensional objects in a space.

In 1904 Charles White wrote:

The studio is again torn up by the annual repairs and alterations. Twice a year, Mr. W. rearranges and changes the different rooms. He says he has gotten more education in experimenting on his own premises, than in any other way. (Letter from Charles E. White, Jr., to Walter Willcox, May 13, 1904, quoted from "Letters, 1903–1906, by Charles E. White, Jr., from the Studio of Frank Lloyd Wright," edited by Nancy K. Morris Smith, *Journal of Architectural Education*, vol. 25, no. 4, Fall 1971, pp. 104–112)

Wright's compulsion to rearrange furniture and objects was also transferred to the interiors that he had designed for clients. On subsequent visits to the Darwin D. Martin House, Wright would rearrange the furniture differently from the plan he had specified on first designing the house (see furniture arrangement of Martin House, fig. 94). Although a definite furniture arrangement plan was frequently part of the designing of his houses, Wright made subsequent changes when possible, always attempting to make his arrangements closer to his artistic idea, which was in a perpetual state of development.

Not all of Wright's clients or friends were agreeable to giving him freedom to arrange or rearrange the furniture. Olgivanna Lloyd Wright described a visit with friends in Chicago who left the Wrights to themselves in the house. Wright suggested to his wife that they change the living room furniture, considering an arrangement by the architect a generous gift to their friends. "So we attacked the work," wrote Mrs. Wright, "I even helped him to pull the piano to another place! We moved every piece of furniture and worked until both of us were exhausted. . . . The old room now contained the magic of harmony" (*The Shining Brow*, pp. 46–47). On their return, however, their hosts were horrified and during the night moved their furniture back as it was.

At Taliesin, arrangements of furniture, tables, and flower decorations were part of the everyday training of the students. New arrangements in the dining room were made weekly and were freely criticized by Wright. Today this practice continues, and attractive flower arrangements are still part of the beauty of Taliesin.

The arrangement of Wright's favorite objects in his own studio (fig. 27) shows his careful attention to details. Again, as in figures 1 and 2, we see an asymmetrical arrangement, with the cluster of objects just to the left of the center. The tall weed holder and urn are discussed elsewhere (see pp. 68–71). The lamp may be of

Wright's design, as it was attributed to him in the 1902 Chicago Architectural Club Exhibition, but John Lloyd Wright stated that it was probably purchased by his father on one of his trips (letter from John Lloyd Wright to the author, 1972).

Since Wright's work received attention through exhibitions, it is not surprising that he was involved in museum installations. Wright's work was shown in The Art Institute of Chicago in 1907 (see *The Early Work*, pp. 101, 102, 103). The photograph of his work exhibited at the Art Institute in 1914 (fig. 28) shows an installation that, as in the 1907 exhibition, was probably done under Wright's direction. Seen in the photograph are models, drawings, plans, and objects, including the art glass windows from the Avery Coonley Playhouse. These stood on the floor in order to let the light flow through rather than hanging against the wall, which might have reflected distracting shadows made from the leading and the colored shapes. Wright also installed at least three exhibitions of Japanese prints: two at the Art Institute, in 1906 and 1908, and one at the Arts Club of Chicago in 1917. Through the years, other exhibitions of his work were installed under his close supervision.

Wright's interest in objects and their arrangement has an interesting parallel in the evident inspiration that he received from objects when designing buildings. Wright's creative and fertile mind received stimuli from a myriad of sources, including objects from the past that he owned and objects that he designed. Objects were always a part of his drafting room as well as his home, for his benefit and that of his students.

27. Studio added to Frank Lloyd Wright House, Oak Park, Illinois. 1898.

Wright's imagination was easily capable of making ascalar transitions—from the object to the building and vice versa. For example, the so-called skyscraper vase was and could become a skyscraper building, and the plan for the Leerdam cup and saucer (fig. 29) was easily transformed into a plan for the Guggenheim Museum (fig. 30). Even Wright's sketch for the inkwell for the Dwight Bank (fig. 31) suggested the plan and elevation of Unity Church, which he was thinking about at the time. These transitions, which, according to Bruce Pfeiffer, Wright playfully or jokingly referred to, were actually made by a logical design process. The concept of Wright's decorative arts' being derived from his architecture helps make the object's transformation into a building easier to understand. The reverse transformation was equally possible: the building could inspire the object. The plan and elevation of a building were always a favorite design motif for Wright and often served as the basis for a graphic (pl. 19) or textile (pl. 23) design.

Wright's interest in arranging objects was reflected in his interest in photography, which could record these arrangements. Although his interest in photography and his ability as an amateur photographer have been mentioned, little attention has been given to this subject. According to David Wright, his father had a hobby of photography. He developed and printed his own pictures in the "vault," which was earlier used as a darkroom in the studio and which later held his collection of Japanese prints (letter from David Wright to the author, May 29, 1977). Wright took many photos of the family in the 1890s and early 1900s, some of which were illustrations in Maginel Wright Barney's book, *The Valley of the God-Almighty Joneses*

28. Exhibition installation of the work of Frank Lloyd Wright, Chicago Architectural Club, The Art Institute of Chicago. 1914.

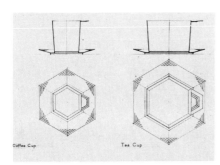

Coffee Cup   Tea Cup

29 (*left*). Coffee cup and teacup (plan and elevation), Leerdam Glass Company, Leerdam, Netherlands. 1930. (Copyright © 1977 The Frank Lloyd Wright Foundation, all rights reserved)

30 (*below*). The Solomon R. Guggenheim Museum, New York (preliminary plan). (Copyright © 1977 The Frank Lloyd Wright Foundation, all rights reserved)

31 (*bottom*). Inkwell (plan, front and side elevations), Frank L. Smith Bank, Dwight, Illinois. 1905. (The Art Institute of Chicago)

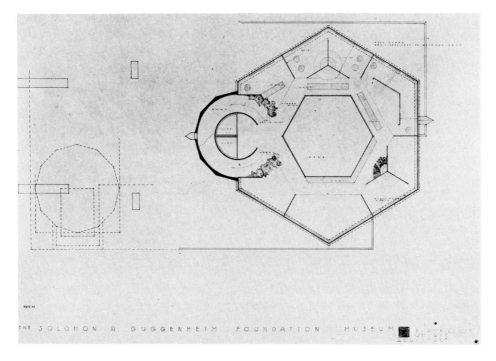

THE SOLOMON R. GUGGENHEIM FOUNDATION MUSEUM

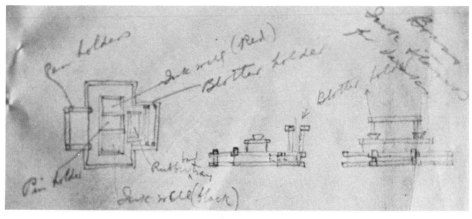

(New York: Appleton-Century, 1965). Wright also took numerous photographs of his own house and studio in Oak Park, many of which are now in the archives of the Frank Lloyd Wright Home and Studio Foundation. Photography was more than a hobby for Wright: it was a means of looking at arrangements of his interiors, which, seen in a two-dimensional medium, could be considered from a completely different viewpoint. And it was only through photographs that Wright's work reached a wider public. When possible, Wright even supervised the photographing of his buildings by professional photographers. However, he recognized the limitations of these photographs: "A building has a presence as has a person that defies the photographer and the color so necessary to the form." He was also critical of scholars and historians who described and assessed his work solely on the basis of a piecemeal analysis of elements seen in photographs. He felt that a true understanding of his aesthetic intent could be gained only by one's experiencing the totality of each building, which was more than a conglomerate of separate parts.

Wright's attention to detail, seen in his arrangements of furnishings, was part of his concern for the unity that an organic architecture required. An article by Elizabeth Gordon in the October 1959 *House Beautiful* ("Wright's Way with Little Things") gives an interesting firsthand account of Wright's attention to detail and love of objects:

> He applied his discriminating eye and mind to the smallest things as well as the biggest. He sought out beauty in all categories—from automobiles and plows to ancient Chinese bronzes or clothes. It was just as important for him to have a beautifully arranged breakfast table as it was to build a beautiful building.

For Wright, making a pleasing arrangement of the salt, pepper, and sugar containers on the dinner table was as worthy of attention as creating a building.

Another instance of Wright's attention to details is seen in the correspondence concerning the Frank L. Smith Bank in Dwight, Illinois, designed in 1905. In regard to designing and executing the furnishings, Wright was involved in every decision, no matter how small the detail. On December 20, 1905, Willy Lau, whose firm was making the lighting fixtures for the bank, wrote Frank L. Smith, president of the bank, that Wright had changed the back plates on all the brackets, which had delayed them. And on February 13, 1906, Lau wrote that he had the lanterns ready but was waiting to hear from Wright regarding the choice of color to be used. In response, R. S. Ludington, an executive of the Dwight Bank, wrote, "As regarding the finish on the brass lanterns we would prefer to have Mr. Wright determine that and we therefore would suggest that if you have not already heard from him that you call him up and have him give you instructions" (letter from R. S. Ludington to Willy Lau, The Burnham Library, The Art Institute of Chicago).

Wright's attention to detail continued in his later houses. One instance of this is the house designed for Mr. and Mrs. Isador Zimmerman in Manchester, New Hampshire (1950). As usual, furniture designs were included in the plans for the house, and the Zimmermans requested certain special forms, such as a music stand that is similar to the one at Taliesin. In addition to designing furniture for the Zimmermans, Wright also designed two tablecloths with accompanying hexagonal napkins, at

Mrs. Zimmerman's request. The drawings, with measurements, were sent, and the tablecloths and napkins were made by Mrs. Zimmerman. Wright also sent a drawing for a tray similar to ones at Taliesin that Mrs. Zimmerman had admired.

■

Wright's concern for the detail required by an organic architecture even occasionally led him to design dresses for his wife and clients. (figs. 32 and 33): "Catherine herself wore so well the clothes I designed for her that it was always a temptation to get new dresses. Designing them was fun" (*An Autobiography*, p. 115). John Lloyd Wright also commented on the dresses his father designed for his mother: "Mother always looked pretty at the parties. She wore the dresses Papa de-

32. Photograph of Catherine Tobin Wright in a dress designed by her husband, Frank Lloyd Wright. c. 1900–1910. (David Wright)

signed for her. . . . Papa designed most of Mama's dresses. Most of Mama's dresses were brown!" (*My Father Who Is on Earth*, New York: G. P. Putnam's Sons, 1946, p. 41). The geometric cut of Catherine's dresses, seen in both photographs, corresponded to the angular lines of his art glass windows. In their cut and folds in angular three-dimensional patterns, they were quite different from the typical dress designs of the early twentieth century as seen in contemporary illustrations. The dress seen in figure 33 was heavy, possibly made of wool, under which she wore a blouse of silk or net. The photograph seen in figure 32 is dated 1908. Since Catherine was born in 1871, she would have been thirty-seven in this picture.

John Lloyd Wright mentioned that his father also designed some of Mrs. Coonley's dresses to harmonize with the interiors. Although Mrs. Coonley appears at a distance in some photographs of the house (see fig. 98), it is difficult to determine whether she is wearing a Wright-designed dress. According to Wesley Peters, Wright also designed dresses for Mrs. Robie and Mrs. Dana, but no photographs to illustrate this have been located, nor are any actual dresses known to have survived. A cape designed by Wright for his mother, however, is still owned by his daughter, Iovanna Wright Schiffner.

33. Photograph of Catherine Tobin Wright in a dress designed by her husband, Frank Lloyd Wright. 1908. (David Wright)

A photograph dated 1910 of Mrs. Darwin D. Martin (fig. 34) in her house shows her in a dress that may have been designed by Wright. She is seen here placing a container of flowers on the ledge above the built-in bookcase/radiator. With her back to the camera, the train of her dress can be seen in full, which would be the greatest artistic opportunity for a designer. The asymmetrical arrangement of the photograph indicates the influence of Japanese prints. The photograph is also reminiscent of James McNeill Whistler's *Portrait of Mrs. Frederick R. Leyland* in the Frick Collection in New York. Here Mrs. Leyland is also seen from the back, the train of her dress in full view, in an asymmetrical composition suggesting a Japanese print. Mrs. Martin's dress is also reminiscent of dresses designed by Van de Velde. The soft folds of her dress are seen in contrast with the geometric design of the rug. Yet the dress is sheared, gathered, and pleated to create a fascinating linear pattern.

Wright's concern for detail is illustrated in many sections of this catalogue and wherever documentary material is available, such as in the Lang correspondence concerning the construction of the Darwin D. Martin House (pp. 90–95), it is clear that Wright's viewpoint included at once the total design and each minute detail.

34. Photograph of Mrs. Darwin D. Martin in her residence in Buffalo, New York. The house was designed in 1904 by Frank Lloyd Wright, who probably also designed the dress worn by Mrs. Martin. c. 1910. (University Archives, State University of New York at Buffalo)

FURNITURE

Frank Lloyd Wright's concept of an organic architecture required that all furnishings of his houses express the spirit of the architectural whole. The scale, proportions, lighting, and furnishings of the interior space, the reality of Wright's architecture, were all calculated to blend and create the effect of freedom and repose. As early as 1894, he proposed, "The most truly satisfactory apartments are those in which most or all the furniture is built in as part of the original scheme considering the whole as an integral unit" (Proposition 6 as recalled in *The Architectural Record*, March 1908). Built-in buffets and bookcases were standard in late Victorian houses, and Wright adopted this convention to assist in fulfilling his organic purposes and also to prevent the use of incongruent furniture belonging to the client. Built-ins helped to make the interior seem as if it had grown naturally. Because he skillfully knitted furniture into the fabric of his architecture, built-in and freestanding furnishings ultimately became hardly distinguishable in Wright's later houses.

Early examples of built-in furniture are seen in the inglenook of Wright's own house of 1889 (fig. 54); in the inglenook, windowseats, and buffet of the George Blossom House of 1892 (figs. 35 and 37); and in the hall seats of the William Winslow House of 1893 (fig. 14). Wright's built-in furniture harmonized with the interior woodwork in material and scale, as seen in the living room of the Blossom House (fig. 35). Built-in furniture provided a connecting link between the interior architecture and Wright's movable furniture, which would not be isolated. This is well illustrated by the B. Harley Bradley dining room (1900; fig. 64).

Commercially available furnishings in the early decades of Wright's practice were often poorly constructed, offensively overelaborate, and totally unsuited to the simple interiors of Wright's houses. The typical late Victorian furniture (fig. 36) was an anachronism in Wright's forthright interiors. The dining room from the Arthur J. Davis House in New York (1905; fig. 44) is typical of the cluttered eclectic interiors of the period.

Wright described his difficulties in finding suitable furnishings:

The trials of the early days were many and at this distance picturesque. Workmen seldom like to think, especially if there is financial risk entailed; at your peril do you disturb their established processes mental or technical. To do anything in an unusual, even if in a better and simpler way, is to complicate the

situation at once. Simple things at that time in any industrial field were nowhere at hand. A piece of wood without a moulding was an anomaly; a plain
wooden slat instead of a turned baluster a joke; the omission of the merchant-
able "grille" a crime; plain fabrics for hangings or floor covering were nowhere
to be found in stock. ("In the Cause of Architecture," *The Architectural Record*,
vol. 23, no. 3, March 1908; reprinted for *In the Cause of Architecture*, New
York: McGraw-Hill, 1975, p. 56)

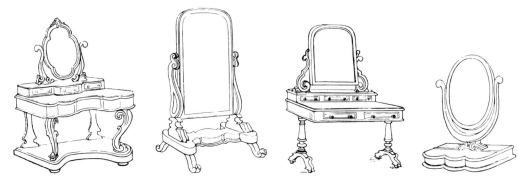

35 (*below*). Living room, George Blossom House, Chicago, Illinois. 1892. (The Museum of Modern Art, New York)

36 (*above*). Rococo revival furniture, illustrated in Christopher Dresser's *Principles
of Decorative Design*. London. 1873.

In the preface to *Ausgeführte Bauten,* Wright again stated his distress with this furniture:

> This feature of development called "the furnishings"—has given most trouble so far and is least satisfactory to myself because of difficulties inherent in the completeness of conception and execution necessary within the usual building—budget and total lack of suitable materials in the market. Suitable fabrics, hardware, furniture and all else has yet to be especially made. All available is senselessly ornate. To make these necessary appurtenances elements, themselves sufficiently light, graceful and flexible features of the informal use of an abode, requires much more time and thought on my part as well as more money to spend than is usually forthcoming in our country at this time. But in time this will be accomplished by improvements in all stock articles. (quoted in *Frank Lloyd Wright: Writings and Buildings,* selected by Edgar Kaufmann and Ben Raeburn, New York: New American Library, 1974, p. 102)

Decades later, when the modern style had gained acceptance, stock items did improve, and partly through the influence of Wright's own work, simple furnishings were designed for commercial production that were appropriate for an organic interior. Of course, Wright continued to design furniture for his later houses, frequently with help from his assistants, but after the 1930s, certain commercially manufactured furniture was more and more acceptable for the completion of his interiors. For example, although Wright designed most of the furnishings for the Herbert F. Johnson House in Racine (1937), a number of the chairs were bought in a local store (letter from Edgar Tafel to the author, June 10, 1977).

The house designed for George Blossom (June 1892) in Kenwood, a Chicago suburb at that time, demonstrates that Wright could compete with his eastern contemporaries in the revived Colonial style. The exterior clapboards, classical portico, and Palladian windows, all part of the Colonial revival vocabulary, were adapted by Wright into his own creative style. The plan also appears to be Colonial revival, with a central hall and flanking rooms. The entrance hall, however, is off-axis and lines up with the living room fireplace. The appearance of the interior belies that of the exterior: it is picturesque and hardly suggestive of a Colonial house. Deep, delicately arched doorways lead from one room to another, with tantalizing vistas. These contemporary photographs of the living and dining rooms (1892; figs. 35 and 37) may be the earliest documentation of completely furnished interiors known to be designed by Wright. The living room has a Wright-designed recessed inglenook—a brick fireplace from which simple geometrically shaped built-in benches of wood continue on either side into the lowest of the horizontal panels of the wall. Also in the living room, a long bench with spindles creating a screen above formed a partition between the stairway and the living room. A woman, perhaps Mrs. Blossom, is seen sitting on the corner of the bench. As early as 1892, Wright's organic intention was clear in the simple, geometric built-in furniture, which was made as part of and scaled to the interior woodwork. Here, as in other early houses, Wright used horizontal paneling of deep width divided by tiny rows of "beading" (to allow for shrinkage). This paneling was also typical of that used in Adler and Sullivan buildings, seen, for example, without the beading, in the trading room of the Chicago Stock Exchange, now reconstructed at The Art Institute of Chicago.

Some of the freestanding furniture may also have been designed by Wright for the Blossom House. If so, it would be the earliest known freestanding furniture designed by the architect. It is interesting that the classical gondolalike chair with the scrolled arms to the left of the table is known to have also been used in the William Winslow House, as a descendant owns an identical chair, which according to family tradition was designed by Wright for the house. Was other freestanding furniture such as the library table with the bun feet also designed by the architect? Or did Wright order the furniture from a local retail shop or from a firm like the Tobey Furniture Company of Chicago, which specialized in custom handmade furniture for architects?

The Blossom dining room (fig. 37) also had built-in furniture, which was no doubt designed by the architect; this included the curved windowseat and the large sideboard–buffet. Although the dining table does not appear to have been designed by Wright, the stepped molding around its top edge is identical to molding used in both the dining and the living rooms. Again, no conclusions can be drawn, but it is interesting to speculate that this may be Wright's earliest furniture designed *before* he turned to the more rectilinear forms with which we are more familiar. Unfortunately all the Blossom dining room furniture that was built in has been removed and

37. Dining room, George Blossom House, Chicago, Illinois. 1892. (The Museum of Modern Art, New York)

presumably destroyed. The freestanding furniture is owned by descendants. The built-in furniture in the living room does remain in situ, although the freestanding furniture has been removed.

The William Winslow House, designed in 1894, also provides an interesting study of Wright's early furniture. One enters the Winslow House by a central hallway (fig. 14), which is flanked by a library and a living room. Behind the hallway is a concealed staircase and the dining room, which, in turn, is flanked by a pantry, a kitchen, and a porch. The entrance hall is strikingly beautiful, with its arcade before the fireplace, which faces the entrance and is reached by three stairs. The spandrels of the arcade are decorated with carved, cutout Sullivanesque foliage. The carved design can be seen as a conventionalized flower when considered part of the column, which serves as the stem. This carving is extremely fine and appears deep until compared with the virtuoso carved leafage of the capitals in the dining room. Andirons apparently similar, if not identical, to those used in the B. Harley Bradley and E. Arthur Davenport Houses (fig. 66) can be seen past the newel post in the foreground; Wright's favorite Indian sculpture by Herman McNeil is placed on the newel post. Built-in benches that can be opened for storage purposes also serve as chests in the inglenook. They are finely crafted, finished on the inside and the back as well as on the front. A stepped molding enframes the panels on each side. The high-backed benches on either side of the front door (one of which is seen in fig. 38) are similar to the inglenook benches. Filigreed, cast-iron sconces are on either side of the arcade. According to the Chicago Architectural Club Exhibition Catalogue of 1902, these were made by Winslow Brothers. Their design of a conventionalized flower is similar to some of those drawn for *The House Beautiful* (fig. 192). Oriental rugs seen here on the stairs may have been used instead of the custom-designed rugs shown in the rendering for *The Architectural Record* (fig. 12). This rendering shows

38. Bench, entrance hall, William H. Winslow House, River Forest, Illinois. 1894.

some of Wright's earliest furniture, and the entire drawing demonstrates his ability to conceive of the total design—architecture, furnishings, floor plan, and details—as a whole. This total viewpoint is reflected in the rugs and furniture, which were custom-designed to harmonize with the interior.

The Isidor Heller House was designed in the summer of 1897, in the Hyde Park community, then a suburb of Chicago. A smaller third story contains an elaborate exterior frieze of winged figures and Sullivanesque ornament very similar to the book cover design for John Keats's *Eve of St. Agnes* (fig. 191). The first-floor plan of the Heller House consists of a row of rooms confined by its narrow lot: the living room and dining room connected by a long hallway that also gives access to the stairway at one side. A drawing for the living room was published in the June 1900 *Architectural Review* (fig. 39) and is one of Wright's earliest surviving renderings for an interior with all the furnishings designed by him to create a harmonious unity. It is not known whether all the furnishings were executed, as only the built-in bookcases remain in the house. These are trimmed with a delicate fretwork of simple square molding in a geometric pattern suggestive of Oriental filigree. The tall lamps shown in the rendering were evidently also made, although they

39. Isidor Heller House, Chicago, Illinois. 1897. (*The Architectural Review*, vol. 7, no. 6, June 1900, pl. XXXV)

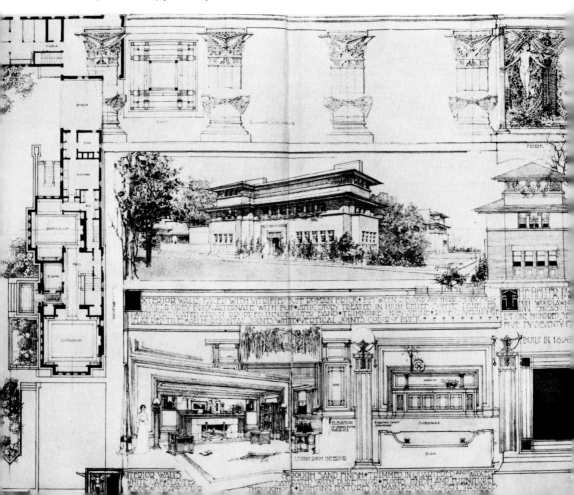

have not survived (the present owners are in the process of reconstructing them).

Wright's will to geometry in his furniture designs was developed quite early and can best be seen in the furniture made for his own house at the time of its remodeling in 1895—severely rectilinear forms characterize this furniture. One of the earliest examples was the "cube chair" (figs. 40, 41). Although it appears in a number of early photographs of Wright's home, no single photograph shows the chair completely unobstructed. Since its present location is unknown, a drawing is used here for illustration (fig. 40). The chair also appears in the photograph used on the cover of the Chicago Architectural Club Exhibition Catalogue of 1902 (fig. 41), with two copper vases and a statue of the architect's son John Lloyd Wright, as a child. John later recalled, "The chair on which stands the statuette goldenrod-holder of his red haired boy John was the first piece of modern furniture made in this country" (*My Father Who Is on Earth*, New York: G. P. Putnam's Sons, 1946, p. 24). This amazing chair, which was a revolutionary design for 1895, represents an uncompromising statement of Wright's ideas about furniture design. Reduced to its basic geometric form, with absolutely no ornamentation, and designed before any possible Secessionist and Scottish influence, the cube chair looks modern even today and stands in strong contrast to the Beaux Arts statue of John. Few designers had approached the extreme geometric severity of this piece, which was totally free of historic references. George Maher, under Wright's influence, designed a similar chair for the Rubens House in Glencoe (illustrated on p. 330 of *Arts and Decoration*, June 1911). Gustav Stickley's craftsman furniture, sold throughout the country by catalogue, was more accessible to the public, but it did not appear until 1900. Although

40 (*below, left*). Drawing by Thomas Heinz (1977) of chair designed by Frank Lloyd Wright. c. 1895.

41 (*below*). Chair, designed by Frank Lloyd Wright in 1895, with the statue of the architect's son, from Catalogue of the Chicago Architectural Club, The Art Institute of Chicago. 1902.

architects contemporary with Wright were designing furniture, few pieces were as straightforward as this chair.

Another important example of Wright's furniture of a very early date demonstrating his severe geometric sense was the library table (fig. 42) designed for the Charles Roberts House remodeling (Oak Park, 1896–1898). Its beading was used on the interior doors as well as other pieces of furniture for this commission. A prototype is seen in the table designed by Philip Webb around 1861 and made by Morris & Co. (fig. 43). Although the form is superficially similar, in Wright's hands it becomes a new and unique piece. Wright's table has an opening between the circular top and the rectangular storage cabinet, which allows the space to flow through and lightens the otherwise bulky look of the table. Each section of the supports is enframed, creating separate units, which are nevertheless unified by the strong geometric form of the table. Casters, frequently used in Wright's early furniture as was traditional in the nineteenth century, are used here in recessed niches (a detail used later with the Robie dining table).

■

Faced with the needs of a rapidly growing family, Wright decided to add to his own house in 1895. He converted the kitchen of 1889, located in the southeast corner of the house, into a dining room (fig. 45) by adding a wide hexagonal bay to the south side. This room was Wright's first known experiment in designing and executing a total environment where the architecture, the freestanding furniture, the lighting, and the ornamentation were all a unified whole. It had been captured in time in the photograph and published seven years later in an article in *The Ladies Home Journal* (January 1903). The stark simplicity of the room was revolutionary. In contrast to the typical rooms of the period (fig. 44), which were still characterized by clutter, Wright's dining room seems sparse. Two articles in which the dining

42 (*below, left*). Library table, Charles E. Roberts remodeled interior, executed gradually over several years, Oak Park, Illinois. 1896. (The Art Institute of Chicago)

43 (*below, right*). Table designed by Philip Webb for Major Gillum, c. 1861, made by Morris & Co. Illustrated in Nikolaus Pevsner, *Studies in Art, Architecture and Design*. vol. 2, *Victorian and After* (New York: Walker & Co., 1968, p. 121).

44 (*above*). Dining room, Arthur J. Davis House, New York. 1905. (Photograph by Byron, The Byron Collection, Museum of the City of New York)

45 (*below*). Dining room, Frank Lloyd Wright House, Oak Park, Illinois. 1895. (*Ladies Home Journal*, January 1903)

room was described appeared in *House Beautiful* magazine, one by an unknown author in February 1897, and one in 1899 (vol. 7), by Alfred H. Granger, who wrote:

> One's first impression of the dining room is its simplicity—no rugs, no curtains, and only the necessary furniture, which, however, is in perfect harmony with the room. One entire end of the room opposite the fireplace is practically of glass, laid in leading of a very delicate design, which was evidently inspired by the lotus flower. . . . The floor and the facing of the high mantel are of a deep red tile laid in an unusual pattern and highly polished. The oak woodwork, which is carried round the room to the height of the window-sills, is designed to emphasize the horizontal line, a very wise thought in a small room, as the horizontal line gives breadth and size, while the vertical line, by accentuating height, contracts. The color of this oak is a golden brown, a happy mean between the very dark of Flemish and the muddy yellow of natural oak.

The article continued to describe the harmonious colors of the room, the browns and red that "give to the entire room a golden tone such as one sees in a rich sunset."

Particularly noteworthy in the room was the intricate perforated wooden screen (fig. 24) in the ceiling, which diffused the light (discussed on p. 16). The bay contains one of the first instances of a band of continuous windows. Originally the panels below the windows, seen in the photograph, were also glazed, but when the house next door was built, they were filled in for privacy.

In contrast to the room's horizontal paneling and the banding of windows, eight high-backed dining chairs gave vertical accents. The dining room furniture was another example of Wright's earliest freestanding furniture. In this ensemble of around 1895–1896, the basic idea of dining was set forth and this was to be repeated in later designs. Tall high-backed chairs gave a sense of enclosure and intimacy as well as the suggestion of the formality of the occasion. Here the Wright family gathered together for meals. The table could be extended by means of sliding supports for the additional leaves needed for Wright's growing family and for guests. The scarf placed across the center of the table emphasized the lines of the table and softened the expanse of the oak top. In the backs of the chairs are "twisted spindles," which would later be replaced by vertical square slats that combined decoration and function.

Although most of Wright's early furniture was not as severe as his "cube" chair, "simple" geometric forms, devoid of applied ornamentation, fulfilled his organic principle. By describing his furniture as "simple," Wright distinguished between the simplicity of his furniture and that of the Mission furniture of Stickley & Roycroft, which was "plain as a barn door," as Wright put it. Wright's furniture was "truly simple"—which implies sophistication and subtleness—the lesson the architect learned from Japanese prints. Careful examination of Wright's early furniture shows that it only seemed simple and was, in fact, complex. For example, the back stile of the Bradley chair (fig. 65) tapers almost sculpturally in two directions, the proportions are refined, and the relationship of the parts is integrated to form a harmonious whole. This is all achieved in a chair that appears fully capable of performing its function under the load of weight.

■

The correspondence between Wright and Colonel Frank Smith of the Dwight Bank commission, already referred to, also illustrates the architect's fundamental concern for simplicity. When he inspected the bank's completed interior, he found that the commercially produced vault molding was disruptive:

> . . . I wish to enter a protest against the overdressed, gaudy, disreputable door frame to the vault. It nullifies the effect of the distinguished simplicity we have tried so hard and spent much money to obtain. The door should have a wide, plain frame, solid and substantial in appearance. Cannot this matter be taken up with the vault company? We would be glad to furnish a design in keeping with the rest of your outfit if it would be of any service to you. (Letter from Frank Lloyd Wright to Colonel Frank L. Smith, February 2, 1906)

A letter of February 3 to Wright in reply indicates that the Dwight Bank agreed to change the vault frame and requested Wright to submit a design.

For Frank Lloyd Wright, each furniture piece was considered part of an organism (structure) that had its own nature (subject to a specific and unique set of principles and needs). Just as Wright removed the barriers between interior and exterior so that the natural world became part of his spaces, so his furniture was not only intrinsic to the space it occupied but became part of the natural world. The living wood became his chosen material, and he used it lovingly and with intelligence. After about ten years of experimentation, Wright produced his first mature furniture designs approximately concurrent with the introduction of his Prairie houses. Respecting the nature of wood, this early furniture rarely used elaborate carved ornamentation, painting, inlay, extensive joinery, or turning. The new woodworking machines of the day, which fabricated furniture rapidly and inexpensively, greatly dictated Wright's furniture aesthetic. The characteristic use of vertical slats in his furniture and as stair balusters, first seen in the Harlan House designed in July 1891, had no precedent in this country; they served not only as integral ornament but as an architectural screening device that allowed space to flow through and yet was of the chair or the wall or the room. The earliest chairs known to make use of vertical slats were probably those designed for his own dining room (fig. 45), which were recently given to the Frank Lloyd Wright Home and Studio by Mrs. Wright. Another early instance of the use of slats are the dining chairs Wright designed for the Husser House (1899), which anticipated the Robie dining chairs (fig. 107). The Husser chairs are highly sophisticated for such an early date, incorporating for the first time stiles that are flared at top and bottom and with the slats extending down the entire back of the chair, details not seen in their prototype, the chairs for Wright's own dining room. The idea of geometrically shaped slats as a decorative motif was probably derived from the Japanese. Arthur H. Mackmurdo's fence for the Century Guild stand at the Liverpool International Exhibition of 1886 (*The British Architect*, November 5, 1886) is an early instance of this idea in the West. Chairs that made use of vertical geometric slats had also been used by English designers in the 1890s (see the armchair designed by Wickham Jarvis illustrated in "Studio Talk," *The International Studio*, vol. 5, 1898). Later, Gustav Stickley's chairs occasionally employed splats and slats. Although the exact date of the dining room furniture for Wright's own house is uncertain, it was in situ for the photograph used in the first *House Beautiful* article, published in February 1897.

Details were also manifested in the thin oak strips that were nailed and glued onto various parts of the Prairie furniture, sometimes in bands of multiple and often intricate formations. The banding, which caught the light and created shadows, added vitality to the wood surface and emphasized the structural elements of the furniture. It also directed the spatial flow echoing and even continuing the molding of the room thereby helping to unify the furniture with its surroundings.

In 1964, in "The Prairie School Furniture" (*The Prairie School Review*, vol. 1, no. 4, fourth quarter), Donald Kalec pointed out the important role of Wright's furniture in arranging the interior spatial flow and creating architectural space. The articulation of the open space of Wright's interiors was often achieved by the movable and built-in furniture as well as by the architecture. For example, the tall-backed dining chairs of Wright's own dining room (fig. 45) had an important function in creating the secondary space of the room. The elongated slatted backs served as screens that defined the eating area, creating a room within the room. In the Robie House dining room (fig. 107) the chairs served the same purpose. In addition, however, lamp standards in the Robie table and in other dining tables that Wright de-

46 (*below, left*). Side chair, Frank Lloyd Wright House, Oak Park, Illinois. c. 1904. Oak, upholstered seat, 40¼" x 15" x 18¾" (102.2 cm x 38.1 cm x 47.6 cm). (Lent by Mrs. Nora Natof, Lovettsville, Virginia)

47 (*below*). Desk, Frank L. Smith Bank, Dwight, Illinois. 1905. Oak. (Private collection)

signed emphasized this demarcation of the dining area in a strongly architectural way. Similarly, freestanding units could mark boundaries, seen, for example, where the built-in desk in the living area of Fallingwater helps to separate and define the spaces. A built-in cabinet that is perpendicular to the wall and has its own terminus is used in the dining room of the Ray W. Evans House. Built-in furniture in such instances functioned as walls. In the Darwin Martin House, the immense space of three large rooms was demarcated primarily by the furniture (see furniture plan, fig. 94), so one could experience the space and yet have the convenience of the specific function of each area or grouping of furniture.

Wright's Heritage–Henredon furniture (fig. 204) was especially important in defining and even *creating* the architectural space when one was attempting to build a Wright environment by means of Wright-designed furniture alone! That much of this furniture tended to be substantial served to express its function not only to be used for storage but also to define space.

■

In discussing Wright's furniture, it is useful to consider the furniture industry in Chicago at the turn of the century and also those manufacturers who were commissioned to make Wright's custom furniture. These forgotten craftsmen must have been extraordinary in their ability to execute Wright's unique and uncompromising designs, as they probably found it easier to add traditional ornament than to omit it. That much of Wright's furniture is very well made is a tribute to the skills of the shops he found to execute his designs.

Most of the furniture for Wright's early houses was made in either Chicago or Milwaukee. Both cities were well located near the Wisconsin forests, which could provide an ample supply of wood, though lumber from the southern states was also shipped to both cities. Oak was the favorite wood for both furniture and house trim in this period. When a good grade of oak log was sawed through its heart, a beautiful graining could be achieved. Some of Wright's furniture was made of "quartered oak." The oak log is sawed into quarters and then lengthwise into boards, producing the beautiful grain of "quartered oak." The diagram in figure 48 (*Masonry Carpentry Joinery*, Scranton, 1899) illustrates the ways in which boards can be cut from a log. If the log is cut into quarters, as indicated here, one can see four ways that a

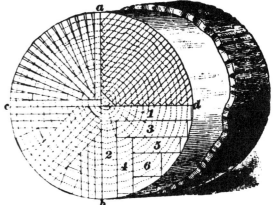

48. Wood sections, illustrated in *Masonry Carpentry Joinery*, Scranton, Pennsylvania. 1899 (reprinted Chicago, 1977).

log could be sawed into planks, according to the purpose for which the lumber is intended and the economy of the material required. The quarter-sawed section, indicated in the diagram as "a" to "c," provides the most beautiful results, since the annual rings of the wood cross the plank at nearly right angles, and the medullary rays, being parallel to this face, exhibited the lines of silver grain, which Wright admired. However, this quarter cut is the least economical in material and labor. After the wood was sawed, the pores of the surface were filled and then stains applied. Fumed oak, characteristic of Wright's early furniture, was achieved by subjection of the wood to very strong fumes of ammonia, which gave it a very dark tone.

By 1890 Chicago had overtaken Grand Rapids as the leading center for the manufacture of furniture; its preeminence as a transportation center made it the leader of the industry. Lumber from Michigan and Wisconsin was available to Chicago via Lake Michigan, by which means manufactured products could also be transported. Freight trains enabled Chicago to deliver the finished products throughout the country. Milwaukee shared some of Chicago's advantages of location and shipping facilities, which encouraged the establishment and growth of furniture factories there also.

Most of Chicago's furniture factories in the late nineteenth century were producing inexpensive, elaborately ornamented furniture to meet the demands of a growing, prosperous middle class. Various styles were popular, including the Renaissance and Rococo revivals, as well as "Eastlake" and "art furniture." The industry strove to meet changing fashions. The cabinetmaker and the small custom shop were exceptional in the furniture industry in Chicago (see David A. Hanks, *Isaac Scott Reform Furniture in Chicago*, Chicago: The Chicago School of Architecture Foundation, 1974). Methods of manufacture varied between the large factory and the small shop, as did the degree of the use of machinery as opposed to hand tools.

According to *The Industries of a Great City* (Chicago: The Little Chronicle Co., 1911) the stages in the furniture manufacturing process were as follows: drying wood; designing, which included making the sketch, planning, specifications, and patternmaking; machine work, which included machining to cut down stock to the desired size, veneering, squaring, smoothing, special shaping such as turning and fretting, nailing, screwing, and gluing; and finishing.

In the early 1890s, when Wright began to design furniture to accompany his interiors, the Chicago furniture industry was already quite advanced technologically. Most Chicago firms employed extensive machine equipment in contrast to Philadelphia, for example, where furniture manufacturers continued to prefer handwork. (For a discussion of the furniture industry in Philadelphia, see David A. Hanks and Page Talbot, "Daniel Pabst—Philadelphia Cabinetmaker," *Bulletin, Philadelphia Museum of Art*, April 1977.) Although Wright felt that the machine must be the normal tool for his simple designs, he was dismayed by the results of the typical furniture factories, which turned out ornamented carcasses in numerous revival styles. It is interesting that Wright turned to a relatively unknown and small shop to produce his first furniture—that of John W. Ayers (see pp. 201–202). Little is known about the relationship between Wright and Ayers. One can only speculate why Wright turned to Ayers for so much of his early work. As mentioned, there were large firms in Chicago that could offer custom-made furniture for architects, such as the Tobey Furniture Company. In *The Architectural Record* of 1907, Tobey advertised that they could offer to the architect their "staff of free-hand artists." Co-operation with the architect would result in a "sympathy of purpose, a unity of conception, and a unity of effort." Ayers's shop, in contrast to Tobey, was much smaller. Ayers seems to have been quiet and unassuming and rarely advertised his services in any of the architectural journals. But in Ayers Wright must have found a man whose shop could produce furniture in a totally new vocabulary. Ayers respected Wright's design ideas and was apparently willing to carry them out without imposing his own will. Wright no doubt benefited from suggestions from the accomplished craftsman, however, in regard to engineering the pieces. Recent research by Irma Strauss has uncovered furniture Ayers made on his own. The quality of the Wright-designed furniture that Ayers made indicated that he was a skilled cabinetmaker who used machinery and finished pieces by hand. When compared with the later work of the Milwaukee firm of George Niedecken, Ayers's craftsmanship is particularly fine.

Wright had proclaimed the machine the "normal tool of civilization." However, an investigation into shop practices at the turn of the century indicates that although machines were increasingly employed to replace handwork, the skills of the cabinetmaker were still needed: "Machines should not displace skilled labor," argued George Ellis in 1902 (*Modern Practical Joinery*, London, 1902; reprinted 1921, p. 87), as a competent joiner-machinist turns out better work than the average laborer. By his "knowledge of the requirements of the specific work in hand, a skilled craftsman often utilises a machine in a manner never dreamt of by the un-technical operator." Combination machines are the type most likely to have been used in a small shop like John Ayers's. Such machines would have been unusual in the large shop, with its larger spaces. Ayers's shop, with its limited accommodations and requirements, would probably have had the following machines: circular saw bench; band saw machine; overhand planes; mortise machine; veneer press; and perhaps a multiple-spindle dovetailer.

■

Most of what has been written about the manufacturers/makers of Wright's early furniture is inaccurate. It has usually been stated that the Milwaukee cabinet-maker George Niedecken made most of Wright's early furniture. First of all, Nie-decken, was not a cabinetmaker. He was an interior decorator who assumed a completely different role from that of manufacturer in the execution of Wright's furniture. Most of the early Wright-designed furniture that can be documented was made by John Ayers's shop.

It has also been said that L. and J. G. Stickley of Fayetteville, New York, executed Wright's furniture for the B. Harley Bradley House of 1900 in Kankakee (see pp. 73–74). This is another inaccuracy since it is known through the Chicago Architectural Club Catalogue of 1902 that John Ayers made both the Bradley furniture and the Hickox furniture (see p. 202). The confusion apparently arose from the fact that in the secondary rooms of the Bradley House, furniture such as bedroom suites, designed, manufactured, and labeled by the Stickley firm, was used. This furniture has nothing to do with the Wright-designed furniture for the Bradley House. L. and J. G. Stickley had opened their factory in Fayetteville, New York, in 1900, and presumably the Bradleys could have bought the furniture in that year. They could also have ordered their furniture from the large catalogue the company issued in 1910.

Gustav Stickley's craftsman furniture like that manufactured by his brothers and competitors L. and J. G. Stickley were appropriate choices for Wright's interiors if the client could not afford all custom-designed furniture. Stickley furniture, for example, was also used in the secondary rooms of the Henry B. Babson House, designed by Purcell, Feick and Elmslie in 1912. The Robies were known to have moved into their Wright-designed home very early in 1910 with an old Mission-style easy chair. It is not known whether Wright recommended or approved of the Bradleys' using the Stickley furniture in their home. Clearly though, this furniture was not incompatible with his interiors, and the geometry and simpleness of the forms were probably preferred by Wright to the typical commercial productions. There is no difficulty in distinguishing the furniture designed by Wright and made by Ayers and the L. and J. G. Stickley furniture; Wright's furniture is far more sophisticated and relates closely to the architecture and interior woodwork of the house.

One must remember that furnishings organic to Wright-designed houses were not necessarily completed in the year the house was built. Even clients like the Coonleys, who could initially afford to furnish their home completely, continued to add furnishings for many years, and of course Wright himself often returned to clients to make architectural changes and to design additional pieces of furniture. To design a building was an ongoing process for Wright, who strongly felt that if the fundamental concept of the building was organic, nothing added to or subtracted from it would disturb its integrity. This is the primary reason that Wright's furniture cannot always be given the date of construction of the house or be explained in terms of a steadily developing chronology.

■

In 1904 Wright turned to another cabinetmaking shop to produce the furniture for the Darwin D. Martin House. According to the contractor's ledger (University Archives, State University of New York at Buffalo), the Martin furniture was manufactured by the Matthews Brothers Furniture Co. of Milwaukee, Wisconsin. The most likely explanation is that Ayers's shop could not handle the manufacturing of all the furniture that was demanded for Wright's growing number of commissions.

In a letter from the studio dated May 19, 1904, Charles White, Jr., states, "The entire Martin (Buffalo) house is regarded as one of W's best opportunities. . . . The Barton House is just about completed. I am now working on the Martin House. Stable plans have just been sent them." Correspondence pertaining to the construction of the Martin House in the University Archives of the State University of New York at Buffalo indicates that the house was under construction from May to November 1905. Ayers could not have handled the large Buffalo commission at that time because he contracted for the Dwight Bank furniture in November 1905. The project seems to have kept his shop fully tied up as, although the Dwight furniture was promised for December 27 when the bank and insurance office building was to open, the furniture was not completed until three months later and then only after daily prodding by the client.

Wright must have been forced to turn to someone else, although one wonders why Wright went to Milwaukee for the manufacture of the Martin furniture.

Clearly furniture shipped from Chicago to Buffalo was a long distance, but working with a firm in Milwaukee when Wright was in Chicago must have presented additional difficulties. Chicago had a good supply of furniture factories, and some, as we have noted, specialized in executing furniture for architects. One can speculate that the Chicago firms, just as most of the Chicago building contractors, were unwilling or unable to execute Wright's special designs, which were deceptively simple and yet required unusual skills. Evidence points to the fact that the contracts to execute much of Wright's furnishings were not let out for bid; rather, Wright came back to the same shops over and over because he had a good working relationship with the cabinetmaker and could be assured of an understanding of his designs and of the quality of work. One such instance was when Wright returned, many years later, to Matthews's successor firm, Gillen Woodwork Corp., to execute the furniture for Fallingwater. (Matthews had gone out of business.) Whatever Wright's reasons for turning to Milwaukee shops, that city was also an important center for the furniture industry and could offer many of the same advantages as Chicago. The large German population in Milwaukee assured it of a number of skilled Old World woodcraftsmen.

The other Milwaukee firm that Wright turned to for supervising the execution of his interiors was the Niedecken–Walbridge Co., which was incorporated in 1907. By this time, Wright's numerous commissions required the services of a relatively new professional—that of the interior decorator—who could supervise all the details of such important and large commissions as the houses for the Coonleys and the Robies. Wright may have met Niedecken in Chicago, where the latter attended the School of The Art Institute of Chicago and exhibited a frieze at the first Chicago Arts and Crafts Exhibition in 1897. In his early career, Niedecken was an artist, and it is for the execution of murals that Wright first turned to him. Niedecken's signature indicated that he executed the sumac mural for the Dana dining room in 1903, and according to Charles White, Jr., in a letter to Walter Willcox, dated May 20, 1904, Niedecken helped out in Wright's studio for a while that year: "Niedecken, the artist, has returned for a few days a week. I am expecting him over this evening. He certainly has great individual talent as a decorative painter. He's just about my age, so we are very good companions. He is to make a few perspectives" (quoted from Nancy K. Morris Smith, "Letters, 1903–1906, by Charles E. White, Jr., from the Studio of Frank Lloyd Wright," *Journal of Architectural Education*, vol. 25, no. 4, Fall 1971, pp. 104–112).

From the evidence of the journal of accounts kept by the Niedecken–Walbridge firm from October 5, 1907, through February 23, 1921, we can now better understand the role Niedecken played in the supervision and execution of Wright's interiors for the Coonley, Tomek, Robie, and Bogk Houses. Niedecken was also in charge of completing the interiors for the Irving and May Houses, which Wright designed before he left for Europe in 1909. Although these were all important commissions, they represent only a small percentage of the Wright-designed houses of the Prairie years.

The most important fact that is revealed by the journal, however, is that the Niedecken–Walbridge firm did not execute Wright's furniture. The company was a *decorating* and not a manufacturing firm. Its role as an interior decorating business was to *supervise* and *coordinate* all the details that went into the execution of Wright's interiors. This included the supervision of the making of the furniture, which was actually manufactured by the F. H. Bresler Co. of Milwaukee. This is documented by entries in the Niedecken–Walbridge journal, which indicate that from time to time the firm paid the F. H. Bresler Co. to supply furniture. The furniture was only one item on an extensive list, however, which included the ordering of rugs, upholstery fabrics, draperies, the execution of a mural, and so forth. The journal accounts indicate the complexity of overseeing the completion of an elaborate interior and why the professional services of an interior decorator were needed by Wright, or any other architect who assumed the responsibility of designing or overseeing every detail of an interior. For example, the Niedecken–Walbridge journal indicates that beginning on September 17, 1909, George Niedecken made numerous trips to Chicago to supervise the execution of the Robie interior. On November 12, 1909, an entry for travel expenses indicates that Niedecken went to Chicago on October 30 "to show Robie drawings" and that he was accompanied by "Herman" on November 3 to measure the Robie House for rugs. On December 10, 1909, an entry indicates that "Goats Hair Satin" was ordered for the Robies from F. Schumacher & Co. in New York. On December 16, another travel expense was recorded for Niedecken to go to Chicago "to superintend color work in Robie house." A December entry noted that Niedecken went to Chicago with Schroeder with embroidery yarns for the Robie spreads, the fabric of which was ordered from Schumacher & Co. All these details and many others were the responsibility of Niedecken as decorator.

Because Niedecken was given these responsibilities, and because he was also in charge of preparing the working and presentation drawings of the furnishings, some have inferred that Niedecken actually designed the furniture for the Robie and other Wright houses. This assumption is inaccurate and does not convey an understanding of the design process and the way Wright worked during this period. Curtis Besinger has pointed out the difficulties that result from confusing concept drawings and renderings and a general misunderstanding of the practice of architects in the late nineteenth and early twentieth centuries. In general, the working drawings and the renderings or presentation drawings were not done by the architect but by draftsmen in the studio who were skilled delineators but were not responsible for the "design" (see *Journal of the Society of Architectural Historians*, vol. 31, no. 3, October 1972, pp. 216–220). The fact that the Niedecken rendering for the Coonley desk was signed by him indicates that he was responsible for executing the rendering but not necessarily for designing the desk.

The exact design process and the extent to which Wright would entrust details to Niedecken are still unclear. One might speculate that Wright would make a rough sketch for Niedecken, giving him the responsibility of developing the idea into a working drawing, which Wright would then review. Niedecken could then execute the rendering, which, subject to Wright's approval, would then be presented to the client. An entry in the Niedecken–Walbridge journal for the first order of furniture for the Robie account, dated February 28, 1910, states, "Designed & made red oak furniture as per specifications of drawings developed by F. L. Wright and G.M.N." By "designing" Niedecken meant "detailing" or preparing the working drawings, but the concept design was Wright's. The same entry indicates that

$936.65 was paid to the F. H. Bresler Co. for making the furniture and to other sources for materials. Niedecken's profit as decorator was $239.30. A second order for furniture, listed as an entry for July 10, 1910, states that Niedecken "designed and made 3 Tabourettes @ 30.50, 2 rockers @ 31.75, and 1 davenport @ 195, also 1 double bed @ 104, 2 straight chairs @ 20.40, and 2 hall chairs @ 36." Niedecken's versatile ability to design furniture that was superficially similar to and suited to mix with that designed by Wright may help to explain this later entry during the year Wright was in Europe from 1909 to 1910. Most of the Robie pieces listed in the July 10, 1910, entry appear different from those in the first entry that were designed by Wright. The davenport, however, is a more faithful copy of Wright's furniture. Its prototype is an armchair designed for the 1903 Little House. Some of the designs for the furniture that Niedecken lists in the 7-10-10 entry therefore may have been discussed with the architect before he left the country.

Comparison with Niedecken's own furniture (figs. 217, 218, and 219) is also revealing, since it is clear that when he was working independently, his designs were quite different. Niedecken's skill as a decorator is seen in his ability to design or detail furniture in any style that the client or the architect desired. An interesting case in point is the furniture that Niedecken made from Wright's designs for the Henry Allen House in Wichita, Kansas (fig. 218). Here we have drawings that were detailed in Wright's studio and given to Niedecken for execution. The Allens accepted most of this Wright-designed furniture, but evidently Mr. Allen needed the comfort of some traditional pieces and went back to Niedecken—no doubt without Wright's knowledge—to commission some Jacobean-styled furniture for his room.

The professional relationship between Wright and Niedecken in the creation of the interiors was documented in an article by Niedecken "Relationship of Decorator, Architect and Client," which was published in the May 1913 issue of *Western Architect.* Niedecken pleaded for professional recognition of the interior designer in the community and urged cooperation between architect and decorator. He argued that the decorator's job was the more difficult one and required the skills not only of a commercial designer but of a designer who was also an artist and could understand the various skills necessary to complete the furnishings of a house. The decorator would require training in architecture and the other arts, including the weaving of fabrics and rugs, decorative plaster, and so forth. The fitness of decorations and furnishings for the house depended on a "harmony between architect, layman and decorator," so that the decorator could contribute to the harmony between the interior and the exterior of a house. He felt that a retail business that carried a large stock of furnishings would not be able to achieve this harmony. The client's role was to make his likes and dislikes known to the architect and the decorator so that the building "can incorporate their individuality and personality in the execution of the structure, design and arranging of the furnishings." The decorator's responsibility was to absorb "the fundamental ideas already laid down." Niedecken was no doubt echoing Wright's sentiments about organic architecture:

> In most of the interiors there will be found a quiet, a simple dignity that we imagine is only to be found in the "old" and it is due to the underlying organic harmony, to the each in all and the all in each throughout. This is the modern

opportunity—to make of a building, together with its equipment, appurtenances and environment, an entity which shall constitute a complete work of art, and a work of art more valuable to society as a whole than has before existed because discordant conditions endured for centuries are smoothed away. ("In the Cause of Architecture," March 1908, p. 60)

It has often been suggested that Wright's superb draftswoman, Marion Mahoney, designed much of the furniture for her employer; the Robie House dining room ensemble particularly has been cited as an example. Inasmuch as Wright was in Europe when the Robies moved into their home early in 1910 and because Mahoney took over the design of his work, with Hermann Van Holst in charge of all the commissions still on the drawing board, this speculation is very easy to accept. Barry Byrne, moreover, has written that on one occasion Wright had taken the statement of her superiority over his draftsmanship "equably." Knowing how Wright respected her abilities and sometimes signed his name to her drawings, it would be logical to infer that he did the same with furniture designs passed on to his talented assistant in the crunch of meeting deadlines. Barry Byrne had personally related to scholars that Mahoney had designed furniture for Wright, and another scholar has suggested this by inference, through the statement of Roy Lippencott, an architect, who claimed to have supervised the construction of the Robie House.

However, there is no known documentation, not even in Mahoney's writings, to indicate that she or anyone else might have designed furniture attributed to Wright. In a letter to Grant Carpenter Manson, dated April 14, 1959 (Manson Collection at the Oak Park Public Library), John Lloyd Wright stated, "Marion Mahoney's rank was more as a delineator of Frank Lloyd Wright's designs and drawings than a 'Designer.' " As in the case of George Niedecken, Wright made the rough sketch, which Mahoney detailed and then, no doubt with Wright's approval, made into a final rendering for the client. Since her own statement testifies to the fact that the Robie House designs were complete before Wright left for Europe and Robie family tradition (conversation between Lorraine Robie O'Connor and Irma Strauss) indicates that Wright designed the furniture before he left, the last recourse to documentation, lacking signed drawings or affidavits to the contrary, is in attribution on the basis of style.

A study of the dining room furniture designed by Mahoney for the David M. Amberg House (*Western Architect*, 1913) reveals it to be in the Prairie School idiom but lacking the graceful stance and authoritative form of the Robie House pieces. The legs of the Amberg chairs are strangely canted toward each other at the side before flaring out again near the bottom, and the design solution of the table is mundane, lacking the finesse of form and detailing that marks the Robie table as such an intelligently conceived design. The vocabulary of the Robie table, on the other hand, is Wright's. The basic table design, often in less elegant versions, had been repeated over and over since Wright's own dining room table, which was built at the time of the 1895 remodeling of his house. Stained-glass standards for dining room tables had been designed by Wright at least as early as 1902 (sketch model dining table standard, item #420 in the Catalogue of Exhibits, Chicago Architectural Club, 1902, The Art Institute of Chicago). Slatted back dining chairs, in an obviously more primitive version, were remodeled for Wright's new dining room of 1895. A careful study of the superior design of the Robie dining room ensemble reveals it as a culmination of all of Wright's Prairie furniture, just as its environment, that of the Robie House, shows Wright's ultimate mastery of the design of the Prairie house. The dining room ensemble is so graced with the consummate authority of line and proportion that resulted from Wright's imagination by 1908–1909 that it is very difficult to believe that anyone other than the master sketched the basic design.

According to Wright, the house of moderate costs was one of his greatest challenges. His development of the Usonian house was one of the major achievements in twentieth-century architecture. The ideal way of constructing a Usonian house and its furnishings was to complete the entire building—both inside and out—in one operation and to eliminate all unnecessary materials and labor. Therefore priorities had to be established as to what was essential to the house. Wright's solution in the Usonian house was to simplify by eliminating all that was not essential. Radiators were replaced by radiant heating and light fixtures by recessed lighting; plastering, painting, and wallpaper were unnecessary; and basements and interior trim were eliminated. Most furniture was built in as part of the walls and simple enough to be constructed on the job site by millworkers or the owner rather than in a cabinet-making shop.

Although Wright eliminated many things by simplifying the design (and then, by extension, the living style of the client), he did consider certain things essential: "We must have as big a living room with as much garden coming into it as we can afford, with a fireplace in it, and book shelves, dining table, benches, and living room tables built in" (*The Architectural Forum,* January 1938, p. 82). It was also absolutely necessary to have the architect oversee the building, including designing the furnishing and planting. Usonian furniture was based on the same module system as its spatial environment and was built in whenever possible. One type of wood, usually redwood or cypress, was used throughout the interior and the exterior of the Usonian house. These were not only more economical than oak, but they offered resistance to moisture—an important consideration in the choosing of an exterior material. The nuances of the Prairie period furniture, which a cabinetmaker had to execute, such as the curve in the molding of the Darwin Martin House table (see fig. 93), were no longer attempted. Usonian furniture often gave the appearance of folded paper and is sometimes referred to as "origami" furniture.

An extensive documentation of the design and execution of furniture for a Usonian house—specifically the first and second houses Frank Lloyd Wright designed for a young journalist, Herbert Jacobs—is in The Burnham Library of The Art Institute of Chicago. Wright's first Usonian house had been designed in 1936 for another client but was built for the Jacobses in 1937 near Madison, Wisconsin. The second was built in 1943 in Middleton, Wisconsin. The collection, which was carefully catalogued by the Jacobses before presentation to the Art Institute, contains correspondence between Jacobs and Wright and a set of blueprints, but more important is the Jacobses' detailed accounts of the building of each house, including the furnishings, which their relatives constructed for their first house. According to their description of the furnishings for that house:

. . . tables, plus a square coffee table, two large armchairs, and six upholstered dining/living room chairs were designed and built by Katherine's cousins, Harold and Clarence Wescott, of Milwaukee, who had power tools and had learned upholstering. Wright saw their plans, and modified the leg and fin design of the dining table, but made no other changes. The brothers agreed to do the job for $300, and they did it so fast that the new furniture was crowded into our small Madison apartment for three or four months before we moved into the new house.

Mr. Jacobs' description of the furnishings for their second house indicates what they did with their furniture from the first house:

We sold the furniture with the first house, but we wanted to duplicate the living room armchairs for the second house. I did the elevation drawing and the dimensions from memory, and had the materials cut from either maple or birch at the lumber yard. Katherine did the upholstery. We built it in the farmhouse and used it a year or two before moving into the second house. We built a second chair during the first winter in the second house. . . . Since I did not have tools or clamps for concealing the dowels I simply ran them in from the top of the arms into the legs, but from the inside, from the bottom rails into the legs.

The furnishings for their second house were a combination of their own work and that of a carpenter, as well as store-bought items. With so many of Wright's houses, the completion of furnishings was sometimes postponed for a number of years—for the Jacobses it was almost a twenty-year wait:

During the winter of 1958–59, with the children mostly gone and more time available, I decided to finish the master bedroom, but it took until April, 1961. I asked Taliesin for detailed plans.

Although the stylistic changes in Wright's furniture forms are touched upon in the chronological section of this catalogue, a brief review and a few observations are appropriate here. Frank Lloyd Wright's furniture of the Prairie years and that custom-designed for a number of later houses have in common a high quality of craftsmanship. The character of the Prairie furniture began to change after Wright returned from Europe in 1910, seen in the furniture for Taliesin at Spring Green (1911) and the Little House in Wayzata (1913). The darker-stained furniture of the Prairie years was replaced by unstained oak furniture that was lighter; the horizontal molding was abandoned; and the terminals of the vertical elements were eliminated. Forms were more straightforward and severely geometric and were often "hung" from four square posts to allow for the spatial flow and to lighten the appearance of a strong form. During the California period, when he was involved with the construction of the Imperial Hotel, Wright placed the architect Rudolph M. Schindler in charge of designing the furniture. Therefore the dining room furniture for the Hollyhock House is among the few pieces Wright designed for the California houses of the early 1920s. With the development of the Usonian house, Wright was more interested in focusing on inexpensive furniture that could be made on the site by the owner or millworker.

■

When Wright designed furnishings for the luxury houses of the 1940s and 1950s, he followed his earlier principles of simplicity and natural materials and at times returned to some of his earliest forms, using, for example, adaptations of the tall rectangular square dining room chair (fig. 45) and the square-spindled barrel chair originally designed for the Darwin Martin House (fig. 92).

Certain forms, such as radiators, were offensive intrusions to Wright, who always attempted to cover them. He wrote, "Consider everything in the nature of a hanging fixture a weakness, and naked radiators an abomination" ("The Modern House as a Work of Art," 1902, quoted in *Frank Lloyd Wright on Architecture*, edited by Frederick Gutheim, New York: Grosset and Dunlap, n.d.). Wright attempted to solve this problem in many ways. He built windowseats to cover the large radiators, as in the Blossom House dining room (fig. 37). He placed the heating element within large supporting piers, as in the Darwin Martin House in Buffalo (fig. 34). He designed rectilinear covers composed of vertical slats around the side and horizontal spindles on the top, as can be seen in the example from the Ray W. Evans House in the collection of The Art Institute of Chicago. Wright also used forced-air ventilation, which requires no radiators. Finally, out of desperation to eliminate the need for imposing these "eye-sores" upon his organic spaces, he developed what he termed "gravity heating" (radiant heating). This forced the circulation of hot water into pipes that were placed in a broken stone bed beneath the concrete floor slabs.

Wright's dining tables were always massive, usually with a thick top that extended considerably over the sides, creating a cantilevered effect. This gave these tables a strong horizontal quality—the long continuous line of the prairie—as well as the appearance that the table was up to the task of holding the weight of the accouterments of dining. The tables were usually supported by four substantial square legs. The introduction of wooden standards with art glass lamps at the four corners, which had containers for flowers, was an early innovation used in at least four Prairie houses (figs. 95 and 107) but was later abandoned because of their impracticality. Storage units were sometimes incorporated into library or dining tables, such as the Roberts library table (fig. 42) and the Booth and Little library tables (fig. 116). In a characteristic manner, Wright attempted to solve the problem of long tables for guest dining in many ways. For the Husser and Dana Houses Wright designed three similar tables that could be placed together for seating many people. These tables contained supports that would slide out from under the tabletop to hold extra leaves. The long single dining table at the Herbert F. Johnson, Jr., House could slide into the kitchen for storage. In the 1930s, with changing life-styles, Wright eliminated the dining room altogether in most of his houses and incorporated the dining area into the large living room, where monumental dining ensembles were no longer needed.

Wright's versatile innovations in artificially lighting his interiors were as dramatic as those of his furniture designs. He preferred recessed lighting (which he became familiar with in working on the Chicago Auditorium designed by Adler and

Sullivan) that was integral to the architecture. Overhead illumination, as in nature, was the inspiration for Wright's favoring the use of ceiling light. He used this type of lighting early and in varied ways, for example, behind a fretted wood grille backed by a sheet of rice paper in the ceilings of his children's playroom and his remodeled dining room of 1895, behind art glass panels in the entrance area of his studio designed in 1898. Indirect lighting behind wooden grilles along the sides of the long living and dining space in the ceilings of the Robie House was adjustable by the use of a rheostat for dimming—a remarkable invention for the time.

Wright also used freestanding movable lamps. Some of the most spectacular table lamps were those designed with art glass shades for the Dana House (see pl. 2). The table lamp designed for the Midway Gardens (fig. 124) was the prototype for a particular type that was used over and over in Wright's later houses. The tall spine-like or flowerlike lamps seen in the Summer Garden of the Midway Gardens (fig. 120) were repeated in variation in some later houses. Indirect lighting continued to be his favorite means of illumination for each of his houses, since it provided softness and thus a feeling of tranquillity.

The most difficult form of furniture for Wright was the chair. As a defense against the criticism that had often been made about the discomfort of his seating furniture, he came to acknowledge what he felt was a failure, blaming the human need to eat or sit in a folded position, which he thought was abnormal to man. In truth, Wright's dining chairs may have implied that a position of strained rectitude was necessary to sit on them, but this critical judgment was not always shared by its users, and the chairs were more comfortable than they appeared. Donald Kalec has pointed out that these straight, high-backed chairs were designed for a different cultural world, where women were highly corseted and straight posture was *de rigueur.* Erectness at the dinner table was a basic, accepted form of etiquette ("Prairie School of Furniture," *The Prairie School Review,* fourth quarter, 1964). Dining chairs have customarily been straight-backed for centuries, and though these chair backs may have been richly carved or decorated and therefore more delicate in appearance, they required the same posture as Wright's straight-backed chairs.

Wright never abandoned his high-backed dining chairs of the Prairie houses, though the slatted backs were generally replaced by solid backs, which must have been easier and more inexpensive to produce. The easy chairs of the Prairie houses, with wooden rectlinear forms that were softened by cushions, gave way to the overall upholstered chairs used in later houses.

A variety of beds were designed by Wright. These included canopied children's beds for his Oak Park house, beds with attached benches at the foot (seen in the Francis W. Little Wayzata House and Paul Hanna's Honeycomb House), and built-in beds.

In the work of his contemporaries in Europe, Wright found sympathetic corroboration of his own ideas about furniture. Wright mentioned them by name, "The Mackintoshes of Scotland; restless European Protestants also—Van de Velde of Belgium, Berlage of Holland, Adolph Loos and Otto Wagner of Vienna . . ." (*A Testament,* New York: Horizon Press, 1957).

Wright was also impressed with the German rooms in the Building of Varied Industries at the Louisiana Purchase Exposition at St. Louis in 1904 and gave his young draftsman Barry Byrne money to go to St. Louis to see them. The building containing the rooms was designed by Joseph Maria Olbrich, an architect and a leader of the Viennese Secession movement, who also designed the interiors of six of the rooms, including the furniture and accessories, which were carried out by Hessian artisans. Charles White, Jr.'s, letter to Walter Willcox, dated May 24, 1904, stated, "You and your wife and I will go to the fair at St. Louis. . . . Mr. Wright has been down and says we cannot miss going. . . . W. says it is a liberal education."

One can speculate on the periodicals that Wright read. It is known that the office of Adler and Sullivan received *The British Architect* and *The International Studio:*

> All that one can say is that the Midwestern Prairie architect did feel a strong kinship with the English Arts and Crafts Movement and its exponents, as opposed to Paris and the Beaux Arts, and certainly did keep abreast of what was published in the English art and architectural magazines. George Grant Elmslie . . . once remarked that . . . *The Studio* (or its American version, *International Studio*) was received with enthusiasm. *The Studio*, then, unquestionably provides the major link between England and America. (David Gebhard, "C.F.A. Voysey—To and From America," *Journal of the Society of Architectural Historians*, vol. 30, no. 4, December 1971, p. 307)

Just as American architectural publications were studied in Europe, progressive periodicals such as *Kunst und Kunsthandwerk* from Vienna and *Deutsche Kunst und Dekoration, Dekorative Kunst,* and *Das Interieur* from Germany, which were interior design and decorative arts publications, were undoubtedly available to Wright and his contemporaries. Wright would have known the work of Leopold Bauer (fig. 49) through such periodicals, just as Bailley Scott might have seen the December

49. Furniture designed by Leopold Bauer, *Das Interieur*. 1900.

1899 issue of *House Beautiful* that described and illustrated Wright's dining room furniture. Any influence that the European movement had upon the designs of Wright's furniture, however, was negligible. The resemblance between the Darwin D. Martin armchair (fig. 92) and the Bauer chair seen here is similar only in terms of the roundness. Wright's furniture aesthetic was his own—as unique to him as his architecture. The differences between Wright's furniture, particularly in its spatial environment, and that of his European counterparts were more noticeable than the similarities. What was important was the shared ideals: "We may differ vitally in manner of expression, in our planning, in our touch, in the way we clothe our work, in our feeling for proportion, but although our problems differ essentially, we are altogether at one in our principles" (preface by C. R. Ashbee for *Ausgeführte Bauten*).

ART GLASS

Perhaps the most important and brilliant of Frank Lloyd Wright's early decorative designs is the art glass used for windows, doors, lamps, and ceiling lighting in his Prairie houses and buildings. One of the earliest examples are the clear leaded-glass doors of the bookcases flanking the fireplace of the Charnley House living room (1891). Additional early examples are seen in the glass designed for Wright's own house (fig. 50) and for the William Winslow House dining room of 1893. The last use of art glass is the Charles B. Ennis House in Los Angeles in 1923, after which time Wright abandoned it in favor of clear plate glass. In the S. C. Johnson Administration Building (1936–1939), Wright used tubular glass in a unique and beautiful way for skylights, walls, and partitions (fig. 165). Colored glass was set into the pierced blocks of the altar of the Florida Southern College Chapel (Lakeland, 1954).

The severely geometric designs in leaded glass had little immediate precedent in Europe or this country but were to become enormously influential and one of Wright's great contributions to American design of the early twentieth century. Thomas Tallmadge was correct in his evaluation in 1908 that Chicago's "minute leading of glass and elaborated texture in cast metals and terra cotta are unknown abroad" ("The Chicago School," *The Architectural Review*, vol. 15, no. 4, April 1908). However, Wright did own a book, *Kunstverglasungen* by H. Carot (Berlin, 1886), that was probably the inspiration for some of his earliest windows (see figs. 51, 52, and 53). The design of the windows for the Winslow House and Wright's own house (fig. 50) are the result of a combination of plates from this book. The alterations on the plate seen in figure 2 may be Wright's own. What Wright *developed* subsequent to these early windows was entirely original. Tallmadge credited the new geometric glass to Wright and explained how quickly his ideas were taken up by commercial glass firms: "while Mr. Wright's creations in leaded glass have been adopted, as their own, by most of the local glass concerns." These commercial designs are seen in numerous Prairie houses, particularly in the Chicago area. Two catalogues of such glass firms are in the Chicago Historical Society (*International Art Glass Catalogue*, Ranson & Evans Co., Chicago, n.d., and *Art Glass Catalogue No. 28*, Chicago Millwork Supply Co., 1910).

The designs of many of Wright's windows were based on nature. Plant forms were highly conventionalized, usually to such a degree that the design became abstract. Although this dependence on organic forms, as has been noted, can also be seen in the ornamental designs of Christopher Dresser, Frank Furness, and Louis Sullivan, none carried the designs to the extreme geometric abstraction or captured the "essence of the plant" that Wright did in his art glass. (See the discussion of the development of Wright's ornament, pp. 1–9.)

Grant Manson theorized that Wright's architectural forms were based on the Froebel blocks, while his two-dimensional decorative designs were based on the "strips of colored paper, glazed and mat, remarkably soft brilliant colors [and] the geometric by-lay of those charming checkered color combinations!" (see Manson, p. 9). Friedrich Froebel believed that the child should understand the geometry underlying natural forms, which was exactly what reformers like Dresser had emphasized in their writings.

The patterns of Wright's Prairie windows tend to be of two types: those that are totally abstract, such as the windows of the stairwell of the Isidor Heller House (1897), and those already mentioned that are based on conventionalized flowers, or plants seen, for example, in the Susan Lawrence Dana House (pl. 3) and the Darwin D. Martin House (pl. 8). One of the earliest examples of the use of conventionalized flowers are the art glass windows designed for the C. E. Roberts House, Oak Park, remodeling around 1896 (see Robert C. Spencer, Jr.," The Work of Frank Lloyd Wright," *The Architectural Review*, June 1900, p. 62). In the Roberts windows, the composition is based on a vertical format, with an erect flower. This verticality provided a contrast to the general horizontality of the Prairie house, and the continuous row of the windows themselves, as a unit, provided a horizontal band. Rather than openings, Wright's windows were conceived more as "light" screens—surfaces with ornamentation that continued the surface of the wall. This can be seen in the sumac windows in the Dana House, which continue the sumac mural on the wall (see fig. 71).

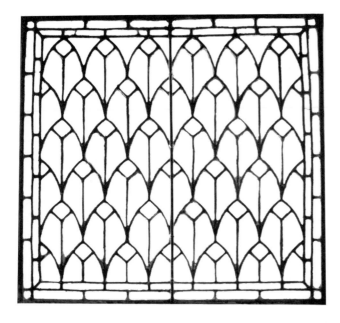

50. Window, Frank Lloyd Wright House, Oak Park, Illinois. 1895. Leaded glass.

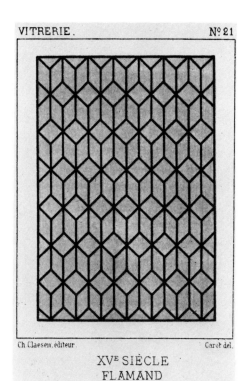

51 (*right*). Plate 21, Vitrerie, from H. Carot, *Kunstverglasungen* (Berlin, 1886). (Collection of Carter Manny, Jr., Chicago) 52 (*below, right*). Plate 72, Vitrerie, *Kunstverglasungen*. 53 (*below, left*). Plate 74, Vitrerie, *Kunstverglasungen*.

Although some windows were conceived as self-contained units in themselves, in some instances the design was carried across a row of windows, seen for the first time in the B. Harley Bradley House in a vertical format (figs. 61 and 62) and in the W. R. Heath House (pl. 9) in a horizontal format, and seen later in the windows for the Francis W. Little House in Wayzata (1913), where a single geometric design continues across eight windows.

Wright's style in art glass changed then from the geometric designs of the Prairie years, most of which remained very symmetrical, to the dramatic, asymmetrical windows seen for the first time in the Thomas Gale House (1909) and subsequently in the Coonley Playhouse windows, where the circle was first introduced, and later in the Midway Gardens and Hollyhock windows.

Rather than imitating the perspective of landscape painting in windows, which was the nineteenth-century practice, Wright designed windows whose patterns acknowledge their flatness of material as glass. Wright wrote:

> The windows usually are provided with characteristic straight line patterns, absolutely in the flat and usually severe. The nature of the glass is taken into account in these designs as is also the metal bar used in their construction, and most of them are treated as metal "grilles" with glass inserted forming a simple rhythmic arrangement of straight lines and squares made as cunning as possible so long as the result is quiet. ("In the Cause of Architecture," March 1908, p. 59)

Long after he had discontinued using art glass, Wright again wrote about his ideas on glass in *The Architectural Record* ("In the Cause of Architecture," 1928). He expressed his dislike of the then-current European art glass, examples of which can be seen in *The International Studio* of the 1890s and the early part of the twentieth century: "Nothing is more annoying to me than any tendency toward realism of form in window-glass, to get mixed up with the view outside. A window pattern should stay severely 'put.' " Wright admired medieval church windows that were pictorial, but glass for the modern building should be "shimmering fabrics—woven of rich glass—patterned in color or stamped to form the metal tracery that is to hold all together to be, in itself, a thing of delicate beauty consistent with slender steel construction expressing the nature of that construction in the mathematics of structure."

The windows in Wright's Prairie houses resulted from the virtuoso skills of able craftsmen. The scheme of the windows throughout the house could be quite complex, as seen in the Dana and Martin Houses, and each window in itself was an intricate design, made up of numerous pieces of glass held together by thin zinc- or copper-plated "leading." Each piece of glass required extremely precise cutting, since the total design had to fit, to the minute fraction of an inch, a specific size of frame. A discussion of how these windows were made is relevant to an appreciation of their beauty.

■

This complex process was described in Arthur Louis Duthie's *Decorative Glass Processes* (New York: D. Van Nostrand, 1908), an account contemporary with a number of Wright's later Prairie windows. The technique of fabricating leaded art glass required the skills of an able craftsman, and the process used in the first decade of the twentieth century was essentially the same as that used by the medieval craftsmen. Instead of using the traditional red-hot iron for cutting the glass, the twentieth-century craftsman used the diamond and the wheel, and he used hydraulic-drawn lead rather than cast lead. Notwithstanding the highly mechanized industries at the time, the process of making leaded glass remained essentially a handicraft, which was revived during the early stages of the Arts and Crafts Movement.

The first step, according to Duthie, was to make a full-sized drawing showing the size of each piece of glass, the lines representing the lead. From the drawing, the glass could be cut to the required shapes. Then the glass was built up into a lead frame, the drawing again serving as a guide. The completed panel then had to be cemented to make it waterproof. The author also described the cutting process and the tools required for cutting. For example, for the cutting of a number of circles, such as were required for the Coonley Playhouse windows, a "circle board" could be used for accuracy. For cutting circles, this was also speedier than cutting by hand, since the machine was able to hold the diamond point with greater steadiness. Straightedges, set squares, and T squares of various sizes were also required for the rectilinear cuts. For pieces of less than three inches, however, Duthie suggested cutting by hand with a paper pattern for the best results. For the numerous elaborate windows of such houses as the Susan Lawrence Dana and Darwin Martin Houses, hundreds of pieces of glass under three inches were required, so that the skills of expert craftsmen were necessary. These windows (like the furniture) also required a combination of machine work and handwork; Wright's geometric design, however, gave the appearance of being entirely made by machine production.

To hold the glass in shape and position while it was on the bench, "laths" of white wood were used. Pencils of French chalk were used to mark the surface of the glass as a guide for cutting and "grozing." In the cutting of very small squares of glass (seen for example in the Martin windows), gauges were necessary to assure the accuracy of the size and angles of the cut pieces. The gauge was held in the right hand, while the straightedge in the left hand was adjusted.

Cutting the glass required great skill, and freehand cutting was recommended as the speediest and most economical for all work where there was no repeated pattern. Allowance had to be made for the leading that separated the pieces of glass, at times to a minute one-sixteenth of an inch. The regularity would affect the neatness and size of the finished window. Pure lead could be used, as it was soft enough to bend easily and was also more likely to withstand the effects of the winter weather in the Chicago area. Wright's windows, however, were usually made with zinc, sometimes copper-plated rather than lead caming, and the term *leading* is used in this catalogue interchangeably with *caming* as a generic description, which refers to any metal used to separate the pieces of glass in the window, whether or not of lead. Wright's zinc leading made a strong, rigid framework and was very appropriate for his simple geometric patterns.

In the designing of windows, both the glass and the leaded part had to be considered. Until the early twentieth century, the lead was regarded as a necessary evil and was kept as small and unobtrusive as possible, used only to define the pattern.

Then lead was considered in itself as an integral part of the design, the dark lines serving as a foil to the glass. Using caming of two or three contrasting widths in one window also became an opportunity in design, and "a style of design thoroughly suited to the nature of the materials and taking full advantage of their opportunities is being evolved," wrote Duthie, an idea that Wright had developed. By varying the thickness of the caming (leading), Wright, working like a graphic artist, could emphasize divisions in the window design. He first did this in the Bradley House (pl. 1), which demonstrates Wright's understanding of the possibilities of the medium of art glass early in his career.

Leaded glass was put together, or "leaded up," by the window flat's being laid on a bench. The working drawing was spread out and "laths" were nailed down along two sides of it. The lead was laid on the bench and the groove was slightly opened on both sides in order to afford easy entrance for the glass. The lead was cut to length and laid against each lath, and then the pieces of glass could be inserted. In the case of a panel of plain squares, seen for example in the Martin window, it was first built up in the vertical direction of the light, working from left to right. As each square was laid in position, it was temporarily fixed by a bench nail placed against the edge of it and driven in by a blow from the loaded handle of the lead knife. As the nails had to be constantly shifted, they had to be easy to withdraw by the fingers without the use of pliers. After the first column of squares had been built up, a length of lead was cut for the vertical line. Then the joints were soldered on one side, the laths were removed, and the panel turned over—in itself a very difficult maneuver. Because the panel was soldered only one one side, it was likely to bend at every lead line. As soon as the second side had been soldered, however, the panel was more rigid. After the application of the cement, the panel was cleaned off and then set aside for a few days to harden.

Duthie refrained from using the term *stained glass* because it conveyed so many different meanings. Technically, all glass that is stained by metallic oxide in the process of manufacture to produce a color is stained glass. In its most general sense, it included many different processes. It was occasionally applied to colored glass and sometimes to glass that was painted with enamels or metallic pigments that were fired in a kiln.

In a discussion of Wright's art glass, another important consideration is an innovation that made his fantasies in glass possible: the casement window. Wright's clients often preferred the double-hung sash windows typical of the period. Yet Wright insisted on the casement window as the only suitable medium for his art glass (a notable exception was the William Winslow House). Wright described his battle against the double-hung window:

> Soon the poetry-crushing characteristics of the guillotine window, which was then firmly rooted, became apparent and, single-handed I waged a determined battle for casements swinging out, although it was necessary to have special hardware made for them as there were none to be had this side of England. Clients would come ready to accept any innovation but "those swinging windows," and when told that they were in the nature of the proposition and that

they must take them or leave the rest, they frequently employed "the other fellow" to give them something "near," with the "practical" windows dear to their hearts. ("In the Cause of Architecture," March 1908, p. 58)

The casement window with simple leaded glass was seen in English houses by such architects as C. F. A. Voysey and Bailley Scott. In this country Robert C. Spencer, Jr., agreed with Wright and argued that the inventive American mind "has strangely failed to note that the casement which swings out would become the ideal and universally popular house window," because this window lent itself to "the beauty of ornamental leading" ("Casements," *House Beautiful*, June 1908, pp. 45, 47).

Wright's most important single window designs were for the Avery Coonley Playhouse (1912; see pp. 111–112). The design of the clerestory windows, contemporary with some of the first European abstract paintings, have affinities with the later paintings of Piet Mondrian. However, Wright's windows were not paintings; they were functional and integral to the structure. Removed from their architectural setting and placed in museum settings or private collections, as indeed all of the Coonley Playhouse windows and many of the Martin windows have been, they lose much of their meaning. The windows are integral ornament and a necessary part of an architectural whole. Stripped of the windows, Wright's Prairie houses lack one of their most beautiful and important components.

In some Prairie houses, the windows vary from room to room, and sometimes, as in the Martin House living room, they vary within the same room. By changing the windows, Wright changed the rooms—the color, the quality and play of light,—each an important consideration. For example, the richly colored "sumac" windows of the Dana dining room screen most of the light out, contributing to the subdued illumination of the room. The screen of windows, with its conventionalized floral motifs, corresponds to the natural landscape outside, and in at least one instance, the W. A. Glassner House of 1905, Wright planned the landscape to be integral with the windows, with trees planted at corresponding intervals.

During his Prairie period Wright often employed beautifully patterned art glass for lighting fixtures and skylights. Although he designed freestanding lamps for his houses, he preferred that the lighting, like the furniture, be integral to the room, "made part of the building, rather than an appliance of an appurtenance, but of the building" ("In the Cause of Architecture," March 1928). The recessed lighting in the ceiling, which had been used earlier by Adler and Sullivan in The Auditorium, corresponded in concept to the built-in furniture. Recessed lighting with art glass was first used in the ceiling of the reception hall of Wright's own studio (1898; see fig. 24) as well as in the dining room ceilings of the Bradley (1900), Willits (1901), and other houses, as well as in the Unity Church. Art glass covering integral lighting became a Wright trademark and was used in most of the Prairie interiors. Leaded art glass windows were also designed for the Midway Gardens, some of the California houses, and for the Imperial Hotel. Beginning with the California houses, however, Wright increasingly used only plate glass, though combinations of clear and ornamental windows were sometimes used in his houses before 1914.

The craftsmen and firms that made Wright's art glass are discussed at the end of this catalogue. Their part in the development of Wright's art glass has been heretofore largely forgotten and ignored. Chief among them were the artisans Orlando Giannini of Giannini & Hilgart and Frank Linden of the Linden Glass Company in Chicago. Documented as being executed by Linden is the glass for the Dana and Martin Houses. In addition, Frank L. Linden, Jr., recalls that the art glass of certain other Wright structures, including the Midway Gardens and the Robie and Coonley Houses, was made by his father's company. Wright came back during a period of time, over and over, to a specific firm with which he was familiar and that he knew could execute his innovative designs, rather than putting the art glass out to bid. Frank Linden, Jr., remembers Wright's coming to his father's studio at 1216 South Michigan and sitting down with the manager, Ernest J. Wagner, to actually work on laying out sample windows. The colored glass was all imported, and bins of it were available for Wright and his artisan to select from.

The brilliance and variety of Wright's art glass windows can be suggested in the color plates. However, seeing the glass in its architectural setting is a moving experience.

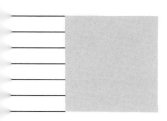

BEGINNINGS: 1887-1900

Elbert Hubbard was almost as picturesque as was Father—they talked arts, crafts and philosophy by the hour.

—JOHN LLOYD WRIGHT,
My Father Who Is on Earth

So Wright summed up his century and went on.

—VINCENT SCULLY, JR.,
American Architecture and Urbanism

Many of Frank Lloyd Wright's earliest principles of architecture and the decorative arts (as expressed in his *Propositions* of 1894) developed from nineteenth-century reform thought, which fed into and culminated in the Arts and Crafts Movement in England and America. This movement was the manifestation of a spirit of renewal in the decorative arts based upon a philosophy or attitude. In its establishment of principles that stressed such virtues as simplicity, propriety, and the honest use of material, Wright found a sympathetic point of view. As H. Allan Brooks has pointed out, the movement also helped to create an artistic environment that made Wright's progressive architecture more acceptable to the client. Wright, however, developed his aesthetic in the context of the capabilities of machine production—a major issue among reformists.

Since a well-documented history of the Arts and Crafts Movement has been written (Gillian Naylor, *The Arts and Crafts Movement*, Cambridge, Mass.: Massachusetts Institute of Technology Press, 1971), it is not necessary to give a history of the movement here. However, a brief survey of some of its sources and concerns regarding a design aesthetic within a social framework, both in England and in America, is necessary to show how Wright would derive certain ideas from the movement and in turn make a substantial contribution to it. The words *arts* and *crafts* were first officially joined in 1888, the year the Arts and Crafts Exhibition Society was founded in London and gave its name to the entire movement. The movement's beginnings can be found, as Edgar Kaufmann, Jr., has pointed out, earlier in the writers of the eighteenth century who were already dealing with concepts of man's right to self-realization through creativity and the expression of form through the honest use of material. The movement began to gain momentum in the early nineteenth century when the promise of utopia through industrialization began to be questioned. Thomas Carlyle, whom Wright admired and quoted, warned of the dangers of the Industrial Revolution and its evil effects. As early as 1829, Carlyle wrote, "Men are grown mechanical in head and heart, as well as in hand. They have lost faith in individual endeavour, and in natural force of any kind" (quoted in Naylor, *The Arts and Crafts Movement*, p. 12).

Another major pioneer reformist was A. Welby Pugin, who in the 1830s and 1840s urged an ethical approach to design based on that Christian faith and spirit that had inspired the great works of the Middle Ages. He developed design principles that became fundamental to the reform of design theory by advocating artistic standards of propriety and the ornamental enrichment of only essential construction. These principles were ascalar and could be applied to all the arts, from the design of a cathedral to that of a wafer box.

The English critic and philosopher John Ruskin made his appraisals within a social framework. He extolled the work ethic, believed fiercely in the dignity of the working class, and pleaded passionately for the right of each workingman to create beauty on his own terms. The development of these doctrines in his chapter "On the Nature of Gothic," published in 1851–1853 in *The Stones of Venice*, formed the basis of the Arts and Crafts Movement and was to lead to the establishment of an aesthetic of individualism. In Ruskin's "The Lamp of Truth," published in 1849 in *Seven Lamps of Architecture*, he was concerned with honesty of expression in material and workmanship:

> For it is not the material, but the absence of human labour, which makes the thing worthless, and a piece of terracotta, or plaster of Paris, which has been wrought by the human hand, is worth all the stone in Carrara cut by machinery. It is, indeed, possible and even usual, for men to sink into machines themselves, so that even hand work has all the character of mechanization.

With London's Great Exhibition at the Crystal Palace in 1851, the criticism aimed at an industrial society came to a climax. Although many thought the exhibition was successful, a growing number of critics saw in the furniture and industrial arts a lack of standards in the excessively elaborate designs. Wood and metal objects had been tortured into unnatural shapes; ornament, applied as a pastiche, was becoming an end in itself rather than an enhancement of design. The question was whether the machine was aiding the production of excessive and imitative designs or was a potential means of producing, more easily, the creative work of the artist.

Among the most influential reformists to follow Carlyle and Ruskin was William Morris, who put their theories to the test in 1862 by establishing an interior design company and workshop in London. The firm initially specialized in ecclesiastical furnishings but soon embraced secular items, such as furniture, fabrics, carpets, tapestries, wallpaper, stained glass, decorated tiles, and metalwork. Morris persuaded friends who were artists, such as the Pre-Raphaelites Dante Gabriel Rossetti and Edward Burne-Jones, to aid in the elevation of the crafts to the fine arts (they painted panels that were inset into the furniture). The idealistic concepts of the Morris firm, based on the spirit rather than an imitation of the Gothic, centered on work of honest craftsmanship and the unification of all the environmental arts rather than only the pictorial arts. This led to a duality in the firm's production of the crafts: works of directness and simplicity as well as richer products that reflected mid-nineteenth-century ornamental thinking.

Morris's design principles, set forth through his lectures and writings, were to form the basis of the Arts and Crafts practice of design. In validating his most fundamental design principle, that of truthfulness, Morris spent the better part of his artistic career learning various craft techniques in order to understand better the potentialities and limitations of the materials with which he worked. He learned to embroider and spent years perfecting his wallpaper and textile patterns, which were hand-printed on wood blocks. He also mastered the art of tapestry, using medieval high-warp techniques, as well as rug weaving and hand tufting.

As a result of his writings and lectures, William Morris became a household name in both England and America. Oscar Lovell Triggs, the champion of Morris in Chicago, evaluated his contribution: "Carlyle announced the doctrine, Ruskin elaborated the system, and Morris gave the first practical example" ("Industrial Art," *The New Industrialism*, Chicago: National League of Industrial Art, 1902, p. 54). Morris's lessons extolling an honest use of materials, simplicity of form, and a return to the principles of organic beauty became very influential on architects in Chicago and craftsmen who were searching for a style more appropriate to modern civilization and who believed in the dignity of each citizen of a democratic republic. Frank Lloyd Wright acknowledged Morris's contribution in 1901: "All artists love and honor William Morris. He did the best in his time for art and will live in history as the great socialist, together with Ruskin, the great moralist . . ."

Morris's prosperous business led him to an increasing awareness of and concern about the exclusiveness of his beautiful handwrought products. Rather than compromise with the perfection of his works, he felt that the system of distribution of goods through profiteering had to change. His philosophy of socialism was based on the ideal of art as redeeming and civilizing man. These socialistic principles were also to travel to Chicago, where Oscar Lovell Triggs was one of the most eloquent defenders of these beliefs. More famous as social reformers were Jane Addams and Ellen Gates Starr, whose Hull House was to become a center for the movement in Chicago. Hull House, on Chicago's West Side, itself was based on Toynbee Hall in London, which Jane Addams had visited before establishing the pioneer social settlement house in 1889.

It was at Hull House that the movement, modeled on the English prototype, was finally institutionalized on October 22, 1897, when the Chicago Arts and Crafts Society was organized. One of the charter members of the society was "F. Wright." Wright's own concern about the decline in craftsmanship and the generally poor quality of design was shared by his fellow members of the society:

At a recent meeting of the Chicago Arts and Crafts Society, a spirited discussion took place as to whether the public taste or the manufacturer's obduracy was most to blame for the shocking commercial furniture in all the large stores, and the fact that it is almost impossible to purchase, for example, a really good chair for a small sum of money. (*House Beautiful*, vol. 3, no. 3, February 1898, p. 103)

■

However, Wright differed from his colleagues in the Arts and Crafts Society in his willingness to abandon the handicraft ideals. What had been a "spirited discussion" with his fellow members of the Arts and Crafts Society soon became a division that resulted in a major split in the membership. This encounter was described by Wright many years later in an article for *The Architectural Record*, "In the Cause of Architecture" (October 1928, p. 217):

> Twenty-seven years ago, under the auspices of Jane Addams, at Hull House, Chicago, an arts and crafts society was formed, and I then wanted to make a study of the Machine as a tool at work in modern materials. I invited Mr. Miller, Mr. Bagley, Mr. Wagner to come to the tentative meeting to represent respectively sheet metal, machined marble work and terra cotta. I wanted them there with us to tell us what we as artists might do to help them. At that time, to put the matter before the proposed society, I wrote (and read) the "Art and Craft of the Machine" since translated into many languages.
>
> It was useless. As I look back upon it, I smile, because the society was made up of cultured, artistic people, encouraged by University of Chicago Professors who were ardent disciples of Ruskin and Morris. What would they want to see, if they could see it in such a programme as mine?

Wright was, of course, referring to his famous speech "The Art and Craft of the Machine" given at Hull House on March 6, 1901. In this lecture, Wright stated his belief that society's workmen and artists had become victims of the machine, which was creating butchered, lifeless forms of the past. The failure, however, according to Wright, was not in the machine but in the desertion of its natural interpreter, the artist.

Wright's departure from his colleagues in the Arts and Crafts Society was suggested in the comment made by Robert C. Spencer, Jr., who described Wright's own house with the "sculptured capitals of the porch . . . the solemn secretary birds have their meaning to the designer who in these caps has enjoyed taking a quiet fling at the reactionary spirits who dominate the 'Arts and Crafts' movement" ("The Work of Frank Lloyd Wright," *The Architectural Record*, June 1900).

One of the University of Chicago professors whom Wright referred to was Oscar Lovell Triggs, whose writings indicate his concern about the machine in an industrialized society. In 1897, he stated, "Among the many subjects claiming the attention of thoughtful minds at the present day none is more importunate than the question of the relation of the machine to our human welfare. We must all agree that this is the age of machinery and organization" ("Arts and Crafts," *Brush and Pencil*, December 1897). In the article, Triggs seems to have come very close to accepting Wright's position advocating use of the machine: "In itself the machine is an object of wonder, one of the special triumphs of the human mind, and worthy of all homage. And it may be that on account of machine-made products we may be obliged to reconstruct our notions of beauty and yield the necessity of having some human content in the product." However, later in the article, Triggs retreats to the position of the handicraft ideals: "The machine products and art products, at least as we now understand them, are as wide as the poles asunder, and there is no possible compromise. . . . But the fact remains that to have beauty in an object the human hand must touch the materials into shape. . . . When a man becomes free he resorts to some form of handiwork."

The division, then, between Wright and the members of the Arts and Crafts Society was in the dispute over whether the machine or handicraft techniques were to be used. Wright wrote in *An Autobiography*: "The Society went 'handicraft' and then soon went defunct" (p. 129). And yet the division was not as wide as the claims of the reactionaries would indicate. The Arts and Crafts Society had stated as one of its aims

> To consider the present state of the factories and the workmen therein, and to devise lines of development which shall retain the machine in so far as it relieves the workman from drudgery and tends to perfect his product; but which shall insist that the machine no longer be allowed to dominate the workman and reduce his production to a mechanical distortion. ("Chicago Arts and Crafts Society," *Hull-House Bulletin*, 1897)

And in the battle within the Arts and Crafts Society, Wright had allies. For example in an article titled "The Machine in Art," in the March 1898 issue of *Brush and Pencil*, Louis H. Gibson, reacting against Triggs's conservative attitude toward the machine, wrote:

> I have a different point of view. I do not see that the machine has anything to do with ugliness. It is but one class of tool. It is the man who makes or directs the machine-tool who is responsible for the ugly product. It is the quality of mind and not the machine which produces the ugliness. The product of the machine is one of the mind. In a brickyard, decorative brick are being made. From the same press there comes beautiful forms and those which are ugly. The man who made the molds is responsible for the beauty or the ugliness.

Wright's championship of the machine in his Hull House speech has been justifiably praised as the strongest statement that had yet been made about the dichotomy between machinery and handicraft. Wright compared the machine to a sphinx, "whose riddle the artist must solve if he would that art live." The solution of the riddle was eloquently stated in Wright's lecture. Wright set out to prove that the machine "was capable of carrying to fruition high ideals in art—higher than the world has yet seen!" Wright not only accepted the machine for the production of works of art, he designed for the machine or at least designed objects that appeared to be amenable to machine production. The key to his designs for machine production was simplicity.

> William Morris pleaded well for simplicity as the basis of all true art. Let us understand the significance to art of that word—SIMPLICITY—for it is vital to the Art of the Machine . . . but the highest form of simplicity is not simple in the sense that the infant intelligence is simple—nor, for that matter, the side of

a barn. . . . Simplicity in art, rightly understood, is a synthetic, positive quality, in which we may see evidence of mind, breadth of scheme, wealth of detail,
and withal a sense of completeness found in a tree or a flower. A work may have
the delicacies of a rare orchid or the staunch fortitude of the oak, and still be
simple. A thing to be simple needs only to be true to itself in organic sense.
("The Art and Craft of the Machine," 1901, quoted in *Frank Lloyd
Wright: Writings and Buildings*, selected by Edgar Kaufmann and Ben Raeburn,
New York: New American Library, 1974, pp. 64–65)

The problem with the machine was that it had been "forced by false ideals to
do violence to this simplicity." Machinery used to imitate wood carving was machinery used for the wrong purpose. But the artist could learn from the machine:

It teaches us that the beauty of wood lies first in its qualities as wood; no
treatment that did not bring out these qualities all the time could be plastic,
and therefore not appropriate—so not beautiful, the machine teaches us, if we
have left it to the machine that certain simple forms and handling are suitable
to bring out the beauty of wood and certain forms are not; that all wood-carv-
ing is apt to be a forcing of the material, an insult to its finer possibilities as a
material having in itself intrinsically artistic properties, of which its beautiful
markings is one, its texture another, its color a third.

The machine, by its wonderful cutting, shaping, smoothing, and repetitive
capacity, has made it possible to so use it without waste that the poor as well as
the rich may enjoy to-day beautiful surface treatments of clean, strong forms
that the branch veneers of Sheraton and Chippendale only hinted at. (*ibid.*, pp.
65–66)

The crux of the Riddle of the Sphinx could be solved by the Artist who would
design for the machine:

Upon this faith in Art as the organic heart quality of the scientific frame of
things, I base a belief that we must look to the artist brain, of all brains, to grasp
the significance to society of this thing we call the Machine, if that brain be not
blinded, gagged, and bound by false tradition, the letter of precedent. For this
thing we call Art is it not as prophetic as a primrose or an oak? Therefore, of
the essence of this thing we call the Machine, which is no more or less than the
principle of organic growth working irresistibly the Will of Life through the
medium of Man. (*ibid.*, p. 71)

Wright's ideal was for the artist to design simple objects that could be made by
the machine. He hoped that the Arts and Crafts Society would be an experimental
station where the artist and the manufacturer would be brought together to work
toward common goals. The attitude of the reformists toward the machine was am-
bivalent—in the beginning, certainly hostile—but this attitude changed as the
movement progressed, and Wright's ideals undoubtedly contributed toward this
change. Although the Chicago Arts and Crafts Society stressed handcraftsmanship,

it also considered the machine, as already mentioned. In their annual exhibition held in conjunction with the Chicago Architectural Club in 1911, rooms of a working-man's dwelling were included to demonstrate "how inexpensively and yet how practically and artistically such a home could be furnished with things made by machinery" ("Chicago Arts and Crafts Society," *American Art Annual*, 1911).

In his friend the English Arts and Crafts leader Charles R. Ashbee, Wright found a colleague who agreed with his philosophy—though with reservations. Ashbee described his meeting with Wright in his own journal, quoting the architect:

"My God," he said, "is Machinery; and the art of the future will be the expression of the individual artist through the thousand powers of the machine,—the machine doing all those things that the individual workman cannot do. The creative artist is the man who controls all this and understands it."

He was surprised to find how much I concurred, but I added the rider that the individuality of the average had to be considered in addition to that of the "artistic creator" himself.

■

In Wright's own house we see many visual reminders of Wright's interest in the Arts and Crafts Movement, which was one of the many sources of his inspiration. Certainly the inglenook in his own living room (fig. 54) represents the spirit of the Arts and Crafts aesthetic, complete with the crafsmanlike motto above the mantel, "TRUTH IS LIFE." (A second motto seen below was added at a later time.)

The 1902 exhibition catalogue of the Chicago Architectural Club (The Art Institute of Chicago) listed a large section of Frank Lloyd Wright's work, which included numerous objects as well as architectural drawings. This catalogue gives credit to some of the early craftsmen and firms who made these objects. This pre-

54. Inglenook, Frank Lloyd Wright House, Oak Park, Illinois. 1899.

ponderance of Wright's objects in an architectural exhibition indicates his concern and that of his contemporaries for the total environment. Included were items as diverse as the furniture made by John Ayers for the Bradley House (Glenlloyd) and the Hickox House in Kankakee; the flower holder, copper lamp, and bowl made by James A. Miller; art glass windows for the Thomas House; and an office chair. The exhibition also included a marble baptismal font for Miss Bryan's private Birdsnest Chapel in Elmhurst made by F. P. Bagley and Co. (Bagley was a client and in the marble business; the present location of this object is unknown, but it was evidently converted into use as a birdbath at an early date); it also included sketches for a model lamp and for model dining table standards made by Giannini and Hilgart for the Husser House.

"Among the decorative things in the Oak Park Studio are some very interesting vessels and flower-holders of sheet copper of Mr. Wright's design, always filled with masses of summer bloom or trophies of autumn fields and woods according to the season" (Robert C. Spencer, Jr., "The Work of Frank Lloyd Wright," *The Architec-*

55 (*below, left*). Pitcher and vase (drawing). 1890–1900. (Copyright © 1977 The Frank Lloyd Wright Foundation, all rights reserved)

56 (*below, right*). Candlestick, repoussé disk, sconce, and urn with two vases (drawing). 1890–1900. (Copyright © 1977 The Frank Lloyd Wright Foundation, all rights reserved)

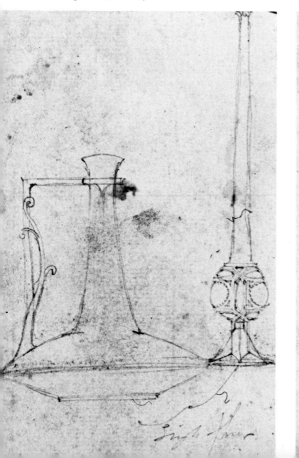
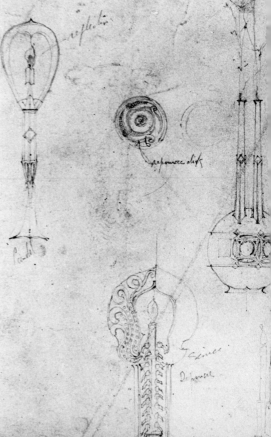

tural Record, June 1900). These copper objects were part of a large group that consisted of vases, urns, candlesticks, and sconces. Only three objects are known to have been produced in copper by James A. Miller; the others are recorded in a collection of drawings in the Taliesin archives, of which three are seen here (figs. 55, 56, 57). These repoussé copper objects were seen frequently in Wright's Prairie houses. Whether Wright commissioned Miller to custom-produce these for the house in which they were to be used, or whether he made them for stock, which would then be available to the client, is not known. In addition to the objects illustrated here, a "skyscraper" vase was also executed and appears in photographs of Wright's 1907 exhibition at The Art Institute of Chicago (see *The Early Work*, pp. 101–103). The present location of this vase is not known.

The drawings in figures 55 and 56 are interesting in the variations on the vase and urn, which were later executed as seen in figures 58 and 59. The scale of each object changes, depending on its placement. For example, the urn, which as executed is rather mammoth, appears quite small at the base of the slender copper vase, which in turn seems quite large. The reverse is seen in the combination of the double vases, which appear to grow out of the urn. The sconces are fascinating objects that are conceived as growing plants. The pitcher in figure 55 is derived from a Near Eastern form. Its rectilinear handle is softened, with the plant entwined around its vertical portion. It is not known whether any of these objects was produced, but they do not appear in photographs.

The copper vase seen in figure 58 was probably designed shortly after 1893, at the start of Wright's independent practice. It appears in a photograph made around 1895 of the octagonal library in Wright's studio (fig. 27) and also as a pair in a photograph in the 1902 exhibition of the Chicago Architectural Club (The Art Institute of Chicago, 1902, #441), (fig. 41), captioned as the "Individual Flower Holder. Made by James A. Miller." According to John Lloyd Wright (*My Father Who Is on Earth*, New York: G. P. Putnam's Sons, 1946, p. 24), his father was "not satisfied with

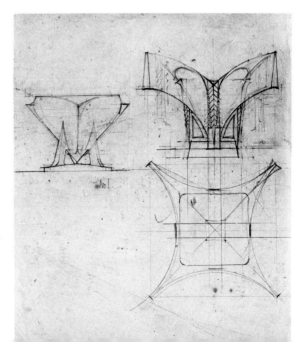

57. Vase No. 1 (elevation) and vase (elevation and plan). 1890–1900. (Copyright © 1977 The Frank Lloyd Wright Foundation, all rights reserved)

the bric-a-brac of the day, so he designed his own. . . . The copper weed-holders pictured to the right and left of the chairs are his early creations. Father liked weeds!" The vase appears in an early photograph of the dining room of the Susan Lawrence Dana House (*The Early Work*, p. 36). It may have been used in the W. E. Martin House, as a descendant of Martin owns an example. Two vases were recently acquired by the Frank Lloyd Wright Home and Studio Foundation, and the vase that was originally in the Oak Park studio is now at Taliesin West. Wright's fondness for the vase continued into the 1950s, as evidenced in a rendering for the Heritage–Henredon furniture (fig. 207) where the vase again appears.

The copper urn in figure 59 is one of a pair made for the Edward C. Waller House in River Forest, which was remodeled by Wright in 1899. It is marked "E. C. Waller" in pencil on the inside of the container. The urns are seen in situ with ferns in the Waller dining room in figure 51 of Hitchcock. An urn was also used in the Waller entrance hall (fig. 60), where it was placed on top of the newel post. Here the circular motifs of the urn were echoed in the circular shapes of the baluster in the

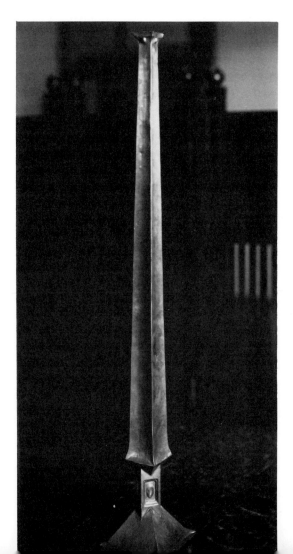

58 (*left*). Weed holder. c. 1890–1900. Copper, 29½" x 4¼" x 4¼" (74.9 cm x 11.4 cm x 11.4 cm). (Lent by Mr. and Mrs. John D. Randall, Williamsville, New York)

59 (*below*). Urn, Edward C. Waller House, River Forest, Illinois. 1899. Copper and galvanized tin, 18½" x 18½" (47 cm x 47 cm). (Lent by Mr. and Mrs. Wilbert R. Hasbrouck, Palos Park, Illinois) 60 (*opposite*). Entrance hall, Edward C. Waller House.

railing of the stair landing. The urn was one of Wright's favorite objects and appears in a number of his interiors. At least six more are known to have been made: two for Browne's Bookstore (one is seen in situ in the photograph on p. 107, *The Early Work*), two for Wright's own studio, and two for the Avery Coonley House (one is seen in situ in fig. 101). A drawing by Wright for the urn is in the collection of the Taliesin archives and is illustrated in *Frank Lloyd Wright Drawings for a Living Architecture* (New York: Horizon Press, 1959), "K. Schneider-/ 352 Southport Ave. Tel- . . ." is inscribed on the back.

According to Hugh Morrison, Kristian Schneider was an artist–craftsman who worked with Sullivan for more than twenty years, modeling almost all the ornament of Sullivan's buildings for execution in iron, terra-cotta, or plaster from the time of The Auditorium in Chicago to the late banks. Schneider's models were then cast by Winslow Brothers. Wright would have known Schneider through his work for Adler and Sullivan. It is not clear, however, what Schneider might have contributed to the production of this urn since the technique employed is that of a rather crude repoussé, with no need of a casting. Perhaps Schneider made the model, which the craftsman later used employing the repoussé technique. One of these urns was

shown in the exhibition of the Chicago Architectural Club in 1902, listed as "*Repoussé* copper bowl. Made by James A. Miller" (see p. 213).

The geometric design, composed of the circle and the square, is repeated on four sides of the urn. The central circle, which echoes the shape of the urn, is enclosed by a square, which in turn is enclosed by a combination of the circle and the square. The cross base is again a variation on the square design, which echoes the square on the side. This geometric object was a complement to Wright's geometric interiors and was prominently placed, either singly or in pairs, usually at eye level or higher. The autumnal color of the copper blended with the prairie color scheme.

As a progressive, Wright was involved with the reforms of the Arts and Crafts Movement, but from there he went on to take these principles further, leaving many of his colleagues behind.

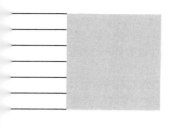

THE NEW SCHOOL OF THE MIDDLE WEST: 1900-1910

By 1900 Frank Lloyd Wright had designed more than fifty houses, and his own distinctive and revolutionary style had evolved, referred to by Robert Spencer as "the new school of the Middle West." Today it is more generally known as the Prairie School—so called because Wright's houses and those of his contemporaries who learned from him were low and flat, and hugged the prairie, the typical midwestern terrain. Wright wrote in 1908:

> We of the Middle West are living on the prairie. The prairie has a beauty of its own and we should recognize and accentuate this natural beauty, its quiet level. Hence, gently sloping roofs, low proportions, quiet sky lines, suppressed heavy-set chimneys, and sheltering overhangs, low terraces and out-reaching walls sequestering private gardens. ("In the Cause of Architecture," March 1908, p. 55)

The two neighboring houses at the south end of Harrison Avenue beside the river in Kankakee, Illinois, built in 1900 for B. Harley Bradley (fig. 61) and his brother-in-law, Warren Hickox, mark the beginning of Wright's Prairie period. The commission was probably secured through Wright's friend Charles E. Roberts, whose wife was Mrs. Bradley's sister. Although the two houses have many common characteristics, the floor plans are different, and the Bradley House, called "Glenlloyd," is larger and more ambitious in terms of its decorative schemes. The low, broad open gables of both houses are dramatic and unusual for the period. Both are similar to Wright's design for a house published in the June 1901 issue of *The Ladies Home Journal*, "A Small House with Lots of Room in It" (illustrated in Hitchcock, pls. 61–63). The Bradley House, with its pronounced cantileverlike gabled roof, suggests a Japanese temple. However, Wright had learned from Japanese prints rather than Japanese architecture what Hitchcock described as "the secret of occult balance which had meant so much to the great European painters Degas and Toulouse-Lautrec."

The plan of the Bradley House is a T, set parallel to the street. The two-story bay gives a vertical accent to the otherwise horizontal house and brings light to the living room and to the master bedroom, which is above. Custom furniture was made to harmonize with the architecture of both houses by John W. Ayers & Co. of Chicago. According to the catalogue of the 1902 Architectural Club Exhibition, a "Hall Table" and "Dining Chairs" from "Glenlloyd" were displayed. The spacious rooms appear to flow into each other because of the wood molding used along the walls. Ayers was probably also responsible for the beautiful and intricate interior wood-work, including an impressive built-in sideboard with leaded-glass windows and lamps for the dining room (fig. 64).

In order to unify the furnishings and the architecture, Wright used similar ma-terials—a fumed oak—for the woodwork, and built-in and freestanding furniture. This is seen in the Bradley living room (fig. 62), where the horizontal molding of the woodwork is repeated in the horizontal molding on the base of the armchair (fig. 63) with a large pillow placed at the back of the chair for comfort, which can be seen in situ to the far right. This five-sided chair also reflects the architecture of the Bradley House—in this case, the floor plan of the bay window area. At least three of these chairs are known to have been made; in addition to the one exhibited here from the collection of The David and Alfred Smart Gallery, two identical chairs are still in the Bradley House, which has now been converted into a restaurant called Yester-year House. Two subordinate areas to each side of the living room contain built-in bookcases.

The living room windows (figs. 61, 62) were also designed to be integral to the architecture. Their design reflects the plan and elevation of the house; the lines of the steep, hipped roof are reflected in the angles of the leading in the window. This design is the most complex and virtuoso of Wright's early windows and is illustrative of his already mature ornamental style in art glass; as mentioned, the design is one of the first to continue over two window sashes from top to bottom separated by the horizontal mullion device. Stylized "tuliplike" flowers were used in the sides of both upper and lower sashes, and double flowers were used in the center of the upper sash, which is stationary, while the lower is a casement window swinging out. The windows also made use of small pieces of clear red and opaque white glass, used very sparingly with the predominantly clear glass in a subtle and harmonious design. The design of the window also suggests a floor plan. The window exhibited, though not illustrated, is from the second floor and is a less ambitious design than that of the living room window seen here.

Although the Bradley House dining room (fig. 64) was a less dramatic space than the well-lighted living room with its projecting bay, it was impressive because of its furnishings, which included a beautiful built-in buffet that extends across the side of an entire wall reminiscent of the Anglo-Japanese sideboard designed by W. E. Godwin. Although the chairs have been dispersed and the table is in storage, the built-in buffet remains in situ, though its leaded-glass windows and lamps have been removed. The side chair seen here (fig. 65) is one of at least six designed by Wright for the dining room and illustrates the sophistication of his early furniture and at-tests to the high quality of craftsmanship of Ayers's shop. The back stiles of the din-ing chair taper in two directions so that, although the design seems simple, it is quite complex. The narrow spaces in the back of the chair isolate a solid plane in the cen-ter and allow space to flow through the back of the chair. In comparison to the "Larkin" side chair (fig. 46), this chair is more refined, with the use of corner blocks and molding being some indication of the skills of a cabinetmaker.

Following soon after the Bradley House was the smaller E. Arthur Davenport House (1901) in River Forest (illustrated in "Global Interior" #9, *Houses by Frank*

61 (*below, right*). B. Harley Bradley House, Kankakee, Illinois. 1900. (Catalogue of the Chicago Architectural Club, 1902) 62 (*above*). Living room, B. Harley Bradley House. (Catalogue of the Chicago Architectural Club, 1902) 63 (*below, left*). Armchair, B. Harley Bradley House. Oak, upholstered seat, 27" x 27½" x 28" (68.5 cm x 69.8 cm x 71.1 cm). (Lent by The David and Alfred Smart Gallery, The University of Chicago, Illinois)

Lloyd Wright 1, edited and photographed by Yukio Futagawa, Tokyo: A.D.A. Edita Co. Ltd., 1975, p. 53). As in the Bradley House, its gabled roof is dramatically extended. It was the first commission of Wright's brief partnership with Webster Tomlinson, which was introduced in a printed announcement dated January 1901 (John Lloyd Wright Collection, Avery Architectural Library, Columbia University, New York). Since this co-partnership was for business purposes only, the design of the Davenport House and its interior is Wright's alone.

Although the house was modest, the pair of spherical andirons (fig. 66) was one of Wright's best and most forceful designs in this form, and in their solid proportions and substantial weight, they contrast with the tall andirons of the Dana House of two years later (see *The Early Work*, p. 82), as well as with the complex fire equipment for some of the later houses. Cast in iron, the andirons project from the small Davenport fireplace onto the hearth, between the two benches that are part of the inglenook (see "Global Interior" #9, p. 54). Because of the smallness of the fireplace, they seem larger in scale when seen in situ, but their shape and extension into the room serve a useful, dual purpose; they not only conveyed the heat from the fireplace, but they also could be used as warm footrests on cold winter nights.

Identical andirons, the present location of which is unknown, were originally in the fireplace of the Bradley House living room (see *The Early Work*, p. 83). Andirons cast from the same mold may have been used in other houses of the period, but they

64 (*below, left*). Dining room, B. Harley Bradley House. (Catalogue of the Chicago Architectural Club, 1902) 65 (*below, right*). Side chair, B. Harley Bradley House. Oak, upholstered seat and back, 45⅜" x 15½" x 18¾" (105.2 cm x 39.4 cm x 47.6 cm). (Lent by Carolynn Mann Brackett, Silver Spring, Maryland)

66 (*left*). Andirons, E. Arthur Davenport House, River Forest, Illinois. 1901. Cast iron, 13" x 13½" x 33" (33 cm x 34.3 cm x 83.8 cm). (Lent by Ellis and Jeanette Fields, River Forest, Illinois)

are not recorded in known publications. Similar andirons were illustrated in the sectional view of the living room for the second *Ladies Home Journal* house (see Hitchcock, pl. 62). A photograph of the Winslow hallway (fig. 14) shows andirons with a similar sphere but without the side supports. They demonstrate Wright's practice of using a similar decorative form that was suitable for a number of interiors of approximately the same date. The rectilinear andirons designed for the Dwight Bank were made by Willy Lau in 1905, but the maker of the Davenport example is unknown.

■

In terms of its extravagant decorative scheme, the Susan Lawrence Dana House in Springfield (fig. 67) was Wright's most important early house. One of his largest architectural commissions to that date, it was completed in 1904 after a two-year building period. In spite of near destruction in 1944, it has survived virtually intact because of the efforts of its present occupant, Charles C. Thomas Publishing Co.

In Susan Lawrence Dana (1862-1946), Wright had found an extraordinary if sometimes eccentric client, who gave him the full power and, apparently, unlimited funds to create a house that would be impressive in any city. Her father was a self-made man who made a fortune in silver and gold mining in Colorado, which he left to his daughter. Mrs. Dana, the social leader of Springfield, was sophisticated and cosmopolitan. She traveled extensively in this country and abroad. For her presentation at the Court of St. James, she commissioned Tiffany's to make a necklace of seventy matching diamonds at a cost of $24,000. Her capricious characteristics seemed to increase with age, and she managed to squander most of her estate during her lifetime. In 1928, without the means for maintenance, she closed the house Wright had designed for her. In her estate, she left safe deposit boxes across the country, which when opened, except for one that contained the deeds to her mining claims, were found to contain only jars of feathers from a favorite parrot.

In *Ausgeführte Bauten*, Wright described the Dana House as "A home designed to accommodate the art collection of its owner and for entertaining extensively, somewhat elaborately worked out in detail." It had an extended cross-shaped plan, set on an open site on a residential street. The house was built around an earlier Lawrence family house, the Victorian study of which was preserved and incorporated into the new building, a unique concession for Wright. The exterior of the Dana House is handsome, but the beautiful, breathtaking interior spaces transport one into another world. One enters through a mysterious arched doorway (fig. 68) of the front vestibule on the Lawrence Avenue side of the house. One can gaze upward toward a ceiling of arched bands of colorful glass windows (fig. 69), which provides the key decorative medium for the house. Through this doorway one also glimpses the terra-cotta statue *The Flower in the Crannied Wall* (fig. 68), designed by Wright and the sculptor Richard Bock and executed by the latter. This fascinating sculpture combines the naturalistic rendering of the female figure, which symbolizes the architect, with the more geometric rendering of the phallic "skyscraper" building she is creating.

The Dana House has amazing spaces created through the existence of several levels. For the first time in Wright's executed work, several rooms are two stories high. To the right of the entrance hall (figs. 70 and 71) the dining room, with its barrel-vaulted ceiling, is one of the most impressive rooms. Its table can be extended to seat forty guests. The tall-backed side chairs with the characteristic slats are similar to those Wright used in his own Oak Park dining room, but here the slats are geometrical cubes, rather than twisted, and descend almost to the floor in a more elegant manner. The Dana dining chairs are of two sizes, the shorter-backed version, according to tradition, intended for women. Illumination is provided by a two-way system of indirect lighting, which runs the length of the room and four "butterfly" lamps, which hang from the ceiling. Strips of dark oak at one-foot intervals articu-

67 (below, left). Susan Lawrence Dana House, Springfield, Illinois. 1903. 68 (below, right). Entrance with statue, The Flower in the Crannied Wall, Susan Lawrence Dana House. 69 (left). Entrance hall, Susan Lawrence Dana House.

70 (opposite). Dining room (perspective), Susan Lawrence Dana House, Springfield, Illinois. 1903. Pencil, pastels, and washes on brown paper, 25" x 20 5/16" (63.5 cm x 51.6 cm). (Avery Architectural Library, Columbia University, New York)

late the shape of the barrel-vaulted ceiling. The walls and the area between the ceiling strips are of sand-finished plaster. A prominent decorative feature is the forty-two-inch-high frieze, which continues around the room at mid-level with a mural decoration of sumac (fig. 71), the major plant motif of the house (see pl. 2), and of fall flowers. According to the *Ausgeführte Bauten* (p. 24), it was painted on a sand-finished background by George Niedecken. A preliminary study for this mural is in the John Lloyd Wright Collection, Avery Architectural Library, Columbia University, New York. In describing this drawing in 1908 Wright wrote: "To avoid distortion in rendering, the side has been shown cut away. The decorative frieze around the room is treated with the Sumac, Golden Rod and Purple Aster that characterize our roadsides in September" (Frank Lloyd Wright, "In the Cause of Architecture," March 1908, p. 109).

The room is important for us today because it remains virtually intact; seeing the harmonious earth color scheme of the prairie, one can experience the rare and great organic beauty of an early Wright interior, as designed. Black-and-white photographs can hardly convey the rich color tones and space of such a room.

An elaborate system of ornamental glass of exceptional craftsmanship and breathtaking beauty, seen in the Dana House windows (pls. 3, 5, 6, 7), ceiling, furniture, partitions, and freestanding and a hanging lamp (pl. 4), repeats the spaces of the Dana interior. Ornamented windows were used on two levels to articulate the space of the dining room (fig. 71). The window in plate 3 is identical to the leaded-glass windows used in the breakfast area of the dining room. It is one of the

"extra" windows, which, according to Wesley Peters, Wright habitually ordered for his houses in case of damage to any art glass. These "extra" windows could also be used for exhibitions. (One of the Dana windows was seen in the exhibition of Wright's work at the Art Institute in 1907.) Wright gave this window to the sculptor Richard Bock, who was responsible for executing the sculpture in the Dana House. Typically the design is based on a plant form—in this instance the sumac—which has been conventionalized into an abstract form, in contrast with the sumac used in the mural, which was treated naturalistically. The amber and green colors are particularly rich and harmonize with the autumnal colors used in the dining room.

Wright described his use of a single motif in a house to achieve unity:

> The differentiation of a single, certain simple form characterizes the expression of one building. Quite a different form may serve for another, but from one basic idea all the formal elements of design are in each case derived and held well together in scale and character. . . . its grammar may be deduced from some plant form that has appealed to me, as certain properties in line and form of the sumac were used in the Lawrence house in Springfield; but in every case the motif is adhered to throughout so that it is not too much to say that each building aesthetically is cut from one piece of goods and consistently hangs together with an integrity impossible otherwise. ("In the Cause of Architecture," March 1908, p. 59)

Compared with a window of the Martin House (pl. 8), those of the Dana dining room have an intense movement that was achieved by the addition of short vertical chevrons of colored glass on the leaves of the conventionalized plant. While the "stems" of the "plants" in the Martin windows are composed of three vertical lines each, the Dana "stems" are of six lines each, contributing to the complexity of the designs. Wright's drawing for the sumac windows (fig. 72) shows one centralized flower, while the window as executed is a double flower. In the drawing, the flower is more naturalistically drawn than as executed in the window.

According to an advertisement in *The Architectural Record* (March 1908, advertising section), all the Dana glass, including the lamps, was made by the Linden Glass Co. of Chicago (see p. 209).

This hanging lamp (pl. 4) is identical to the four designed for the Dana dining room, which are seen in situ in the rendering (fig. 70) and photograph of that room (fig. 71). The drawing indicates the complexity of the design, where numerous planes and angles form an abstracted "butterfly." Identified by Wright as "butterfly" lamps, these hanging lamps were used by other Prairie School architects, though the Dana example seems to be the first use of this unique form. The elevation drawing of half of the shade indicates the intense colors—orange, yellow, red, and green—as well as the type of glass—sandblasted, clear, colored, and iridescent. To the right of the half elevation are sketches, probably in Wright's hand, of the lamp in plan from above and below, as well as an indication of its placement in the Dana dining room. This lamp was an extra, which Wright apparently gave the sculptor Richard Bock. When acquired by Greenville College, it was in pieces but has now been carefully restored.

■

It is not surprising that the house designed for Mr. and Mrs. Francis W. Little in Peoria (fig. 74) has many furnishings that are similar to those of the Dana House since they were built at about the same time. The Littles commissioned their first Wright house, located at 1505 Moss Avenue in Peoria, Illinois, in 1902. In 1908 Little joined the Federal Reserve Banking System as a vice-president of the Minnesota Trust Company, which led to his commissioning Wright to design a second house for him (fig. 115) in Wayzata, Minnesota, a suburb of Minneapolis.

When the Littles moved to Wayzata, they took some of the furniture from their Peoria house with them; consequently it was used side by side with the furniture designed for their new house. Some of the furniture left in the Peoria house remains

71 (*right*). Dining room, Susan Lawrence Dana House, Springfield, Illinois. 1903. 72 (*below, left*). Window (drawing), Susan Lawrence Dana House. (Copyright © 1977 The Frank Lloyd Wright Foundation, all rights reserved) 73 (*right, below*). Hanging lamp (elevation), Susan Lawrence Dana House. (Copyright © 1977 The Frank Lloyd Wright Foundation, all rights reserved)

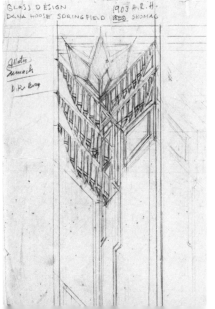

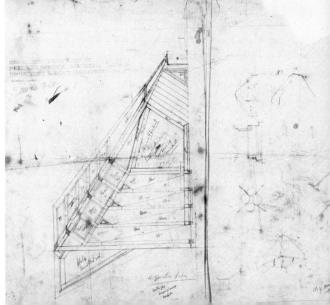

there today, including an armchair, similar to the Bradley chair (fig. 63), which incorporates slats instead of panels; beds; a side chair similar to the Bradley dining chairs; a library table; and an armchair with a reclining back. The remaining Peoria furniture was acquired by The Metropolitan Museum of Art when it purchased the rooms from the Littles' Wayzata house.

A considerable number of pieces of the Littles' Peoria furniture have survived, including an intriguing print table (fig. 75). At least three more of these tables are known to have been made; one that is now owned privately and was used in Wright's Oak Park house, and two made for the Susan Lawrence Dana House (one of which is seen in situ in the gallery, illustrated in *The Early Work*, p. 43). This unusual gateleg table was designed specifically for the viewing of Japanese prints, since the top was hinged in the middle so that half of it could rest against a wall in a vertical position, or both sides of the top could be folded upright in the center and lowered into the fitted middle section of the table itself for storage. Prints could also be viewed on the flat tabletop, which could also function as a table or a desk. The gatelegs could fold in on both sides for compactness. This concern for efficiency anticipated some of Wright's later furniture designs.

When the gatelegs are open, as seen here, the table resembles, in form, the typical square table, with the vertical slats enframed on two sides, that Wright used in a number of examples of his early furniture (see *The Early Work*, p. 38). The tall vertical supporting piers, which anticipate the standards for the Martin, Boynton, and Robie dining tables, are articulated by means of thin horizontal moldings spaced evenly, one at the center, one near the base, and a double row at the top. Middle and lower moldings continue the horizontal line of the moldings above and below the slats, visually unifying the standards with the table. A rectangular "capital" and base define the bottom and top of the standard, and there is an "either end up" aesthetic that was characteristic of furniture of the aesthetic movement (see Marilynn Johnson Bordes's discussion in *19th-Century America: Furniture and Other Decorative Arts*, introduction by Berry Tracy, furniture texts by Marilynn Johnson Bordes, New York: The Metropolitan Museum of Art, 1970, cat. nos. 209–211).

This same aesthetic was characteristic of the built-in buffet and post designed for the Little dining room, a drawing of which is seen here in front and side eleva-

tion, in plan, and in section (fig. 76). The proportions and form are surprisingly similar to those of the print table. The lamp posts in the sideboard stand vertically in the manner of the piers for the print table. The idea of incorporating lamps into a buffet was not new, as Wright also designed lamps for the buffet in the Bradley House (see fig. 64), and these two buffets show similarities in form. For the Coonley desk (1907; fig. 103), Wright used lamps with shades. The Coonley desk is similar in proportions to both Little pieces shown here, with the tall verticals contrasting with the horizontal, cantileverlike top. The mammoth sideboard–buffet designed for the E. E. Boynton House in Rochester, New York (1908), represents the culmination of Wright's designs in this form; it incorporates elaborate leaded-glass windows and a lighting system.

■

Although Wright's residential commissions occupied most of his time, these were interspersed with several commercial commissions. The most important dur-

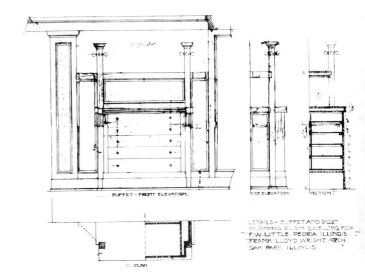

74 (opposite). Francis W. Little House, Peoria, Illinois. 1903. 75 (right). Print table, Francis W. Little House. Oak, 45⅜" x 37⅜" x 44 1/16" (115.2 cm x 95 cm x 112 cm), closed. (Lent by The Metropolitan Museum of Art, New York; Purchase, Emily C. Chadbourne Bequest, 1972) 76 (above, right). Buffet and post, dining room (elevation, plan, and section), Francis W. Little House. Pencil and colored pencil on paper, 19½" x 22" (49.5 cm x 55.8 cm). (Lent by The Metropolitan Museum of Art, New York; Emily C. Chadbourne Estate, 1972)

ing this early period was the Larkin Administration Building of 1904 in Buffalo, New York (fig. 77), which was distinguished for its furnishings as well as its architecture. This tall brick structure, which was demolished in 1949–1950, served as the administrative offices of the Larkin Company's large mail-order house, which sold the company's soap products. The building was among a large group of factories adjacent to the New York Central Railroad and, because of the smoke, noise, and dirt of the area, was designed to be isolated from its environment. Fresh air was taken in high above ground in shafts extending above the roof surface. The design of the building and its furnishings was based on utilitarian considerations of efficiency. Because its heating and ventilating systems and stairways were placed outside the building in the four corners, the inner area (fig. 78) was free for working spaces. The magnificent central court rose the full height of the five-story building and was lit by a skylight, creating what Vincent Scully termed "an industrial cathedral that should have delighted Viollet le Duc." The main floors were galleries that opened to this court, with windows placed high so that the view outside would be upward. Boxes were provided for growing plants and flowers, creating a pleasant and cheerful environment for the Larkin employees. The solid geometric severity of the exterior was protective, and the interior was light, healthful, and well ventilated. Flexibility was provided in the open planned office area. The space beneath the windows of each story was used for built-in steel filing cabinets, among the earliest vertical file systems (see fig. 84). The metal vertical files and furniture as well as all the interior furnishings were custom-designed by Wright for the building. Wastebaskets were designed but not executed, and a drawing in the Taliesin archives indicates that desk equipment was designed, including lamps, "telephone travellers," and rubber-stamp holders (apparently none was executed). In *An Autobiography* Wright described some of the many innovations:

> All the furniture was made in steel and built into place . . . Magnesite was a new material then. We experimented with it—and finally used it—throughout the interior. And I made many new inventions. The hanging partition. The automatic chair-desk. The wall water closet were several among them. All were intended to simplify cleaning and make operation easy. (p. 152)

Floor and trimmings were of Magnesite of the same color as the desk tops, expressing the ideal of architectural continuity and unity. The cream color of the interior brick created a subtle harmony. The fifth floor was a restaurant for employees, with a conservatory in the mezzanine over a kitchen and bakery at either end (fig. 79).

Wright claimed that the Larkin furniture was the first metal office furniture; it was the first to express the nature of its material. Metal furniture was quite common in the nineteenth century, but it was rarely used for office furniture until the turn of the century. In the 1896 catalogue of the A. H. Andrews Company of Chicago (*Furniture and Fittings*), quarter-sawed oak "curtain" desks were the most popular item. However, the "Andrews Metal Chair" was a specialty of the firm, and various forms of this steel-rod office furniture were offered, many with adjustable backs and seats. After 1900 more firms began to include metal furniture in their lines of office furniture. For the Larkin Company's metal office furniture (figs. 80–82), Wright went to the Van Dorn Iron Works Company of Cleveland, Ohio, a firm that specialized in metallic vault and office furniture and fixtures. A drawing in the Taliesin archives (0403.26) for a "Continuous Desk Interchangeable Fittings" for the Larkin Building bears the note "Made by Van Doren [*sic*] Co., Cleveland FLW." These custom desks had drawers of various sizes designed to provide space for specific forms and papers. A blueprint at Taliesin for a "special steel office chair" also has the note "The Van Dorn Iron Works Co. Cleveland." The Van Dorn catalogue of around 1900 claimed that

work can be enameled in any color to suit the taste of the purchaser, and the trimmings can be finished in oxidized copper, nickel plate, or antique brass. In the construction of our metallic furniture we use only the best pickled and cold rolled sheet steel, which is thoroughly cleaned before enameling, and we guarantee our enameling to not scale off or crack. If you have drawings of any metallic furniture wanted, forward them to us and we will quote you prices, or

77 (*bottom, left*). Larkin Company Administration Building, Buffalo, New York. 1904 (razed 1949–1950). 78 (*below, right*). Interior court, Larkin Company Administration Building. 79 (*below, left*). Fifth floor, Larkin Company Administration Building.

forward us a pencil sketch of such an arrangement as would suit your requirements with sizes of books and papers, and we will prepare drawings, specifications and submit propositions for the work. We respectfully solicit your
correspondence for further information. (*Metallic Vault and Office Furniture
and Fixtures Manufactured by The Van Dorn Iron Works Company, Cleveland,
Ohio,* Chicago Historical Society collection, n.d.)

Some of the working drawings for the Larkin Company furniture are dated March,
April, June, and October 1906, so the furniture can be more accurately dated to that
year.

Three variations of the metal office chair are seen in photographs of the Larkin
Building interiors: the armchair seen here (fig. 81) with a central pedestal base and
four flanking supports, a double one in the back, and two in the front. The study at
Taliesin for the chair (fig. 83) shows Wright's intention more clearly. The arms and
legs form a continuous line around the back—a forerunner of the tubular steel furniture designs of Marcel Breuer and Ludwig Mies van der Rohe almost two decades
later. The chair as executed (fig. 80) was more rectilinear than the drawing indicates.
The adjustable back in both versions of the Larkin armchair is perforated—in a geometric design much favored by the Vienna Secessionists (see Otto Wagner's chairs
for the Vienna Postal Savings Bank Building of 1904–1906). This gave comfort to the
sitter as well as visual interest to the back of the chair. Similar perforated backs
were also used in chairs designed by Charles Rennie Mackintosh (see armchairs for
the Board Room of the Glasgow School of Art, 1900, Filippo Alison, *Charles Rennie
Mackintosh as a Designer of Chairs,* Milan: G. Milani, 1973; Eng. ed. 1974, p. 39).
Similar rectilinear supports of four columns are seen in a design for chairs for a
Friseurladen by H. Stubner (*Das Interieur III,* Wien: Verlag von Anton Schroll,
1902, p. 67). The third Larkin metal chair was attached to the desk (fig. 82)—an innovation that was in keeping with the overall concern for efficiency of the

80. Office, Larkin Company Administration Building, Buffalo, New York. 1904.

building. The attached chairs would automatically fold in, so no furniture had to be moved when the office floors were cleaned—a not-insignificant consideration in the cleaning of an office of many desks and chairs. The seats of the chairs either were upholstered in leather (fig. 80) or were of wood (fig. 81). Furniture entirely of wood was also designed for the Larkin Building, and the chairs with the back made of a solid wooden splat that extends from the stretcher to the crest are seen in situ in a Larkin office (fig. 84). This wooden chair was also used in the Larkin restaurant, and although a number of these were used in Frank Lloyd Wright's own house (see fig. 46), the chair may have been designed for the Larkin Building first. The Larkin chair

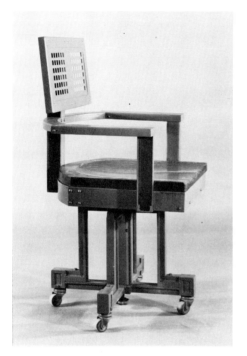

81 (above, left). Armchair, Larkin Company Administration Building, Buffalo, New York. 1904. Painted steel, oak seat, 37½" x 24 11/16" x 21⅛" (95.2 cm x 62.7 cm x 53.6 cm). (Lent by The Museum of Modern Art, New York) 82 (above, right). Desk and chair, Larkin Company Administration Building. 83 (right). Armchair (drawing), Larkin Company Administration Building. Pencil on paper. (Copyright © 1977 The Frank Lloyd Wright Foundation, all rights reserved)

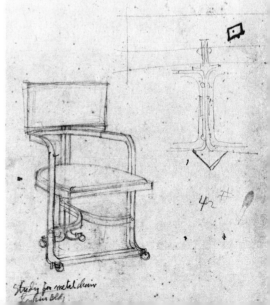

seen here, however, differs from the ones in Wright's house in that its solid back extends much higher above the crest rail and the seat lacks the rectangular terminals
seen on the Oak Park chair.

The Larkin Building was a building of many "firsts," one of which was the
wall-hung water closet (fig. 85), a convention common today but designed first for
the Larkin Building to facilitate cleaning. The architect's son described the
invention:

> He found a way to cantilever the bowl from the cast-iron soil pipe in the wall
> behind. The underside of the bowl was then clear of the floor for better sanita-
> tion. Every time I see a porter swinging his mop under one of these closets, I
> wonder why Dad didn't patent the idea. He would not patent any of his many
> inventions. (John Lloyd Wright, *My Father Who Is on Earth*, New York: G. P.
> Putnam's Sons, 1946, p. 134)

Ornament was used sparingly in the Larkin Building—as capitals for the tall
piers of the interior court (fig. 78) and on the exterior piers at the side of the building
(fig. 87), for which the ornament in figure 86 was designed. It is the original plaster
model for the terra-cotta that was presumably destroyed with the building. This
model was kept by the sculptor Richard Bock, who was in charge of creating the
sculptural ornament on the front of the building as well as executing the ornament
designed by Wright for the building. A highly conventionalized floral pattern is the
basis of the design here. It is related to the ornament of Unity Temple a year later
(see *The Early Work*, pp. 12–13).

■

Wright's second major commission in Buffalo was for a residence: the Darwin
D. Martin House of 1904 (fig. 88). As with the Dana House, Wright had a great op-

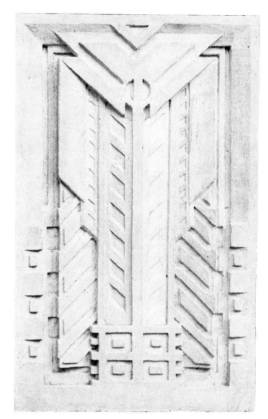

84 (*opposite*). Office, Larkin Company Administration Building, Buffalo, New York. 1904. 85 (*above*). Water closet, Larkin Company Administration Building. (*The House Beautiful*, April 1908) 86 (*above, right*). Model for ornamental relief made by Richard W. Bock, Larkin Company Administration Building. Plaster, 17¾" x 11⅜" x 1⅜" (45.1 cm x 28.9 cm x 3.5 cm). (Lent by Greenville College, Illinois; The Richard W. Bock Sculpture Collection) 87 (*below*). Larkin Company Administration Building.

portunity to design all the furnishings of a house with no strict limit on expenditures. With the exception of rugs, all interior details—windows, lighting fixtures, lamps, and furniture—were designed by the architect, who was also consulted on the choice of Japanese prints and ceramics. Wright had designed a house for William E. Martin in 1902 in Chicago, and it was through his brother's enthusiasm that Darwin Martin came to Wright. Darwin Martin was vice-president of the Larkin Company, which was founded by John Larkin and Elbert Hubbard. The officers of the company were related by several marriages. W. B. Heath, for whom Wright also designed a house, was the attorney for the Larkin Company and married to Elbert Hubbard's sister. When Hubbard retired from the company in 1895, to establish the Roycroft Community in nearby East Aurora, he was succeeded by Darwin Martin.

88 (below) and 89 (left). Darwin D. Martin House, Buffalo, New York. 1904.

The Martin House complex on the Jewett Parkway included the small house designed for George Barton, Darwin Martin's brother-in-law. A greenhouse and a garage were shared by both houses. The plan of the Martin House is impressive. Built on a long axis that was parallel to Jewett Parkway, it has an open porte cochere at one end and an open porch outside the living room at the other end. The large dining and living room areas form the T of the plan and were an immense interior space. Beneath lower and upper eaves on the front and rear are continuous rows of windows—both clear and ornamental—separated by brick mullions. Two wide chimneys break the line of the hip roof. The amazing concrete birdhouse (fig. 90) seen in situ in figure 89 corresponds in its form to the table seen in figure 93. The rows of squares, as we have noted, were a favorite motif of Wright's.

In the *Ausgeführte Bauten,* Wright described the interior with its groups of freestanding piers, which contained the radiators and the lighting fixtures. Outward-swinging bookcases were placed between the piers (see fig. 34), and the open spaces above were used as cabinets, from which the heat could pass into the rooms. The brick walls and reinforced-concrete floors made the house fireproof. The interior brick with bronze joints was used in a decorative sense as a mosaic. The woodwork throughout was a fumed white oak.

The execution of the elaborate interior of the Darwin D. Martin House (fig. 91) is well documented. Not only are there original Wright drawings for some of the furniture (see figs. 95 and 96), but there is also a letter book kept by O. S. Lang, contractor and builder of the house, which contains correspondence from May 9 through November 1, 1905, pertaining to the construction of the house (Frank Lloyd Wright Collection, the University Archives, State University of New York at Buffalo; Gifts of Darwin R. Martin and Dorothy Martin Foster, cat. nos. 1–35). Lang, a local contractor (170 Norwalk Avenue, Buffalo), could well have been recommended to Wright by Darwin D. Martin. The correspondence reveals Lang to be an extremely patient person, who had the responsibility of coordinating all the details of the various trades involved in creating a large house with lavish interiors, in which almost all the furnishings were custom-made. Lang's responsibilities included more than what we today think of as those of a building contractor; they also included the responsibilities of an interior designer. These duties for the Coonley and Robie Houses were turned over to an interior design firm in Milwaukee: the Niedecken–Walbridge Co. George Niedecken's profession—that of interior designer— was relatively new at the time. Lang's responsibilities included the interior and exterior; this *total* architectural responsibility was more in keeping with Wright's ideal, but it may have been too much for one person for the Coonley and Robie Houses.

Numerous letters from Lang to Wright and the various contractors involved in executing interior furnishings show that Matthews Bros. Manufacturing Co. of Milwaukee, Wisconsin, was responsible for almost all the interior trim, the furniture, and the cabinetwork. The trim was cut to order in Milwaukee and shipped to Buffalo, where it was installed by either Lang's or Matthews's men on the job. In one letter, Lang asked Matthews to send a sample chair to Mr. Martin, and this seems to have been the usual method of "testing" the furniture designs, a practice that must have been expensive and not necessarily common for other Wright houses. The correspondence also indicated that Wright made a number of changes as the building

90 (*left*). Birdhouse, Darwin D. Martin House, Buffalo, New York. 1904.

91 (*below*). Living room, Darwin D. Martin House.

progressed. A letter to Matthews of June 20, 1905, reveals that Wright decided to put fumed-oak trim on the front veranda ceiling, a change in what was specified. Wright also closely supervised the entire construction of the house in minute detail, both exterior and interior. This illustrates that while Wright was concerned with the total unity, he was also interested in each minute detail. For example, on June 21, 1905, Lang wrote Wright asking him if he would approve of using a cement base on the pergola piers instead of carrying down the brick piers. And on June 21, 1905, Lang wrote to Wright asking him to approve or disapprove the detail for the kitchen sink arrangement. A letter of September 12, 1905, to Wright asked him whether plate glass (as shown on the drawing) or art glass was to be used at the sides of the front vestibule doors. Wright responded almost immediately via his secretary, Isabel Roberts, that the windows should be plate glass as marked on the detail.

Interestingly enough, these interchanges, which today might take several days or more by mail, were then carried out so efficiently, mail could be sent and received in a single day.

A letter of July 10 to Matthews requested a quart can of the mahogany stain so that Lang could match the stain of the fumed-oak trim; therefore one

92 (*below, left*). Armchair, Darwin D. Martin House, Buffalo, New York. 1904. Oak, upholstered seat, 32" x 23" x 23" (81.3 cm x 58.4 cm x 58.4 cm). (Lent by Albright–Knox Art Gallery, Buffalo, New York; Gift of Darwin R. Martin) 93 (*below, right*). Table, Darwin D. Martin House. Oak, 26¼" x 27" x 27" (66.7 cm x 68.6 cm x 68.6 cm). (Lent by Albright–Knox Art Gallery, Buffalo, New York; Gift of Darwin R. Martin)

can conclude that the trim was sent from Matthews in a finished state. On August 22, Lang wrote Darwin Martin notifying him that Matthews had worked eleven weeks thus far on cabinetwork in the house, indicating that Matthews's craftsmen or carpenters probably came to Buffalo to install some of the more complex cabinetwork rather than the trim or the freestanding furniture. (Paul Warnecke of Matthews signed the work sheets for Matthews, and it was by the job rather than on contract.) Since Matthews was also responsible for the window sash, they furnished Linden Glass Co. of Chicago with the size of the windows in which the art glass would be set. On October 3, Lang wrote Matthews about the furniture: "How are you getting along with the furniture for house? Mr. Wright says he has given you details for same: As Mr. Martin will move Nov 1st. they are anxious about above. You no doubt understand that all upholstering will be done in Buffalo." And on November 1, Lang wrote Matthews about the wardrobe in bedroom no. 1, as they wanted the men to set it before they completed the job.

The Lang letter book also reveals the identity of the other manufactur-

94. First-floor furniture arrangement (plan), Darwin D. Martin House, Buffalo, New York. 1904. Pencil on paper, 23⅞" x 25⅜" (60.7 cm x 64.5 cm). (Lent by University Archives, State University of New York at Buffalo)

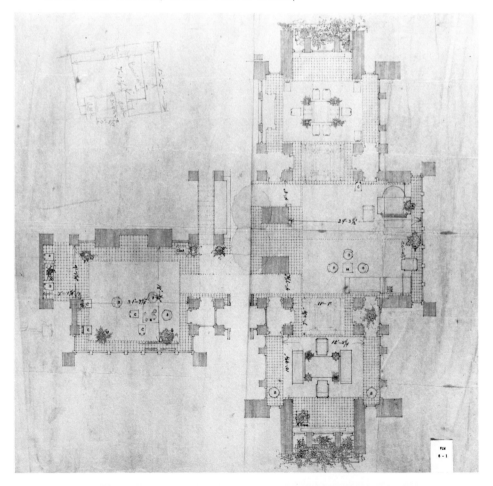

ers/craftsmen. Wright's characteristic monolithic floor was supplied by the American Monolith Co. of Milwaukee, Wisconsin; these floors were continuous and helped give the room its unity and harmony. The very beautiful glass mosaic fireplace in the Martin House living room was executed by Giannini and Hilgart of Chicago. In a letter of September 12, Lang wrote to Wright saying that he had sent Giannini a detail with measurements marked on it and that Wright should see about it. Giannini evidently was slow in getting the mosaic fireplace executed, as Lang had to remind him twice that they were ready to install it. The mosaic as executed was quite beautiful, as photographs indicate. However, only a few pieces of glass mosaic survive. The wisteria mosaic, in the manner of Tiffany, is quite different from the geometric design that Wright had submitted. Its flowing lines and softness were a contrast to the otherwise rectilinear room, but Wright undoubtedly approved it. Giannini was also responsible for the glass to go over the Martin sideboard.

The correspondence indicates that all the art glass was supplied by the Linden Glass Co. of Chicago. Frank Linden must have been very pleased to receive Lang's letter of September 24 placing an additional order and praising the glass: "Your glass has many compliments. It is beautiful," a remark that indicates Lang's aesthetic appreciation for the house he was building. The clear plate glass, which was used between art glass windows, was furnished by the Pittsburgh Plate Glass Co. The only work given to John W. Ayers in Chicago was the trim for the pergola.

In its introduction of circular and semicircular forms, the armchair in figure 92 marks a notable departure from Wright's severely rectilinear furniture of the prairie years. A chair of a similar form, though different in detail, was designed by the German architect Leopold Bauer and was published in *Das Interieur* (1900, p. 171) (fig. 49). The Martin chair differs from Wright's other early furniture in its craftsmanship, which is further refined. The joinings of the wood are extremely tight; the outwardly flared crest rail is made of six sections of wood, layered horizontally and joined so tightly that the joints are almost invisible. The flared crest and curved incline of the arms are designed for comfort—very different from the usual rectilinear back and arms. However, the splats extending from the base to the crest are characteristic of the early furniture. Another fine detail is the circular seat. The bowed support under the seat indicates that it originally was crowned below as above, so that the appearance was that of a suspended disk. The original upholstery was probably of dark brown or black leather, since fragments of this were found underneath the chair.

The drawing for this armchair (fig. 96) shows it in elevation and plan. A drawing of the plan of the furniture arrangement (fig. 94) indicates that three of these chairs were to be used in the living room, three in the dining room, and two in the library.

According to Edgar Tafel, Wright's interest in this chair was revived when he visited the Martin House in 1936. Versions of the chair were used at Taliesin North and at Wingspread, the Herbert F. Johnson House in Racine, Wisconsin.

The extraordinary table seen in figure 93 equals the Martin armchair in its fine quality of craftsmanship and design. Framed by molded supports, the cantilevered shelves appear to float and echo the cantilevered roofs of the exterior of the house. This table is apparently unique to the Martin House. As is the armchair, it is on ball-bearing casters for ease of movement and was also made by the Matthews firm.

As in the Dana House, the windows for the Martin House formed an important part of the decorative and architectural scheme. Several designs were created, the most dramatic being the so-called Tree of Life window (pl. 8), the design for which was based on three conventionalized flowers with seven leaves or branches each. The majority of the glass of this window is clear, separated by both zinc and copper caming of varying thicknesses. Small facets of colored and iridescent glass have been inserted that change color with the light source. As are the windows in the W. A. Glassner House in Glencoe, Illinois, it is iridescent only on the side with the greatest amount of light, that is, outside during the day and inside at night. The Tree of Life window was used in the upstairs rooms and in the reception area. For the living–dining–library area, geometric windows (without conventionalized flowers) flanking clear plate glass windows were used. Geometric windows were used in the study.

In addition to the Lang ledger, drawings for the Martin furniture designed by Wright provided additional documentation for the furnishings. A number of drawings are now in the University Archives of the State University of New York at Buffalo, from which three are illustrated here (figs. 94, 95, and 96). Additional drawings are in the collection of Darwin R. Martin. Characterized by their delicacy, these light pencil drawings show the furniture in elevation and plan.

The plan for the placement of furniture in the first floor of the Martin House

95. Dining room table and chairs (elevation and plan), Darwin D. Martin House, Buffalo, New York. 1904. Pencil on paper, 23⅞" x 25⅝" (60.6 cm x 64.5 cm). (Lent by University Archives, State University of New York at Buffalo)

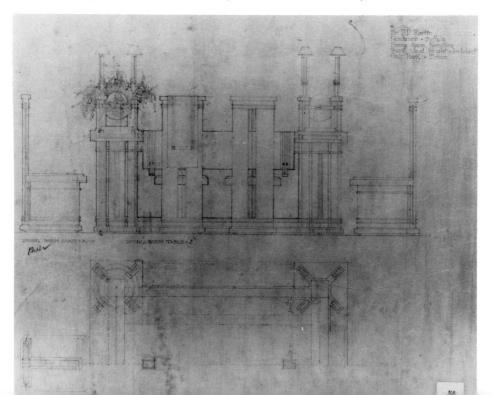

(fig. 94) is an indication of Wright's meticulous consideration of every aspect of the interior space within the framework of his overriding concept of the whole. In the living area, one table is even set for tea! As evidenced in photographs and surviving pieces, most of the furniture was executed and placed as shown in the plan. The tall clock, shown here in the living area rather than on the stair landing, where it now is located, is one of three known examples designed by Wright. A number of the numerous plant stands shown in the plan survive in the house today.

Wright's drawing for the Martin dining table (fig. 95) indicates that the original design incorporated light standards, which, according to Martin's daughter, Dorothy Martin Foster, were executed but removed because they were an impediment to serving. A fragment of one of these standards remains in the Martin House. Wright's drawing for the Martin dining table is important because it is the only record of the Martin dining table as originally conceived. Foliage and flowers intended for all standards were drawn for the left example and were indicated but not drawn for the right standard. Two small lamps for each standard are indicated on the drawing rather than the single lamps used in the Boynton and Robie standards. According to Mrs. Foster, the heat from the lamps killed any foliage placed in the containers underneath. This table with four standards (and the earlier Husser dining table of about 1899) served as the prototypes for later dining ensembles, such as for the W. E. Boynton House (1908) in Rochester, New York, and culminating with the Robie dining room table and standards (fig. 107). Table and chair scarves

96. Living room couch, table, chairs, and stand (elevation and plan), Darwin D. Martin House, Buffalo, New York. 1904. Pencil on paper, 23⅞" x 25⅜" (60.6 cm x 64.5 cm). (Lent by University Archives, State University of New York at Buffalo)

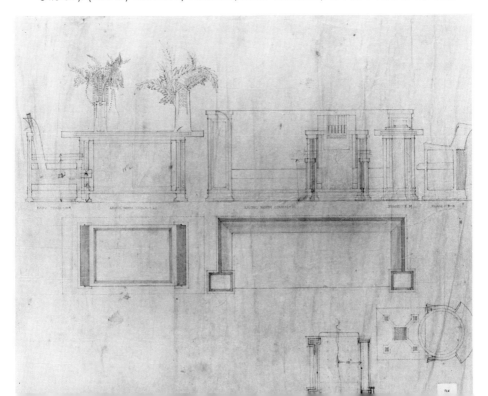

are indicated in the drawing to complete the ensemble. The dining chairs were un-usual in that instead of the vertical slats or the single-boarded back, a combination of the two was used with two broad slats separated by an open space, which is artic-ulated by three narrow slats. These chairs apparently were never executed.

The drawing of the living room furniture (fig. 96) includes a table (in elevation and plan) with two variations of the "skyscraper" vase, each filled with flowers and foliage and placed at each of the corners. All the furniture was designed with casters for ease of movement. The armchair is shown in profile by the table and in front of the sofa with its back toward the viewer. The barrel chair is shown to the right of the sofa with an occasional table in front. This overlapping and juxtapositioning served the purpose in the drawing of determining scale and establishing interrela-tionships. The use of horizontal molding and the horizontal proportioning of the furniture to unify the various pieces become significantly apparent in these studies.

■

A discussion of Wright's work during this period is hardly complete without a consideration of Unity Church (1906; fig. 97) in Oak Park, Illinois, where the archi-tecture, ornament, and furnishings become absolutely one. The only furnishings not part of the wall screens are the simple pew seats and the four impressive electric lamps that hang from a cantilevered support attached to the ceiling. The wiring, similar to that of the ceiling lights designed for the Dwight Bank (1905), is set in a wood trellis and exposed for several feet from the support to the fixtures below. The idea of exposing electric wires was probably based on Arts and Crafts principles of propriety, where, in the example of light fittings, designers were exhorted to express the true nature of the electric fixture and not create it in the mold of the gas lamp.

The great strides made in this building, however, are seen in the remarkable

97. Unity Church, Oak Park, Illinois. 1906.

space of the interior by which Wright felt he had finally brought the room through to the outside. Beautiful art glass coffers in shades of amber break through the roof slab and open the interior space to the sunlight above. The sides of the room are plastic so that the feeling of wall enclosure is thoroughly dissolved. The pulpit side is a three-dimensional tapestry in which the pulpit stand and organ keyboard behind the pipe screen are combined with the art glass clerestory, pipe screen, lamp stand, lamps, and tufted leather sofa (not the traditional high-backed minister's chair). All these threads along with the colors and the striking rhythms of decorative wood molding achieve such a complete integration with the architecture it would be disruptive to discuss each separately.

■

Wright felt that the Avery Coonley House (fig. 98) was the most successful of his Prairie houses. According to Elizabeth Coonley Faulkner, her mother had seen Wright's work exhibited (probably initially at The Art Institute of Chicago), and she wanted him to design their house. Mrs. Coonley was an educated woman who was in the vanguard of the progressive ideas at the turn of the century, especially in education, which was her primary interest. It was natural that she would come to Wright and find in his principles and architecture an expression of her ideas. The Coonleys must have been ideal clients; after expressing what they required in a house, they gave Wright the freedom to create a design that he felt would meet their needs.

Of his first meeting with the Coonleys, Wright wrote in *An Autobiography*:

> About this time Mr. and Mrs. Avery Coonley came to build a home at Riverside, Illinois. Unknown to me they had gone to see nearly everything they could learn I had done before coming.
>
> The day they finally came into the Oak Park workshop Mrs. Coonley said they had come because, it seemed to them, they saw in my house "the countenances of principle." This was to me a great and sincere compliment. So I put the best in me into the Coonley House. I feel now, looking back upon it, that building was the best I could then do in the way of a house. (p. 164)

According to Elizabeth Coonley Faulkner, her mother was sincerely impressed with the rational planning behind Wright's buildings. She was a Christian Scientist and therefore believed that

> the inner concept which expresses itself in something tangible, is the reality on which the tangible is based. If the principle is sound, its expression is likely to be sound,—and vice versa. I believe that Mr. Wright did work from a basic principle in his designs, and that my mother's comment recognized this. (Letter from Elizabeth Coonley Faulkner to the author, August 9, 1977)

Wright's designs for the Coonley House were included in the 1907 exhibition of the Chicago Architectural Club and construction was begun in 1908.

Since the principal rooms of the house are on the second floor, one has the feeling of looking out above the gardens and pool. However, because of the strong horizontal lines, the house appears to hug the ground so that there is no feeling of height. The plan is basically a U in shape, which is "zoned" for service facilities, living and dining areas, and family and guest bedrooms. With its garages and service building, the house rambles over the Coonley estate, becoming part of its setting and presenting no single view. The large playroom (below the living room) was the only major room to be located on the ground floor, and soon after the house was completed, a row of French doors that gave direct access to the garden from the playroom were installed where there had originally been three tall windows. The polychrome tiles on the exterior with their abstracted tulip design gave relief and interest to the exterior wall (fig. 99), the first instance of Wright's use of this medium.

98 (*below*). Avery Coonley House, Riverside, Illinois. 1908. 99 (*left*). Avery Coonley House (detail showing lamp). 100 (*opposite, below*). Living room, Avery Coonley House. 101 (*opposite, right*). Living room and hall looking toward dining room, Avery Coonley House.

The exterior lamp seen here had been used earlier on the exterior of the Unity Church.

The most spectacular space in the Coonley House is the great living room (fig. 100), which one reaches by either of twin staircases on each side of the entrance. Hipped ceilings are used in each of the hallway areas and in the living room, where wood-framed skylights are integral to the building. In contrast with their geometric spaces is the naturalistic mural wall painting of fern and birch motifs designed and executed by George Niedecken (see fig. 101). Its rich autumnal color scheme—predominantly green with cream and orange tan and accents of blue—contrasts with the plain white oak trim, stained soft brown, and the rough plaster walls, stained brown tan with accents of soft green.

The Coonley House was one of Wright's most elaborate houses in terms of its decorative scheme, all of which was executed. The interior was supervised by the Niedecken–Walbridge firm of Milwaukee, whose records indicate the original color scheme of the house. George Niedecken made numerous trips to Riverside to take care of the details involved in ordering and executing all the furnishings (see pp. 43–44), but he was working under Wright's direction, and the overall scheme of interior decoration is the architect's. The white oak furniture matched the woodwork. The trim gave sharp linear definition and articulation to the space and also screened the ceiling lighting with tracery. Bronze fixtures on the sides with tracery tops reflected the designs on the surrounding surfaces. The carpets (figs. 100, 101) were hand-tufted in Austria to Wright's design to harmonize with the scheme. The living room carpet was a brown tan in color with a tobacco brown border, with accents in green, blue, and red outlined in soft gray. A design for a rug apparently not executed is seen in figure 102. The window draperies were made of soft ecru silk and wool casement cloth, embroidered in color and design to match the rugs. Table scarves were also designed to harmonize with the room. The richness and softness of these specially designed accouterments contributed to the sense of harmony and repose in the room.

Unfortunately few pieces from the luxurious and extravagant furnishings of the interior have survived. When the Coonleys moved to Washington, D.C., in 1917, they reluctantly left their beloved house and all its furnishings behind. Elizabeth Coonley Faulkner explained that her parents were very sad to leave their house in Riverside:

> But my father, who was also a Christian Scientist, held a very interesting position in Chicago for the State of Illinois, a kind of public relations position, opposing the enactment of laws to which the Christian Scientists were opposed, and correcting what they considered misstatements in the press. He also did some public speaking. He was offered this same position in the District of Columbia, and felt that he could be useful there. It was a sacrifice to leave the house, but they felt that it was important.

They did not commission Wright to design a house for them in Washington because

> Newly arrived in wartime Washington [1917] just to find a house to live in was difficult. I do not believe that they could have found the proper site, or even the building materials required to build again. Even adding a second bathroom to the house they bought . . . was difficult. It was not a moment for creativity! (Letter from Elizabeth Coonley Faulkner to the author, August 9, 1977)

The Coonley House was purchased by the Kroehler family, who lived in the house much longer than the Coonleys, thus giving rise to its being referred to in many instances as the Kroehler House. When the Kroehlers moved out, a sale of the contents of the house resulted in the dispersement of almost all the Wright-designed furnishings. The hand-woven carpets custom-made to Wright's designs are no longer in the house, and no movable furniture remains. Particularly fragile, the curtains, table scarves, and other textiles, with the exception of the linen dinner napkins, were probably discarded long ago. The complete unity of exterior and interior that was part of the greatness of the Coonley House can now be sensed only through photographs. The dresses that Wright designed for Mrs. Coonley to complete the unity have also disappeared and are apparently not even recorded in photographs (Mr. and Mrs. Coonley appear to the far right in fig. 98). The few pieces of furniture and the linen napkins designed for the house that have survived are in private and museum collections.

The desk designed for the rear guest room of the Coonley House (fig. 103) reflects the exterior architecture of the house (fig. 98) in its intersecting geometric forms. A comparison of the desk's facade with that of the house shows the use of similar composition and devices. One of Wright's most striking architectural features—the emphatic cantilever—is used forcefully in this desk. Another relationship is evident in the small doors along the front of the desk; their vertical format and horizontal arrangement echo the banding of the living room's casement windows. The door panels are also articulated in a manner similar to that of the exterior wall tiles. Bandings of applied molding are also used in both desk and house facade.

102 (right). Rug design (drawing), Avery Coonley House, Riverside, Illinois. 1908. (The Frank Lloyd Wright Foundation). 103 (below). Desk, Avery Coonley House. Oak, glass, metal, 44" x 42" x 26" (111.8 cm x 106.7 cm x 66 cm). (The Art Institute of Chicago; Gift of The Graham Foundation for Advanced Studies in the Fine Arts)

A watercolor rendering (fig. 104) confirms the provenance of the desk, which had been acquired from the Coonley House. The rendering is signed by the Niedecken–Walbridge Co. and was probably executed by George Niedecken, who was in charge of executing the Coonley interior to Wright's plan. Niedecken's delicately drawn ink and ink-wash rendering shows a strong influence characteristic of Japanese prints. The asymmetrical composition and the use of vertical floating panels to the left and right are typical devices of Japanese prints, where such areas are usually filled with calligraphy. The panel to the left in the Niedecken rendering contains a meandering Oriental vine with flowers, similar to the clytemnestra plant. The composition is reminiscent of Japanese prints in its use of overlapping planes, which suggest a theatrical rather than a real setting. A low Japanese bowl with flowers is placed just to the left of the center of the top of the desk. The larger planter with the vine, however, is a form derived from American southwestern Indian pottery, of which its geometric banding is characteristic. This banding is connected to the picture plan by an extension of the outside lines, a critical element of the composition that has been placed outside and overlapping the picture frame, yet another device of Japanese prints.

The rendering was made for presentation to the Coonleys for approval before the desk was executed. A working drawing, which may date from slightly before, is in the collection of the Prairie School Archives in the Milwaukee Art Center. Although almost identical to the rendering, some of the details have been omitted, and architectural guidelines and measurements indicate its purpose as a working drawing. Additional desks almost identical to this example are known to exist; these apparently have no connection with the Coonley House (one is on loan to the Elvehjem Art Center, Madison, Wisconsin). One can speculate that Niedecken made similar desks on his own for his clients. A working drawing for a desk for guest room no. 2 is also in the Prairie School Archives. It is a variation on the desk seen here, with the drawers placed along the side rather than across the top and the lamps placed facing each other on the standards.

"The Avery Coonley estate was one of Papa's most complete creations. He designed everything in and about the house including table service and linens—even some of Mrs. Coonley's dresses to harmonize with the interiors" (John Lloyd Wright, *My Father Who Is on Earth*, pp. 41–42). Family history confirms that Wright designed the table linens for Queene Ferry Coonley, whose initials are embroidered in monogram with cotton thread on the dinner napkin in figure 105. Rather than the usual square-shaped napkin, Wright designed the Coonley napkin in the form of a long rectangle, which he felt was more suitable for use in the human lap (interview of Elizabeth Coonley Faulkner by the author, March 19, 1977). The napkin was folded four times when placed at a dinner setting, the monogram facing out. All four sides of the napkin are hemmed and a double row of crocheting was originally worked at each end. According to Mrs. Faulkner, there were probably twelve napkins in the original set, which may have been all that were needed since her mother did not like large dinner parties. Her mother very much

liked the initials "Q.F." but found the third letter such a distraction that she returned to her maiden initials, in spite of the great happiness and congeniality

PLATE 1 (*left*). Window, B. Harley Bradley House, Kankakee, Illinois. 1900. Leaded glass, oak frame, 49" x 30" (124.5 cm x 76.2 cm). (Lent by Yesteryear, Inc., Kankakee, Illinois)

PLATE 2 (*below*). Table lamp, Susan Lawrence Dana House, Springfield, Illinois. 1903. Bronze, leaded glass.

PLATE 3 (*opposite, above*). Window, Susan Lawrence Dana House, Springfield, Illinois. 1903. Leaded glass, wood frame, 46¼″ x 31½″ (117.5 cm x 80 cm). (Lent by Greenville College, Greenville, Illinois; The Richard W. Bock Sculpture Collection)

PLATE 4 (*opposite, below*). Hanging lamp, Susan Lawrence Dana House, Springfield, Illinois. 1903. Leaded glass, 19″ x 23½″ x 23½″ (48.2 cm x 59.7 cm x 59.7 cm). (Lent by Greenville College, Greenville, Illinois; The Richard W. Bock Sculpture Collection)

PLATE 5 (*below*). Entrance hall, Susan Lawrence Dana House, Springfield, Illinois. 1903.

PLATE 6 (*opposite, above*). Door with art glass window, hall, Susan Lawrence Dana House, Springfield, Illinois. 1903.

PLATE 7 (*opposite, below*). Windows and lamps, hall, Susan Lawrence Dana House, Springfield, Illinois. 1903.

PLATE 8 (*below*). Window, Darwin D. Martin House, Buffalo, New York. 1904. Leaded glass, wood frame, 41½″ x 26¼″ (105.4 cm x 66.7 cm). (Lent by Grey Art Gallery and Study Center, New York University Art Collection, New York)

PLATE 9 (*above*). Window, W. R. Heath House, Buffalo, New York. 1905. Leaded glass.

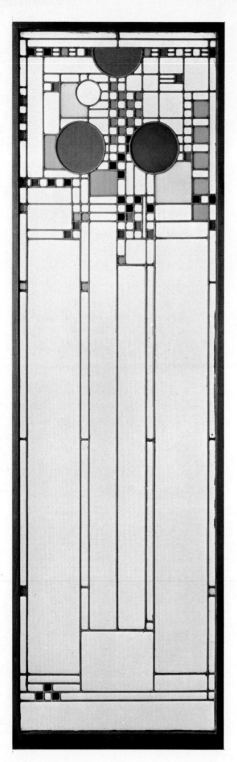

PLATE 10 (*left*). One of three windows, Avery Coonley Playhouse, Riverside, Illinois. 1912. Leaded glass, wood frame, 86¼" x 28" (219 cm x 71.1 cm) each. (Lent by The Metropolitan Museum of Art, New York; Purchase, Edward C. Moore, Jr.; Gift of Edgar J. Kaufmann Charitable Foundation Fund, 1967)

PLATE 11 (*opposite, above*). Rug, F. C. Bogk House, Milwaukee, Wisconsin. 1916. Wool, 76½" x 142¾" (194.3 cm x 363.4 cm). (Lent by Mr. and Mrs. Robert R. Elsner, Jr., Milwaukee, Wisconsin; Courtesy of The Prairie Archives, Milwaukee Art Center, Wisconsin)

PLATE 12 (*opposite, below left*). Cream pitcher, Imperial Hotel, Tokyo, Japan. 1916—1922. Silver, 3" x 3" x 3⅝" (7.6 cm x 7.6 cm x 9.2 cm). (Lent by Mrs. Frank Lloyd Wright, Taliesin West, Scottsdale, Arizona)

PLATE 13 (*opposite, below right*). Dinner service, Imperial Hotel, Tokyo, Japan. 1916—1922 (examples are from the 1960s). Ceramic, cup: 3½" (8.9 cm) diam.; saucer: 5⁵/₁₆" (13.5 cm) diam.; plate: 10½" (26.7 cm) diam.; bowl: 5¾" (14.6 cm) diam. (Lent by Mr. and Mrs. Roger Kennedy, New York)

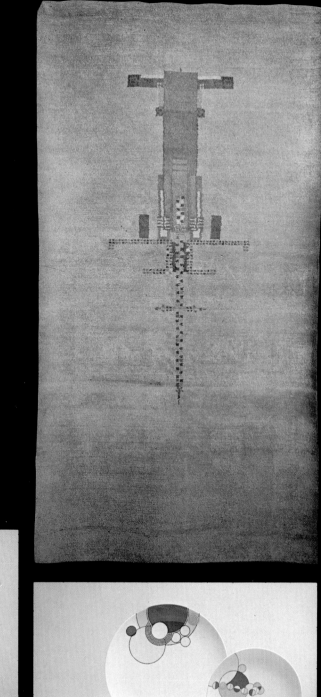

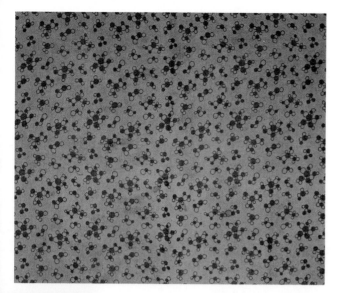

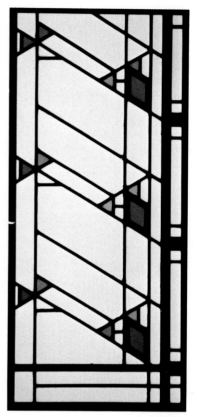

PLATE 14 (*above*). Upholstery fabric (detail), Imperial Hotel, Tokyo, Japan. 1916–1922. Silk, 33" x 36" (83.8 cm x 91.4 cm). (Lent by Mrs. Frank Lloyd Wright, Taliesin West, Scottsdale, Arizona)

PLATE 15 (*left*). Hollyhock House, Los Angeles, California. 1920.

PLATE 16 (*right*). Window, Aline Barnsdall Hollyhock House, Los Angeles, California. 1920. Leaded glass, 26¾" x 12⅝" (68 cm x 32 cm). (Lent by Southern California Chapter, American Institute of Architects, Los Angeles)

PLATE 17 (*right*). Living area, David Wright House, Phoenix, Arizona. 1952. Side chair, Philippine mahogany, 31⅜″ x 19¼″ x 19⅛″ (79.7 cm x 48.9 cm x 48.5 cm). (Lent by Mr. and Mrs. David Wright, Phoenix, Arizona)

PLATE 18 (*above*). Living area, David Wright House, Phoenix, Arizona. 1952.

PLATE 19 (*opposite, above*). Brochure of *The Taliesin Fellowship*. 1933. Red and black ink on paper, 8¾" x 17¼" (22.2 cm x 43.8 cm) open. (Lent by Donald Kalec, Oak Park, Illinois)

PLATE 20 (*above*). Cover of *Town and Country*. July 1937. Ink on paper, 13½" x 9¾" (34.3 cm x 24.7 cm). (Lent by Mrs. Nora Natof, Lovettsville, Virginia)

PLATE 21 (*opposite, below*). Cover of *The Architectural Forum*. January 1938. Ink on paper, 11⅞" x 8¾" (30.2 cm x 22.2 cm). (Lent by Curtis Besinger, Lawrence, Kansas)

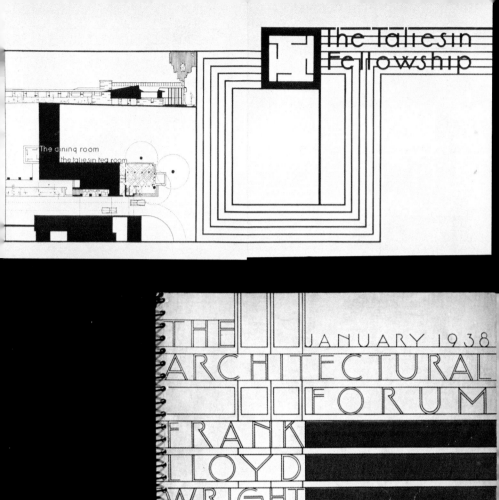

The Taliesin Fellowship

The dining room
the taliesin tea room

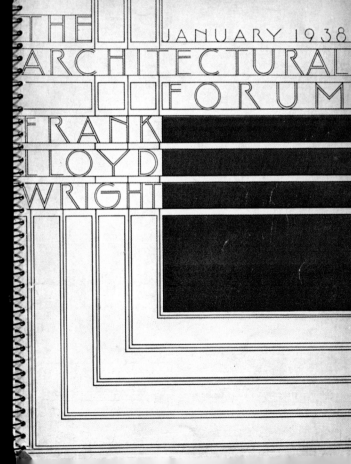

JANUARY 1938

THE ARCHITECTURAL FORUM

FRANK LLOYD WRIGHT

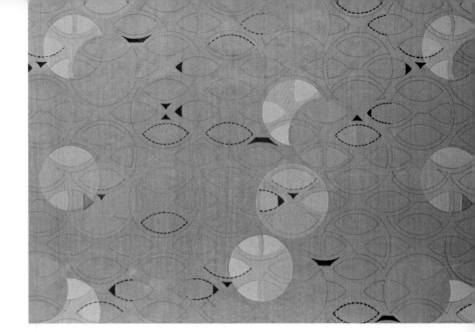

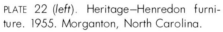

PLATE 22 (*left*). Heritage—Henredon furniture. 1955. Morganton, North Carolina.

PLATE 23 (*above*). Fabric design No. 104. 1955. F. Schumacher & Co., New York. Silk and Fortisan, 24½" x 52" (62.2 cm x 132 cm). (Lent by Donald Kalec, Oak Park, Illinois)

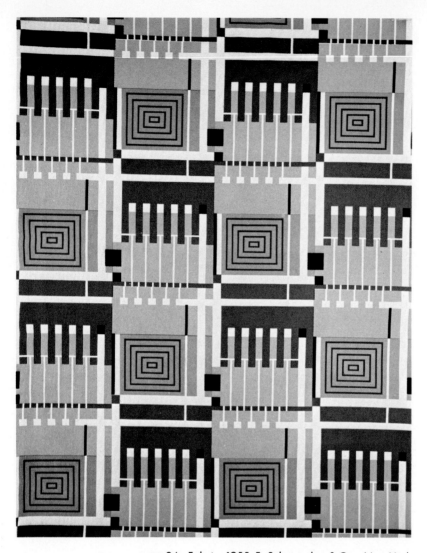

PLATE 24. Fabric. 1955. F. Schumacher & Co., New York.

of her marriage. My father, who teased her affectionately, used to say that the kitchen plated flat silver was marked Coonley, but the really good things were marked "Q.F." (Letter from Elizabeth Coonley Faulkner to the author, March 24, 1977)

Nevertheless the *C* is incorporated into this fine linen napkin, surrounding the *Q* and the *F*. The coloration of white on white is quite subtle and goes well with the white dinner plates, which Wright may also have designed. They are marked "Durant -/ 1913." The design of the monogram is unusual for Wright and is more typical of the work of Charles Rennie Mackintosh and the Glasgow School. Instead of a severe rectilinear format, curves and arcs were introduced to soften the geometric design. However, the arcs forming the initials were drawn from the strike of a compass.

■

Whereas the Coonley House rambled over the countryside, the Frederick Robie House (fig. 106) on Woodlawn Avenue in Hyde Park (1908) is contained within a city lot, and the more sober materials of brick and concrete replace the ephemeral plaster and tile walls of the Coonley House. The tightness of the Robie plan makes it seem more like a ship than a house. Its huge chimney acts as a mast,

104 (*below, left*). Desk for rear guest room (watercolor rendering by George Niedecken from a design by Frank Lloyd Wright), Avery Coonley House, Riverside, Illinois. 1908. Pencil, ink, and wash on tracing paper, 10⅞" x 15½" (27.6 cm x 39.4 cm). (Lent by The Burnham Library, The Art Institute of Chicago, Illinois; Gift of Mr. and Mrs. James W. Howlett) 105 (*below, right*). Dinner napkin, Avery Coonley House. Linen, 10" x 24½" (25.4 cm x 62.2 cm). (Lent by Mr. and Mrs. Waldron Faulkner, Washington, D.C.)

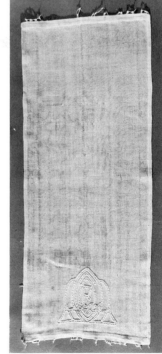

balancing and weighting down the rest of the house, which would otherwise seem suspended. The plan of the second floor is open and fluid, with the living room and dining room as one area separated by the fireplace and the central stairs. Each of these rooms has a triangular-shaped bay, and these bays appear as bows of a ship. The family bedrooms are in a smaller area on the third floor. The ground floor reflects the first, with the billiard room and playroom beneath the living and dining rooms. Each major room has access to the porches and balconies, which are lined with flower boxes.

Although not nearly as large as the Coonley House, the Robie House also had a complete decorative scheme for the interior, which was supervised, as already noted on pages 44–45, by the Niedecken–Walbridge firm in Milwaukee. Again, George Niedecken, under Wright's direction, was responsible for supervising the execution of the interior, including developing the designs for furniture from concept sketches to presentation drawings.

Fortunately much of the Robie furniture has survived and is now owned by the University of Chicago, which uses the house as their development office. Extensive remodeling of the interior from 1967 to 1968 made use of a few pieces of the furniture, while most, including the dining room ensemble, is kept at The David and Alfred Smart Gallery. Although the dining room was altered drastically, with the removal of the dining room table and chairs as well as the built-in buffet, it still retains its trim, which defines the space, and its original light fixtures, which can be regulated by a dimmer. The custom-designed hand-woven rugs were removed from the house long ago, though the working drawings and even the yarn color samples are in the Niedecken collection at the Milwaukee Art Center. Most of the windows still remain in the house, and the example in figure 110 is typical. Its design is based on two conventionalized flowers on both sides of an angular composition that reflects the floor plan of the house.

106. Frederick C. Robie House, Chicago, Illinois. 1908.

The Robie dining room table and six chairs (fig. 107) formed Wright's most important furniture ensemble. Whereas Wright was uneasy about the disarray that a living room seemed to require, a dining room was for him "always a great artistic opportunity." The occasions of "dining" and of "living" were different. Norris Kelly Smith has pointed out the symbolic significance of this ensemble, where a family "at dining" could participate in a great oneness of purpose:

> In his early houses Wright consistently treats the occasion almost as if it were liturgical in nature. His severely rectilinear furniture, set squarely within a rectilinear context, makes these dining rooms seem more like stately council chambers than like gathering places for the kind of intimate family life we usually associate with Wright's name. They declare unequivocally that the unity of the group requires submission and conformity on the part of its members. (*Frank Lloyd Wright: A Study in Architectural Content*, Englewood Cliffs, N.J.: Prentice-Hall, 1966, p. 74)

107. Dining room, dining table, and six side chairs, Frederick C. Robie House, Chicago, Illinois. 1908. Oak, metal, glass, and ceramic, 55⅜" x 96¼" x 53½" (141.3 cm x 244.9 cm x 135.9 cm) table; 52⅜" x 17" x 19¾" (133 cm x 43.2 cm x 50.2 cm) each side chair. (Lent by The David and Alfred Smart Gallery, The University of Chicago, Illinois)

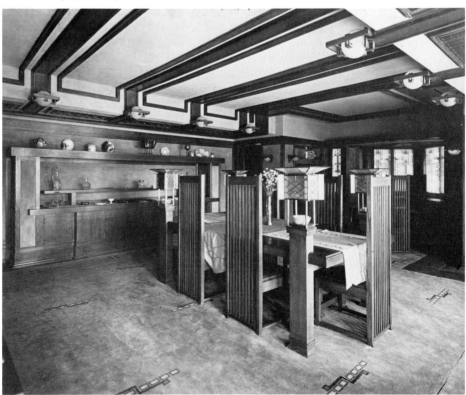

This type of formal family dining requiring conformity must not have appealed to the Robies, since according to their daughter Lorraine Robie O'Conner, her parents preferred to dine at the smaller table in the "prow" of the dining room, and the formal table was reserved for guests. The formal dining was Wright's idea about his family at dining, not the clients'.

The Robie dining ensemble is an impressive and moving aesthetic experience, especially when seen in the context of the original setting, where it achieves even greater power. The visual relationships between the dining furniture, conceived in its vertical and horizontal lines, and the interior architecture contributed to the overall unity of the room. The strong horizontal thrust of the extended top of the dining table and of the built-in buffet had their exterior counterpart in the cantilevered roofs. The vertical lines of the high-backed chairs were echoed in the buffet.

According to the account book kept by H. Barnard, contractor for the Robie House, cash disbursements were recorded from April 15, 1909, through June 21, 1910. The documentation for the completion of the Robie interiors is in the journal kept by George Niedecken between August 4, 1909, and December 31, 1910 (Prairie School Archives, Milwaukee Art Center). Clearly Niedecken, as interior decorator, supervised the execution of the Robie dining room. His account book indicates that the furniture was made by the F. H. Bresler Co. of Milwaukee and that leather for the chairs was purchased from the Federal Leather Co. (Niedecken's role in the design of this furniture has been discussed on pp. 43–44).

The dining table originally could be extended, which explains the extra set of legs. The piers and end sections could be moved and extra leaves inserted for larger dinner parties. The table was drastically altered some time after the Robies left in 1911. The four piers and lamps were removed, probably in order to shorten the table or because they were in the way; these presumably were destroyed. In 1972 they were reconstructed from drawings photogrammetrically plotted from original photographs of the dining room for the traveling exhibition "The Arts and Crafts Movement in America 1876–1916" (an exhibition organized by The Art Museum, Princeton University, and The Art Institute of Chicago; catalogue edited by Robert Judson Clark, Princeton, N.J.: Princeton University Press, 1972). Recently this preliminary restoration has been refined. The Robie dining room furniture represents a culmination of Wright's efforts in designing integral furnishings, the beginnings of which had been seen in earlier houses.

The watercolor rendering of the rug plan (fig. 108) gives the floor plan of the first floor, with varying patterns indicated for different rooms. Although shown here as wall-to-wall carpeting, area rugs were actually executed, as seen in figure 107.

A thorough documentation of the execution of the Robie House is possible through the Niedecken journal and the Barnard account book. The latter includes an entry that indicates that the South Halsted Iron Works had the contract for the metalwork, which probably included the gates seen in figure 109. Frederick Robie, Jr., also is seen here in his toy automobile. The design for the now-demolished gate reflects the windows almost exactly.

In the fall of 1909, after twenty-two years of successful architectural practice, Frank Lloyd Wright, feeling that he had reached a creative plateau, left family and

108 (*below*). Living room, dining room, and hall rugs (plan), Frederick C. Robie House, Chicago, Illinois. 1908. Watercolor on Kraft paper, 15⅛" x 40⅜" (38.4 cm x 102.5 cm). (Lent by Mr. and Mrs. Robert L. Jacobsen, Milwaukee, Wisconsin; Courtesy of The Prairie Archives, Milwaukee Art Center, Wisconsin) 109 (*above, left*). Frederick C. Robie, Jr., in front of the gate to the garage of his father's house. 110 (*above, right*). Window, Frederick C. Robie House. Leaded glass, wood frame, 49" x 30¼" (124.5 cm x 76.8 cm), with frame. (Lent by The David and Alfred Smart Gallery, The University of Chicago, Illinois)

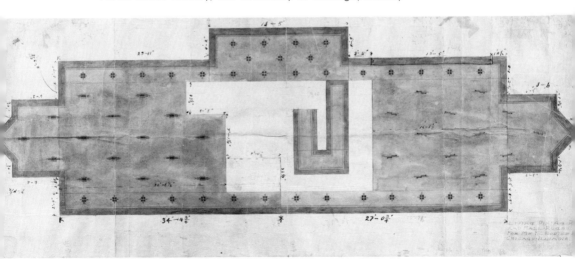

practice to go to Europe. After a sojourn in Berlin, Wright moved to a small villa at Fiesole near Florence, Italy. There he worked on preparing a retrospective publication of his work. This departure marked the close of Wright's first remarkable and productive period of work.

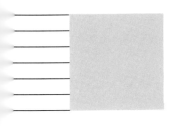

FROM THE MIDDLE WEST TO JAPAN AND CALIFORNIA: 1911–1930

The publication in Germany in 1910 of the portfolio *Ausgeführte Bauten und Entwürfe von Frank Lloyd Wright* ("The Wasmuth Portfolio") made Wright's work of the first decade of the twentieth century known to Europeans and was of great influence in the development of modern architecture abroad. The change in Wright's work on his return in 1911 resulted more from his own personality than from his contact with European architecture, which only encouraged his own instincts. The work of the period 1911–1930 does not represent any cohesiveness as a total group, but various germane developments can be seen. During the second and third decades of the century, Wright's work was no longer to be concentrated in the Middle West. Important commissions in California and Japan were to take him away from Chicago. And a new house for himself in Spring Green, Wisconsin, Taliesin, built in 1913, was to be his home and studio rather than in Oak Park.

On his return from Europe, however, Wright was to receive a number of commissions in Chicago, including a second important commission from the Avery Coonleys. The kindergarten or "playhouse" (figs. 111, 112), which stands on the Coonley's extensive Riverside estate some distance from the house, is a completely independent structure. Unlike the house, which rambles, the kindergarten is tight and symmetrical, with a formal cross plan, and whereas the house has a hip roof, the kindergarten has a flat slab roof.

The three tall windows, which were originally placed above a flower box stylobate in the front of the Coonley Playhouse (fig. 111), are one of Wright's most important single decorative achievements; although integral to the architecture, they are self-contained artistic expressions. Although derived from different sources, Wright's design relates visually to nonobjective experiments in European painting at the time, such as the paintings of Francis Picabia and Frank Kupka. Wright called the building a "playhouse" because it had a stage at one end and could be used to present plays. However, it was actually a school; according to Elizabeth Coonley Faulkner, calling it a playhouse distressed her mother "because the school was one of the 'Progressive' Schools of the period, and these were always accused of substituting play for work" (letter to the author, January 17, 1977). Mrs. Coonley's interest in education is seen in the four schools she began and financed. She was particularly interested in the kindergarten, and "the workshop" began with that level and added a grade each year through eighth grade. According to Mrs. Faulkner, Wright's idea for the windows was inspired by his observing a parade with balloons, flags, and confetti. It is not surprising then that Wright sometimes called these colorful windows his "Kindersymphony." Wright's fascination with balloons is also seen in the playroom he designed for his children in his own house. The glass globes of the light fixture that were suspended from the ceiling at different lengths resembled balloons. John Lloyd Wright recalled that "he bought colored gas balloons by the dozen—released them in the playroom—arranged and played with them by the hour" (*My Father Who Is on Earth*, New York: G. P. Putnam's Sons, 1946, p. 27). The observation of these balloons against his own earlier geometric windows may have been the inspiration for these windows. They were to inspire Wright's later murals for the Midway Gardens. The bright primary colors were unusual for Wright, who preferred earth colors.

The drawing (fig. 113) for one of the horizontal windows seen in figure 112 shows that narrower windows were planned than were ultimately used, and the design as first conceived was more compressed, with the balloons and confetti filling the entire format.

■

Plans for a second house for Francis W. Little, called "Northome" (figs 114, 115), were begun in 1908, but were interrupted by Wright's departure for Europe. On his return in 1911, he began building Taliesin and also returned to the plans for the Little House in Wayzata, near Minneapolis. Taliesin and Northome, built not on a suburban plot but in open land, are similar in their dependence on their sites. Taliesin was built into (not on) the brow of a hill, and the Little House was built along the crest of a hill. Each house is marked by emphatic horizontality. At Northome, Wright could not experiment as freely as with his own house inasmuch as the Littles had very specific wishes. However, the light-colored, unstained furniture and woodwork of both houses have much in common.

The library table for Northome (fig. 116) demonstrates the change in Wright's

furniture style after his return from Europe in 1911. The delicacy and elegance of his earlier-designed furniture is replaced here with a boldness and severity seldom seen before or even subsequently in Wright's domestic oeuvre. An interesting comparison can be made between this table and the table designed for the Darwin D. Martin House in 1904 (fig. 93). The refined Martin table is a tight composition contained within a molded frame, while the Little table is free and open. The forceful cantileverlike top and shelves beneath on the Little table, which reflect the building's external forms, are far more daring than on any earlier tables. The cabinet section, which is separated from the top by an open space, has doors like casement windows on both sides and is "hung" between the two shelves. This open space allows spatial flow, whereas the table otherwise would be heavy and compressed. The four strong post supports cut through the corners of the top and cabinet. The

111 (*opposite*) and 112 (*bottom*). Avery Coonley Playhouse, Riverside, Illinois. 1912. 113 (*below*). Window (drawing), Avery Coonley Playhouse. (Copyright © 1977 The Frank Lloyd Wright Foundation, all rights reserved)

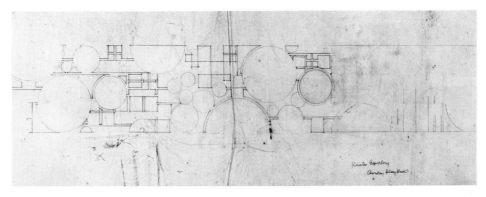

only concession to "ornament" on the Little table is the molded edge on the top and bottom of the cantileverlike top. Although it was customary to use veneers on Wright's furniture, apparently none was used on the Little table. Instead of the traditional dark stain, this table has a blond finish that is waxed. The only hardware is the hinges on the doors. Elimination and simplification have been taken to a logical conclusion; even the traditional "pulls" are gone, and in their place "slits" in the wood serve as handles, so that they are "of" rather than "appurtenances to" the table. What might have been a cumbersome piece of furniture becomes, in Wright's hands, a masterpiece of plasticity—dynamic and strong yet weightless. A variation of the Little library table was used later in the desks for the S. C. Johnson Administration Building (fig. 167), where metal replaced wood, but the concept of the cantileverlike top with a space and shelf beneath, as well as a "hung" drawer section, was essentially the same.

In the Little table, one sees Wright's influence on the furniture of Gerrit Rietveld inasmuch as this table served as the prototype for a sideboard designed by Rietveld in 1919, now in the Stedelijk Museum in Amsterdam.

The drawing of the bedroom furnishings from the Little House (fig. 117) illustrates the same boldness as the library table. They have the same extended tops and open space between the drawers and top. Although the proportions are similar to that of earlier furniture, in detail they are starkly simple and are in outline like abstract Constructivist paintings.

■

114 (*opposite, above*). Francis W. Little House, Wayzata, Minnesota. 1913.   115 (*opposite, below*). Living room, Francis W. Little House.   116 (*bottom*). Library table, Francis W. Little House. Oak, 26 5/16" x 72" x 27" (66.8 cm x 182.8 cm x 68.6 cm). (Lent by The Metropolitan Museum of Art, New York; Purchase, Emily C. Chadbourne Bequest, 1972)   117 (*below*). Dressing table and highboy (elevation and plan), Francis W. Little House. Pencil and colored pencil on tissue, 19" x 40" (48.2 cm x 101.5 cm). (Lent by The Metropolitan Museum of Art, New York; Emily C. Chadbourne Estate, 1972)

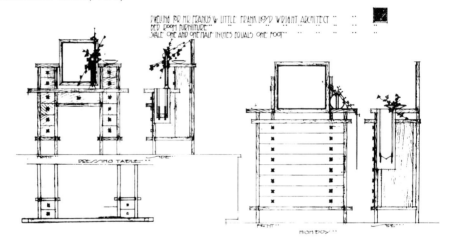

The Midway Gardens in Chicago (figs. 118 and 119) provided Frank Lloyd Wright the opportunity to design an elaborate complex with a rich decorative scheme of great variety and innovation. In *An Autobiography,* Wright described the story of the building of the Gardens as if it were a tale of the architectural Arabian Nights (pp. 178–179). The sponsor, Edward Waller, Jr., son of one of Wright's earliest clients (see p. 70), came to Wright in the late autumn of 1913 with the idea of providing an entertainment center, modeled after the outdoor garden restaurants of Germany, on Cottage Grove Avenue at 60th Street to be built on a 200-square-foot block near The University of Chicago. The resulting plan provided a variety of spaces, both interior and exterior, for purposes of eating, drinking, ball-room dancing, listening to symphonic music, and viewing the ballet. As originally conceived, the Gardens included plans for landscaping with trees, sunken gardens, and flowers and vines covering the trellised towers. Only plants in various containers, placed on the masonry walls of the various terraces and balconies, were ultimately used. It was the beginning of the age of the automobile, still a relatively rare possession, and one could drive to Midway Gardens, where ample parking space was provided, or use public transportation to the door, since the electric streetcar stopped at the main entrances. The Gardens were the showplace of the area, where one could spend the entire evening dining, dancing, or being entertained. Although balconies sheltered some of the tables, most were out of doors.

The Midway Gardens included a long rectilinear building with a multistoried series of indoor terraces and promenades. This served as a year-round restaurant and was known as the Winter Garden (figs. 118, 124). It faced Cottage Grove Avenue to the east. On the opposite, or west, side it faced the large outdoor bandshell from which it was separated by a vast series of open masonry terraces, known collectively as the Summer Garden (figs. 119, 120). Enclosing the Summer Garden to the north and south stood two long and low arcaded buildings that extended to the street where they were capped by large, flat towers and flanked the Winter Garden. These buildings held three stories of balconies and terraces and, although roofed, stood in the open air overlooking the Summer Garden. Promenades were placed around the open areas and the kitchen, reached by ramps, was located under the Winter Garden. A tavern, which was included to help support the complex, was located on the ground floor at the northeast corner of the Winter Garden building.

The buildings were clad on the inside and outside in concrete blocks of various geometric patterns that were cast at the site. These alternated with Roman brick. The vertical elements, which countered the strongly horizontal masses of the buildings, were four "sky" towers located at the corners of the Winter Garden and the so-called electric needles. Wright described the latter (*An Autobiography,* p. 185) as "electric needles that I made out of wrought-iron pipe punctured to let the lamps through thickly at the sides."

John Lloyd Wright reported in *My Father Who Is on Earth* (pp. 71, 72) that his father initially sketched the entire conception of the plan of Midway Gardens in one hour. The architect's son was responsible for detailing the finished drawings, supervising the construction and even painting the murals on the tavern walls. Paul F. G. Meuller was the general contractor.

Frank Lloyd Wright wrote (*An Autobiography,* p. 181) that he had based his

118 (*below*). Midway Gardens, Chicago, Illinois. 1914 (razed 1929). 119 (*above*). "Summer Garden," Midway Gardens.

designs for the painting and sculpture of Midway Gardens on "abstraction" although he was not sure about the public's possible reception to it: "Would Chicago respond to adventure into the realm of the abstract in the sense that I wanted to go into it?" The Armory Show of 1913 held first in New York and later in Chicago was the first formal exhibition to introduce abstract European art to Americans. The exhibition was received with great interest and enthusiasm although many of the more avant-garde paintings had been initially greeted with shock and derision. Wright wrote: "Fortunately, human beings are really childlike in the best sense when appealed to by simple, strong forms and pure, bright color." He considered his characteristic "straight line" and "flat plane" to be already abstract and, abandoning plant forms, chose "pure form" with the circle, the square, and the triangle as the decorative design motif throughout. Since Froebel blocks symbolized child's play in Wright's recollection, he probably committed these shapes to every aspect of the design of Midway Gardens as metaphors for playfulness and fun.

The use of basic geometric shapes as a decorative motif also helped to give unity to the vast complex. The cords of the lights hanging from the Winter Garden ceiling were strung with small, geometric-shaped blocks of spheres, cubes, and tetrahedrons. These terminated in the large, glass light globes that resembled balloons and had been used in this manner in the Wright children's playroom (1895.) Geometric shapes were used in the patterned concrete blocks, the painted wall murals, the large stone reliefs, the carved ceiling panels, and the floor, as well as the art glass windows, the table linens, and the ceramics. Even the sculpture of human figures was modeled in flat planes and not in rounded naturalistic forms as was the common artistic practice of the day.

Another decorative motif used to give unity to the vast complex was the row of squares, favored by Japanese wood-block and Viennese Secessionist designers as well as Richardson, Sullivan, and Wright (the Secessionists were a group formed in 1897). Wright had used this motif on the furniture and trim of the Husser House (1897). It was also used by Wright as early as the cornice of the Charnley House (1891). The Midway Gardens was a masterpiece in planning. By integrating the various functions of this complicated building with its ingenious decorative system, not only unity but a sense of a lighthearted and festive spirit were achieved.

In the Midway Gardens, Wright attempted an artistic synthesis on a scale never before accomplished for the purpose of providing food and entertainment (baroque stage designs for opera had included the integration of sculpture, painting, and architecture as a setting for music). Architecture, sculpture, landscaping, painting, and music and dance were all conceived and determined by the architect. After plans for the building were completed before the beginning of 1914, Wright proceeded to commission sculptors and painters to help him execute his artistic ideals for the building. The artistic collaboration that sounds so effortless as an idea was not so easy to achieve. Wright felt that although architecture was the most important of the arts, painting, sculpture, and music should harmonize with it. In recalling his difficulties in integrating the arts in the Midway Gardens, Wright later wrote:

. . . I found musicians, painters, sculptors were unable to rise at that time to any such synthesis. Only in a grudging and dim way did most of them even understand it as an idea. So I made the designs for all to harmonize with the architecture; crude as any sketch is crude, incomplete as to execution, but in effect sufficiently complete to show the immense importance of any such attempt on any architect's part and show, indeed, that only so does architecture completely live. ("Organic Architecture," *Architect's Journal*, August 1936; quoted in Frederick Gutheim, *Frank Lloyd Wright on Architecture: Selected Writings 1894–1940*, New York: Grosset and Dunlap, 1941, p. 188)

Some of Wright's decorative details were never completed, such as the inlaying of the concrete relief blocks with scarlet and green flashed glass. When the Gardens opened in August 1914, even without the clouds of colored balloons that were to fly from the needles and the towers, the effect of the whole setting was apparently spectacular.

120 (*right*). Sculpture by Alfonso Iannelli and lamp designed by Frank Lloyd Wright, "Summer Garden," Midway Gardens, Chicago, Illinois. 1914. 121 (*below*). Garden terrace lamps (front and side elevations), Midway Gardens. (The Frank Lloyd Wright Foundation)

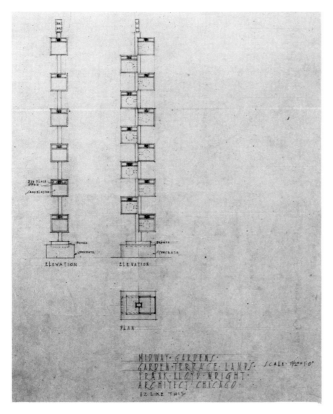

122 (*above left*). Midway Gardens, Chicago, Illinois. 1914. 123 (*above, right*). Block, Midway Gardens. Concrete, 17¾" x 20¾" x 2¾" (45 cm x 52.7 cm x 7 cm). (Lent by The Museum of Modern Art, New York) 124 (*below*). "Winter Garden," Midway Gardens.

Wright described the opening of the Gardens:

> . . . the Gardens, though unfinished, had opened in as brilliant a social event as Chicago ever knew. . . . The atmosphere aimed at was there. In a scene unforgettable to all who attended, the architectural scheme of color, form, light and sound, came alive with thousands of beautifully dressed women and tuxedoed men. This scene came upon the beholders as a magic spell. All there moved and spoke as if in a dream. . . . Chicago marveled, acclaimed, approved. And Chicago went back and did the same again and again and again. It was "Egyptian" to many, Maya to some, Japanese to others. Strange to all. It awakened a sense of mystery and romance in them all to which each responded with what he had in him to give. (*An Autobiography*, p. 186)

The glory of Midway Gardens was short-lived, notwithstanding its successful first season. Its opening was followed closely by the beginning of World War I in Europe. In 1916 the Gardens were sold to the Edelweiss Brewing Company, which turned the beautiful complex into a beer garden and altered it extensively by painting the ornamentation. Wright himself was so upset that he hoped someone would "give them the final blow and tear them down" (*An Autobiography*, p. 188). In 1920, with the introduction of Prohibition, the Gardens could not even succeed as a beer garden, and in 1929 they were demolished. John Lloyd Wright, who had supervised the construction of the Gardens, noted sadly that "the people of Chicago lost a fantasy. . . . It became a skating rink, then a dime-a-dance casino—and finally it was razed" (*My Father Who Is on Earth*, New York: G. P. Putnam's Sons, 1946, p. 88).

The Armory Show of 1913, first in New York and later in Chicago, introduced contemporary European art to Americans for the first time in a formal showing, but Wright's abstract murals for the Midway Gardens were developed separately as a part of a new architecture.

Wright's two Midway Gardens murals, called *City by the Sea*, one of which is seen here (fig. 125), were a development of the idea first expressed in the Coonley Playhouse windows (pl. 10). A myriad of colored balloons were incorporated into a complex composition in the mural, and the confetti motif, seen in the Coonley windows, was replaced with vertical rows of small circles.

The design of the mural extended beyond the painted frame and even the architectural molding, blending the pictorial with the structural. Nonperspectival space was built up by the overlapping, transparency, and juxtaposing of the circular forms (and, possibly, also by their colors). These techniques incorporated advanced theoretical ideas at the time (Wassily Kandinsky overlapped circles in paintings in 1926 in much the same manner), although Wright had been committed to flat-pattern designs. The painting, however, successfully suggested a cloud of balloons bobbing back and forth amid showers of confetti. Although there is no record of the colors employed, Wright stated his preference for "pure, bright color," and it is likely that the exuberant primary hues seen in the Coonley windows were also used here. The murals were executed by three painters from The Art Institute—William Henderson, John Norton, and Jerry Blum—and it is possible they or Wright suggested alterations in the design, as the mural as executed was quite different from the drawing illustrated in plate 295 in Drexler (Arthur Drexler, *The Drawings of Frank Lloyd Wright*, New York: Bramhall House, 1962; see also Dimitri Tselos, "Frank Lloyd Wright and World Architecture," *Journal of the Society of Architectural Historians*, March 1969, pp. 62–66).

The sculpture for Midway Gardens was a joint effort of the architect and the sculptors Alfonso Iannelli and Richard Bock. According to Iannelli, Wright designed the female winged sprite holding the cube aloft at the entrance (fig. 122), which was substantially carried out as he had sketched it (see Drexler, pl. 294). The sprites in the Summer Garden (figs. 119 and 120) were designed by Iannelli in collaboration with Wright. The figures in the main dining room (fig. 124) holding the cube, sphere, triangle, and octagon were a joint effort of the sculptor and the architect. In *An Autobiography* Wright described his inspiration for the sprites: "The lovely human figure might come into the scheme but come in only to respect the architecture, dominated by a proper sense of the whole" (p. 181). Iannelli made scale drawings and models before they were then finally approved by Wright for execution by Iannelli. In each instance, Wright evidently followed the development of the design and the execution carefully (letter from Alfonso Iannelli to Grant Manson, May 13, 1957, Oak Park Public Library). According to Edgar Kaufmann, Jr., the statues by Iannelli were very close to those in the Kunstschau designed by Joseph Hoffman in 1908, which Wright may have seen in publication or when he was in Europe. Some sprite statues and heads survive today in a number of private collections. Richard Bock modeled a large relief that was cast in concrete for the four huge pier capitals seen in photographs in the interior of the main dining room. According to Bock,

125. Mural, Midway Gardens, Chicago, Illinois. 1914.

these were actually located on the walls of the inside stairway. Bock's models and the reliefs have apparently been destroyed.

According to Iannelli, the art glass windows were carried out by the Temple Glass Co. of Chicago; however, Frank Linden, Jr., stated, in conversation with the author in July 1977, that the glass was done by the Linden Glass Co. The strongly diagonal and asymmetrical designs appear to be a new departure in Wright's art glass, and it is unfortunate that apparently none of these windows has survived. The Midway Gardens glass design is similar in composition to that used in the Hollyhock House (pl. 16).

With Midway Gardens, Wright had the opportunity to design all interior furnishings, some of which were executed. They included the ceramics, which were produced by the Shenango China Company of New Castle, Pennsylvania, to Wright's design. Two drawings for the furniture in the Taliesin archives (figs. 126b and 127) show the teacup and saucer in elevation and plan. Although designed with a double row of squares and a square handle, the cup and saucer as executed contain only a single row, and the handle is rounded, a practical concession to the manufacturer. In the drawing of the table and chairs (fig. 126a), one sees the plates set for dining with tablecloth, napkins, and lamp. This illustrates Wright's attempt to create a unity by the repetition of the square or confetti motif on the rim of the cup and saucer, the edge of the napkin, and at random on the tablecloth and lamp. For variation, the row of squares is arranged diagonally in some instances. The square motif is echoed in the floor design and, in three dimensions, in the shape of the legs and the stretchers of the chairs and table. Even the base of the centerpiece that contains the salt and pepper shakers is square. The drawing at Taliesin also indicates that these too incorporated the square design.

The cup and saucer here are among the few ceramic pieces (which originally must have been ordered by the hundreds) known to have survived from Midway Gardens. With its demolition in 1929, most of the contents were sold or destroyed. This cup and saucer were saved by Wright's son, John Lloyd Wright. He recalled, sadly, the demise of the great gardens when he wrote:

> To me, all that marks the spot is a single white cup and saucer. Dotted around the rim of the saucer and mouth of the cup is a design of square confetti—like vermilion beauty spots. Dad designed it especially for the Gardens—I drew it—Shenango China made it. I love to drink from its lips. (*My Father Who Is on Earth*, p. 89)

John Lloyd Wright used the cup and saucer every morning for coffee, as a reminder of the great Midway Gardens. It is marked "SHENANGO CHINA / NEW CASTLE, PA.," with a seated Indian decorating a vase stamped in ink on the bottom.

Wright's interest in concrete has already been noted, but the textured blocks for the Midway Gardens (figs. 122, 123) represent one of his first efforts in articulating the wall surface by means of precast "textile" blocks, which were characteristic of most of his California houses. A similar treatment is seen in the tiled facade of the Coonley House (fig. 99), where ceramic sections were inserted, whereas in Midway Gardens the design was entirely dependent on the relief. Wright considered this block so important that he gave the example here to The Museum of Modern Art in 1947. Its pristine condition indicates that it was an extra block never used in the building. Another block in the collection of The Art Institute of Chicago shows the wear of exposure to weather.

The drawings for the Midway Gardens furniture (figs. 126a, 127, and 128) show that three different chairs were designed, though apparently only one was produced. The chairs in figure 126a appear to be designed for production in metal. They are a development of the designs for chairs for the Larkin Building (see fig. 81). Cushions appear to be tied to the seat with long tassels hanging at the side. The vertical slats forming the back were seen in the chairs from many of the Prairie houses. Figures 127 and 128 show two additional chair designs, a hexagonal-backed chair that was not executed for Midway Gardens but was adapted for the Imperial Hotel. The second chair, shown in figure 128, may have been produced since a similar oval-backed chair appears in the photograph of the dining room (fig. 124). It also was apparently designed to be produced in metal, and in more recent years these chairs were made for the dining room at Taliesin West.

The table lamp that Wright designed for Midway Gardens is seen in situ in both the drawing of the dining table ensemble (fig. 126a) and in the photograph of the Winter Garden dining room (fig. 124). This lamp served as the prototype for most of Wright's later table lamps. As most of the lamps were apparently destroyed or have been lost, this example is a rare survival. Its decoration of the row of squares is integral to the vertical support and relates to other ornaments in the building. The horizontal member is adjustable so that the octagonal-shaped opaque glass shade can be raised and lowered. This cantilevered construction as well as the use of the exposed electrical cord was seen in the hanging lamps in Unity Church (fig. 97).

■

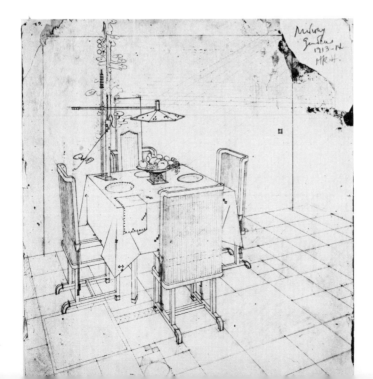

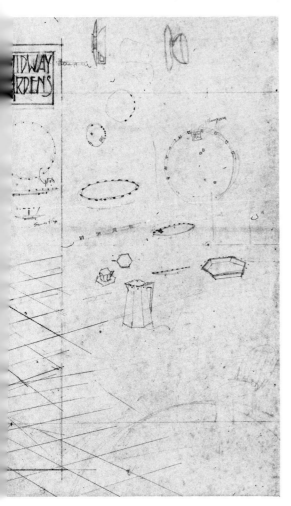

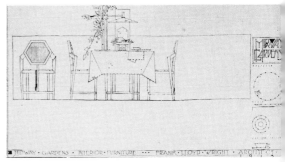

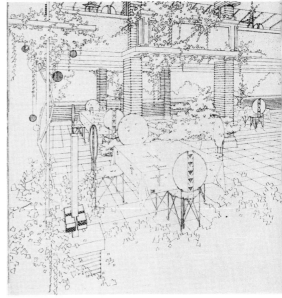

126a (*opposite*). Dining table, chairs, and ceramics (rendering), Midway Gardens, Chicago, Illinois. 1914. 126b (*top, left*). Ceramics (rendering), Midway Gardens. (Figs. 126a and 126b were originally one rendering.) 126c (*top, right*). Cup and saucer, Midway Gardens. Cup: 4″ (10.1 cm) diam.; saucer: 6 1/16″ (15.5 cm) diam. (Lent by Mrs. John Lloyd Wright, Del Mar, California) 127 (*above, right*). Dining table, chairs, and ceramics (elevation and plan), Midway Gardens. 128 (*right*). Dining table, chairs, and light standard (rendering), Midway Gardens.

In its richly ornamented and complex facade of Roman brick and concrete, the F. C. Bogk House is reminiscent of the Midway Gardens. Built in 1916 in Milwaukee, Wisconsin, its square plan can be seen in the illustration of the rug plan (fig. 130). Since most of the rugs that Wright designed for the early houses have been lost or destroyed, the survival of the original carpets for this house is remarkable. Although reproductions were made of the original rugs used in the living room, dining room, and entrance hall, the original hand-knotted wool rugs were saved, including this original stair rug (pl. 11) used between the dining and living rooms. The drawing for this rug is seen in figure 131. It reflects the interior and exterior architecture of the Bogk House. Its design of overlapping squares and rows of squares was seen in

129 (left). Stairway to dining room, F. C. Bogk House, Milwaukee, Wisconsin. 1916. 130 (below). Rugs (plan), F. C. Bogk House. Pencil on paper, 30¾" x 30¼" (78.1 cm x 78 cm). (Lent by Mr. and Mrs. Robert L. Jacobsen, Milwaukee, Wisconsin; Courtesy of The Prairie Archives, Milwaukee Art Center, Wisconsin)

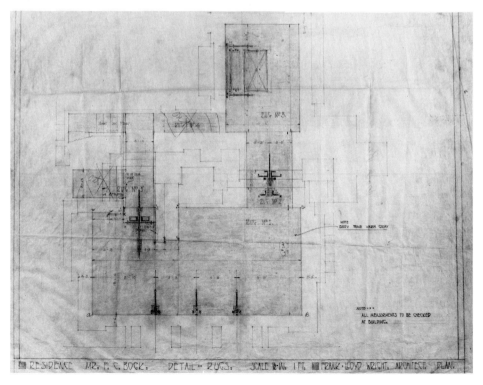

the ornamental scheme of Midway Gardens. The row of square design was also used on the top edge of most of the Bogk furniture. The decoration of the dining room rug (fig. 132) reflects the elevation of the exterior of Midway Gardens if it is placed adjacent to the built-in sideboard, the form of which it reflects in a shadowlike fashion. This rug, placed on axis with the dining room table, also reflects the plan of the table in its design. A rendering of the Bogk living room in a private collection shows an alternative decorative scheme: a circular pattern used in all draperies, rugs, and table scarves, similar to motifs seen in the Midway Gardens murals and the Imperial Hotel ceramics.

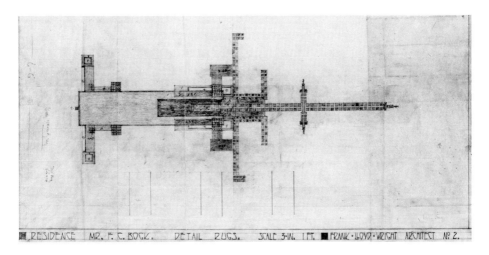

131 (above). Rug for hallway (plan), F. C. Bogk House, Milwaukee, Wisconsin. 1916. Pencil on paper, 22″ x 35″ (55.9 cm x 88.9 cm). (Lent by Mr. and Mrs. Robert L. Jacobsen, Milwaukee, Wisconsin; Courtesy of The Prairie Archives, Milwaukee Art Center, Wisconsin) 132 (below). Rug for dining room (plan), F. C. Bogk House. Pencil on paper, 22″ x 34¾″ (55.9 cm x 88.3 cm).

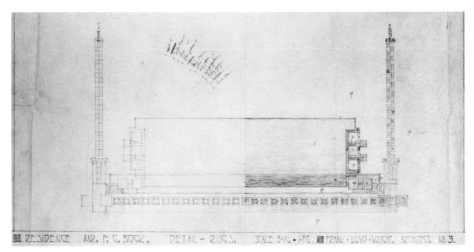

■

A Prairie house designed during the years that Wright was working on the Imperial Hotel was the Henry J. Allen House (1917) in Wichita, Kansas. Its L-shaped plan, which encloses a garden courtyard and reflecting pool, is different from that of the typical Prairie house. The execution of the furnishings designed by Wright for the Allen House was under the supervision of the Niedecken–Walbridge Co., and their journal records the business transactions. Some of Wright's beautiful drawings for the furniture, sketched in colored pencils, were kept by the Niedecken firm. The dining room light standard (fig. 133), seen in front and side elevation as well as in plans on a fragment drawing, is a graceful and beautiful design that incorporates two functions—lighting and a plant stand—in one form. The lamp form is adapted from earlier Wright designs for light standards that were a part of dining tables. The drawing for the Martin dining table (fig. 95) and the photograph of the Robie dining room (fig. 107) illustrate tables with lamps that served as the prototype for this example. The notation on the drawing indicates that two of these light standards were made. A very similar tall lamp was designed for the Sherman M. Booth House (1915–1916) in Glencoe, Illinois (see pl. 92 of exhibition catalogue *The Arts and Crafts Movement in America, 1876–1916*, edited by Robert Judson Clark, Princeton, N. J.: Princeton University Press, 1972). Whereas the Booth lamp enframes the en-

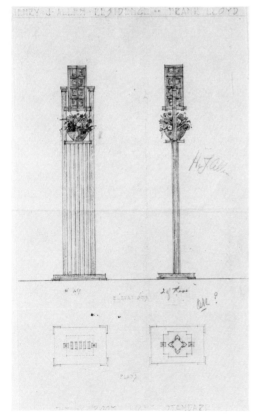

133 (*left*). Dining room light standard (front and side elevations and plans), Henry J. Allen House, Wichita, Kansas. 1917. Pencil on paper, 14¾" x 7½" (37.5 cm x 19 cm). (Lent by Mr. and Mrs. Robert L. Jacobsen, Milwaukee, Wisconsin; Courtesy of The Prairie Archives, Milwaukee Art Center, Wisconsin) 134 (*opposite*). Dressing table and chair (front and side elevations and plans), Henry J. Allen House. Pencil on paper, 14⅝" x 17⅞" (37.1 cm x 45.4 cm). (Lent by Mr. and Mrs Robert L. Jacobsen, Milwaukee, Wisconsin; Courtesy of The Prairie Archives, Milwaukee Art Center, Wisconsin)

tire shade, the Allen lamp is held by side supports; an extra step at the base is included in the Booth example. In the drawing for the dressing table and chair in Mrs. Allen's boudoir (fig. 134), the furniture is placed in a partial architectural setting so that one sees the relation of the furniture to the room as well as to smaller objects. The leaded-glass window to the left of the dressing table mirror is balanced by the tall vase with flowers to the right. This furniture drawing, which, as noted, was detailed on December 20, illustrates Wright's interest in scale for his furnishings and interiors, which he achieved by drawing these elevations, where different pieces of furniture could be seen in relation to one another. The design for the curtains and the table scarf is based on circle motifs. These drawings, which were sent to Niedecken from Wright's studio, were probably developed further into working drawings.

■

The commission for the Imperial Hotel (fig. 135) was another great opportunity for Wright to create a total unified design that included all the decoration details, from the furnishings and carpets to ceramics and silver. The design was begun in 1915, construction started in 1917, and the hotel opened in 1922. The plan, structure, and ornamentation were the most ambitious and complex of all Wright's work:

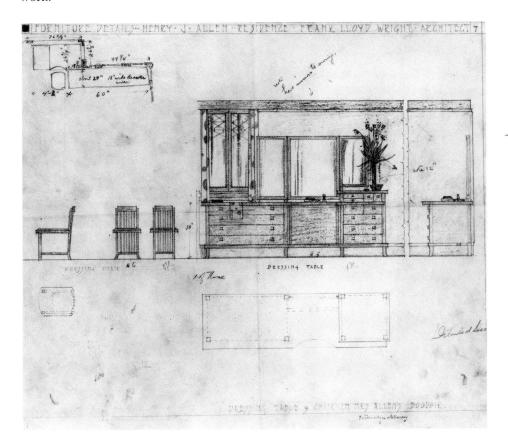

We had a hundred or more clever stone "choppers" beating out patterns of the building on the greenish, leopard-spotted lava, for that period.

On an average we employed about 600 men continually for four years. As a large proportion of them came from the surrounding country they lived round about in the building as we built it. . . . And we tried faithfully—sometimes frantically and often profanely—to teach them how to build it, half-way between our way and their way. . . . How skillful they were! What craftsmen! How patient and clever. (*An Autobiography*, p. 217)

The large building, which was H-shaped in plan, rested on concrete piers. Large garden courts and pools surrounded the hotel. The lavish and rich ornamentation of the grounds and the structure itself was made possible in part by the use of native Oya stone, which could be cut so easily into elaborate decoration for the structure itself; ornament of terra-cotta and copper was also used on the structure, both inside (fig. 136) and outside (fig. 135). The copper section (fig. 137) is part of the exterior cornice and in its use of a combination of triangular, hexagonal, and rectilinear shapes reflects the shapes of the structure itself. The section of terra-cotta ornament (fig. 138) was part of the exterior and interior facades, which created a rich mosaic effect (fig. 139) similar to that used at the Midway Gardens and on the California houses.

The interior spaces of the Imperial Hotel were also richly ornamented and spe-

135. Imperial Hotel, Tokyo, Japan. 1916–1922 (razed 1968).

136 (*below*). Interior, Imperial Hotel, Tokyo, Japan. 1916–1922.   137 (*above*). Architectural fragment, Imperial Hotel. Copper, 12″ x 49″ x 5″ (30.5 cm x 124.5 cm x 12.7 cm). (Lent by the State University of New York at Buffalo)   138 (*top, left*). Architectural block, Imperial Hotel. Terra-cotta, 8″ x 8½″ (20.3 cm x 21.6 cm). (Lent by the State University of New York at Buffalo)   139 (*top, right*). Imperial Hotel (detail of interior).

cial furniture was designed for the entire building. Hexagonal-backed chairs were used throughout the hotel. Most of the early versions were caned in the back and seat and on the sides, as seen in the chairs in situ (fig. 140), so that the structure of the chair was revealed. The chair seen in figure 141, however, was originally uphol- stered, as there is no evidence of caning. Photographs of the Imperial Hotel show chairs upholstered as well as caned, and the caned version frequently had cushions attached to the back or seat. When the hotel was demolished in 1968, the furniture was distributed to various museums and collections, some given to American muse- ums, such as The Museum of Modern Art, the Cooper–Hewitt, and the Philadelphia Museum of Art. These chairs were covered with a leatherette that was evidently a later upholstery. The Philadelphia chair had evidence of an earlier upholstery; rem- nants of a dark blue fabric were found beneath original tacks in the hexagonal back. The original finish of the chair, which was quite light as indicated in areas of pro- tected wood, has now turned yellow with age. A wood analysis of the Philadelphia chair indicated that the chair was primarily oak, with a seat frame of sweet gum and seat blocking of elm.

The design of the chair echoes the interior architecture, with its hexagonal- shaped forms in the cornice and the ceiling (fig. 136). Variations of the hexagonal shape were used in the back, seat, and sides of this chair; the legs are canted in- wardly and outwardly to form half a hexagon. One is surprised to find that the chairs are so fragile and small in scale. They may have been too delicate for the stature of foreign guests to the Imperial Hotel, and chairs were undoubtedly frequently bro- ken. Repairs and replacements must have been common, and therefore it is difficult to give an exact date to this chair. One of the drawings in the Taliesin archives for an "overstuffed chair" at Taliesin is dated February 15, 1921, which would be a more specific date for when the furniture was first produced.

Occasional tables were also used throughout the hotel. The example in figure 142 demonstrates the use of integral ornament (rows of squares around the edge) to give emphasis to the structure. This device was used earlier for the Bogk furniture and later for the Heritage–Henredon furniture. The stepped terminus used for each leg here was also used in the dining chairs of the Hollyhock House.

Wright's only known design in silver was for the three-piece coffee service (fig. 143) for the Imperial Hotel. The cream pot and sugar bowl are seen in elevation and plan, the coffeepot in elevation, and the tray in quarter plan. A detail of the per- forated handle is to the far right. The hotel's rectilinear monogram "IH" echoes the plan of the structure itself. The hexagonal forms of the sugar bowl, coffeepot, and cream pot are those seen throughout the hotel. At least one silver coffee service was executed to this design, as it appears in a photograph of the dining–living room at Taliesin II in Spring Green (Hitchcock, pl. 177). The cream pitcher (pl. 12) is the only piece to survive today. Of fine craftsmanship and raised with the use of hand tools, its hexagonal shape gives the impression that it could easily be machine-made. The monogram seen in the drawing was not executed. A Japanese maker's marks are stamped on the bottom of this piece.

Various fabrics and rugs were especially designed to complete the unity of the Imperial Hotel. Upholstery fabric is seen on some of the bedroom furniture in plate 229 of Hitchcock. A section (pl. 14) is one of three samples to have been preserved at

140 (below). Interior, Imperial Hotel, Tokyo, Japan. 1916–1922. 141 (above, right). Side chair, Imperial Hotel. Oak, upholstered seat and back, 38" x 16" x 17" (96.5 cm x 40.6 cm x 43.2 cm). (Lent by Cooper–Hewitt Museum, the Smithsonian Institution's National Museum of Design, New York) 142 (above, left). Oak table, Imperial Hotel. (Cooper-Hewitt Museum, the Smithsonian Institution's National Museum of Design, New York)

Taliesin. As in the Midway Gardens murals, the design is based on disks and over-lapping circles.

The Imperial Hotel provided Wright with a second opportunity to design a dinner service in ceramics for an important public building (see pl. 13). The use of circles was seen in the Coonley Playhouse windows (pl. 10), where they were intro-duced into an otherwise rectilinear design. The more direct prototype for this de-sign is seen in the Midway Gardens mural (fig. 125)—Wright's first experiment with overlapping circles. Two variations in the circle design, both asymmetrically placed on the plate, were used in this dinner service, two pieces of which are illustrated here. In a small circle on each piece of the setting is the abstracted Imperial Hotel monogram "IH"—reminiscent of Wright's own early monogram signature but quite different from the rectilinear monogram designed for the silver coffee service. The circular motifs are also reflected in the ornamentation of the interior architecture of the hotel.

Ceramics designed by Wright were produced for the Imperial Hotel to Wright's designs from the 1920s until the 1960s (production of the china was inter-rupted by World War II). The early versions were of a finer, thinner porcelain, which evidently did not hold up to the heavy use in the hotel. In this version, the circle design continued from the outside to the inside of the cup—a particularly nice detail that is seen in japonisme-styled ceramics. According to Bruce Pfeiffer, the large red circle that overlaps the edge was intended to hide the lipstick marks, but the underlying design principle embodied in this aesthetic technique was to en-hance the organic and sculptural quality of the vessel by allowing the design to complete itself over and beyond the cup's rim.

Overlapping circle designs appear also on Viennese ceramics of the early

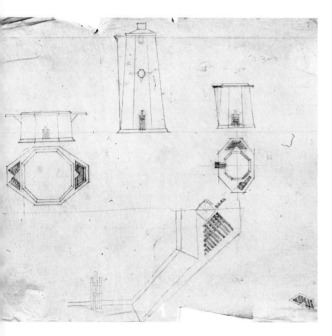

143. Coffee service (elevation and plan), Imperial Hotel, Tokyo, Japan. 1916. Pen-cil on paper. (Copyright © 1977 The Frank Lloyd Wright Foundation, all rights reserved)

twentieth century, seen for example in porcelain designed by Josef Böck (pls. 153 and 154 of Waltraud Neuwirth's *Österreichische Keramik des Jugendstils*, exhibition catalogue published by Österreichisches Museum für angewandte Kunst, Wien; München: Prestel-Verlag, 1975). The underlying aesthetic interest, however, is different from Wright's. In the Secessionist example, the flower of the cup is continued into the saucer, unifying the two, but Wright's intent was to finish the design *over* the lip of the cup, and therefore he began the design high so that it had to overlap in order to "dematerialize" the wall of the cup and to give continuity to the design— all architectural considerations applied to a decorative object.

The drawing for a hanging lamp for the Imperial Hotel (fig. 144) shows the same interest in the complex interaction of planes seen in the Dana House lamps (fig. 71). The form of this lamp is compressed and has a delicate vertical appearance in comparison to the Prairie prototype.

■

While Wright was working on the Imperial Hotel, his major commission in this country was for Los Angeles oil heiress Aline Barnsdall (1882–1946). Born in Bradford, Pennsylvania, Aline Barnsdall was one of two sisters to inherit the family oil fortune. She studied drama in London and was managing a little theatre in Chicago when she met Wright. She moved to Los Angeles around 1915 and managed a theatre there too.

Hollyhock House was to be a natural house that responded to its region of California, as had the Prairie houses to the Middle West (pl. 15). The commission included the client's home in Hollywood as well as two other houses, which were subsequently demolished. Projects for a theatre and a terrace of shops were designed but not built. Wright devoted ample space in *An Autobiography* to discussing Hollyhock House:

> So, when called upon by Aline Barnsdall—her metier the theater—to build a house for her in Hollywood, why not make architecture stand up and show itself on her new ground, known as Olive Hill, as Romance? A bit sentimental,

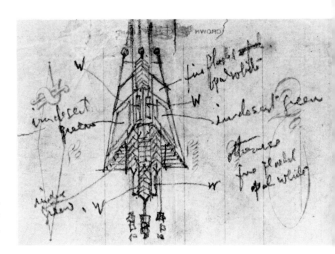

144. Hanging light fixture (rendering), Imperial Hotel, Tokyo, Japan. 1916. Pencil on paper, 2¾" x 3⅝" (7 cm x 9.3 cm). (The Frank Lloyd Wright Foundation)

Miss Barnsdall had pre-named the house for the Hollyhock she loved for many reasons, all of them good ones, and called upon me to render her favorite flower as a feature of Architecture how I might. (p. 226)

The house was, for Wright, an expression of individuality and democracy:

Individuality is the most precious thing in life, after all—isn't it? An honest democracy must believe that it is. . . . In any expression of the human spirit it is principle manifest as character that alone endures. And individuality is the true property of such character. No . . . not one house that possessed genuine character in this sense but stands, safe, outside the performance of the passing show. Hollyhock house is such a house. (*An Autobiography*, p. 232)

Wright described the difficulties in designing and constructing the house. Since both he and Miss Barnsdall were traveling at the same time, "Hollyhock House had mostly to be built by telegraph so far as client and architect had anything to do with it or each other" (*An Autobiography*, p. 228). Designed in 1918, the house was not built until 1920–1921, under the direction of Wright's superintendent, Rudolph M. Schindler.

Hollyhock House was one of Wright's most ambitious residential endeavors. Built near the top of Olive Hill, the main block of the house surrounds a central courtyard. Most of the windows are small (pl. 16) and the wall surface is solid to keep out the heat and light. Wright used exposed poured concrete for the walls, and near the mansard-type roof are the ornamental rows of poured-concrete hollyhocks (figs. 145, 146), the integral theme of the house.

In 1927 Aline Barnsdall gave her house and eleven acres of what is now Barnsdall Park to the City of Los Angeles to be used for recreational and cultural purposes. The house is now open as a museum. Most of the original furniture was

designed by Rudolph M. Schindler, and it was replaced in later years. However, the dining room table and chairs (fig. 147) were of Wright's design. The hollyhock motif, highly conventionalized, was used as the basic decorative ornament for the six dining chairs, which are unique to this house, two of which are illustrated here (fig. 148). The tall spine of the hollyhock has replaced the slats of the earlier chairs; its small flowers seem to grow up the back of the chair, beginning above the base and extending above the crest rail. The back of the chair is also divided into horizontal rectilinear panels, which act as a trellis for the hollyhock and are echoed in smaller scale in the block course in the dining room walls. These panels are also repeated to scale on the triangular base of the hexagonal dining table.

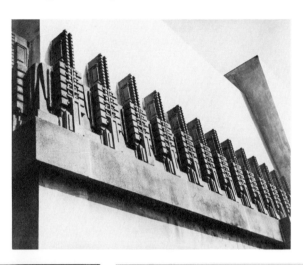

145 (*opposite*). Aline Barnsdall Hollyhock House, Los Angeles, California. 1920. 146 (*right*). Hollyhock House (detail of hollyhock frieze). 147 (*below, left*). Dining room, Hollyhock House. 148 (*below, right*). Two side chairs, dining room, Hollyhock House. Oak, upholstered seat, 45¾" x 17¾" x 20" (116.2 cm x 45.1 cm x 50.8 cm). (Lent by Los Angeles Municipal Art Gallery, California)

Although the motif of the hollyhock is clearly suggested, the abstract design of rows of squares that seem to grow like a plant was a favorite of Wright's. It appeared quite early, in the design of the birdhouses for the Martin House (fig. 90), in the ornament of the Larkin Building, and of the Unity Church, to name a few instances.

The design of the windows of Hollyhock House (pl. 16) was based on an asymmetrical composition, an idea first seen in the windows for Midway Gardens. What was apparently new to the Hollyhock windows was the color palette, composed of purple and green, Wright's response to a new environment—"beautiful in California in the way California herself is beautiful," as Wright put it. The windows wrap around the corner with no mullion, and the narrow windows are used vertically and horizontally to create an interesting pattern.

One of the most interesting features of the Hollyhock interior is the fireplace, with its reflecting pool, relief mural, and skylight above (fig. 149), a development of the idea expressed in the Dana House. The mural is based on several Wright motifs: the overlapping disks and the square, as well as motifs unique to Hollyhock House. In contrast are the symmetrical and rectilinear reflecting pool and skylight. The Hollyhock House interior also included "carpets woven in Austria for the inside floors," according to Wright, and "she brought 'home' a few choice objets d'art from Europe to add to others built into the walls of the rooms themselves, and to go with the furniture that was made part of the house design itself" (*An Autobiography,* p. 233).

It is not known whether the two lamps seen in elevation and plan in the drawing in figure 150 were executed, but they have not shown up nor do they appear in

149. Living room fireplace and reflecting pool, Hollyhock House, Los Angeles, California. 1920.

any known photographs. They represent a new and innovative form in lamps for Wright; in their complex angular shapes they are reminiscent of furnishings for the Imperial Hotel. The two lamps are identical except in height. The complexity of the cast-brass base and supports is reflected in the shades, which, as the detail indicates, were to be of sand-blasted and clear glass within a cast frame that had a repoussé sheet brass added to it. The detail of this framing seen in the lower right-hand corner anticipates some of the designs for later perforated Usonian panels.

■

Wright's other California houses of the 1920s were characterized by their use of textured concrete blocks, reinforced by steel rods. In *An Autobiography*, Wright described his desire to get some system of building construction as a basis for architecture:

> Form would come in time if a sensible, feasible system of building-construction would only come first.
>
> The concrete block? The cheapest (and ugliest) thing in the building world. It lived mostly in the architectural gutter as an imitation of "rock face" stone.
>
> Why not see what could be done with that gutter-rat? Steel wedded to it cast inside the joints and the block itself brought into some broad, practical scheme of general treatment then why would it not be fit for a phase of modern architecture? It might be permanent, noble, beautiful. It would be cheap. . . . steel

150. Lamps (elevation, plan, and details), Hollyhock House, Los Angeles, California. 1920. Pencil on tracing paper, 26⅝" x 34⅜" (67.6 cm x 86.7 cm). (Lent by Municipal Arts Department, City of Los Angeles, California)

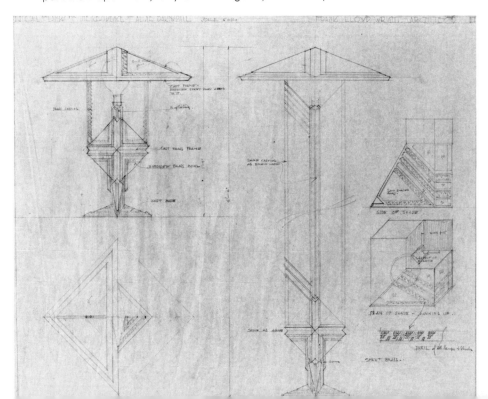

would enter into inert mass as a tensile strength. Concrete was the inert mass and would take compression. Concrete is a plastic material—susceptible to the impress of imagination. I saw a kind of weaving coming out of it. Why not weave a kind of building? . . . I had used the block in some such textured way in the Midway Gardens upper walls. If I could eliminate the mortar joint I could make the whole fabric mechanical. I could do away with skilled labor. I believed I could and began on "La Miniatura." (p. 235)

An exterior view of part of Mrs. Madison Millard's house (fig. 151) shows two types of textured blocks—one perforated, the other not. The Millard blocks are amazingly close in concept to their prototype—the Midway Gardens block seen in figure 123. Each has the same complex relief design, based on overlapping squares and rectangles that are both contained within a single block and continued from block to block. These intricate patterns break up the solid surfaces of the exterior and interior walls and provide a continuous play of light and shadow. A corner block from the Millard House (seen in fig. 152), which originally would have had sharp edges, is now worn from exposure to the weather.

Another variation on the textured block is seen in the majestic 1924 Charles Ennis House in Los Angeles (figs. 153, 154), located prominently on one of the Hollywood hills. The house recalls Mayan architecture in the massing of both the exterior and the interior, with its varying heights of rooms. Rudolph M. Schindler was responsible for supervising and designing the furnishings of this and Wright's other California houses.

When Taliesin at Spring Green burned a second time in 1925, Wright set about

151 (*opposite*). Mrs. George Madison Millard La Miniatura House, Pasadena, California. 1923. 152 (*above, left*). Block, Mrs. George Madison Millard La Miniatura House. Concrete, 15½″ x 7½″ x 8″ (40.6 cm x 18.8 cm x 20 cm). (Lent by Randell C. Makinson, Pasadena, California) 153 (*below*). Charles Ennis House, Los Angeles, California. 1924. 154 (*above, right*). Interior, Charles Ennis House.

again to rebuild his house for the third time on the same site. Taliesin III contains
some of Wright's most spectacular and moving interior spaces. The living room (fig.
155) is particularly beautiful and mystical. Its breathtaking juxtaposition and overlapping of angular and horizontal lines are complex, and yet the effect is one of repose. Oriental objects are combined with furniture designed by the architect in a
carefully controlled, yet relaxed space. The furniture for Taliesin is severely geometric and is related to that designed for the Francis W. Little House in Wayzata. Two
types of armchairs are seen at the dining table, one of which is the high-backed,
slatted type (fig. 155), which is reminiscent of the Prairie furniture and armchairs,
but is quite different from the earlier furniture. The second type (fig. 156), which is
severely rectilinear, recalls the "cube" chairs of Wright's Oak Park studio. A single
broad horizontal splat forms the back, while the space below is open, corresponding
with the vertical board placed between the side stretchers and the arms with a vertical space on either side. The seat is cantilevered. Despite its uncompromising design, the chair is surprisingly comfortable. Feeling that the chair was an important
example of his viewpoint, Wright presented it as a gift to The Museum of Modern
Art in 1949. Before 1932 most of the furniture at Taliesin was made by William H.
Weston (see pp. 222–223). The table lamps designed around 1925 for Taliesin and
used in many later houses were made by Ralph Reeley.

In the 1930s, changes made in the living room included substituting circular
chairs for the rectilinear versions (fig. 157). These chairs were originally designed for
the Darwin D. Martin House and were adapted later for the living area of Wingspread. Another important earlier Taliesin chair is seen in the loggia (fig. 158). This
chair is related to the living room chairs but has broader proportions and an unusual

155 (*opposite*). Living room, Taliesin III, Frank Lloyd Wright House, Spring Green, Wisconsin. 1925. 156 (*above, left*). Armchair, Taliesin III, Frank Lloyd Wright House, c. 1925. (The Museum of Modern Art, New York) 157 (*below*). Living room, Taliesin III, Frank Lloyd Wright House. Remodeling in the mid-1930s. 158 (*above, right*). Loggia, Taliesin II, Frank Lloyd Wright House. c. 1914.

series of square blocks on each side of the back. A discussion of Taliesin's decorative designs would not be complete without a mention of the magnificent curtain designed by Wright in 1933 for the Hillside Theatre (fig. 159). This is a highly conventionalized rendering of Taliesin itself and is related to some of Wright's graphic designs of the period. When this curtain was destroyed by fire in the 1950s, it was replaced by another made of felt and yarn appliquéd on fabric in rich greens, golds, reds, and brown. Executed by the women of Taliesin while Wright was away on a trip, it was presented to him as a birthday surprise.

Wright's commissions of the late 1920s and early 1930s were important because of the seminal ideas contained in the buildings of that period, even though the Depression prevented their being executed. This is also true of Wright's furniture designs, seen in drawings of this period, which were to find expression in Wright's next great creative period.

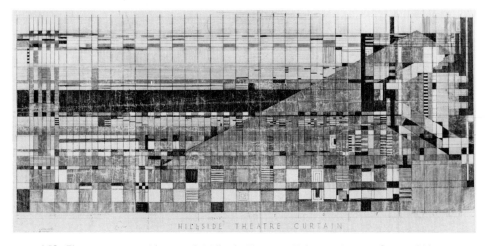

159. Theatre curtain (drawing), Hillside Theatre, Taliesin, Spring Green, Wisconsin. 1933. Colored pencils and gold and white paint on tracing paper, 30¾" x 58½" (78.1 cm x 48.6 cm). (The Frank Lloyd Wright Foundation)

RENAISSANCE:
1930-1959

After the Imperial Hotel, Wright, with other architects, had few architectural commissions because of the Depression. Wright's own personal life had been in turmoil, because of both financial difficulties and a disastrous second marriage. Wright's remarkable recovery began with his relationship with Olgivanna Milanoff, whom he married in 1928. She helped him to organize the Taliesin Fellowship in 1932 and encouraged him to write his autobiography, which was published in the same year. Amazingly Wright, who was in his sixties, began a new career and what can be termed an architectural renaissance, which placed him as the most daring of American architects. In 1936 Wright designed two major works of architecture—Fallingwater and the S. C. Johnson Administration Building—with innovations as staggering as those of the Prairie houses. In 1937, at the age of seventy, Wright designed his first Usonian house, the Herbert Jacobs House in Madison, Wisconsin. Wright's development of this prototype of an inexpensive house for the middle-income family was another major contribution to architecture.

Wright's new winter headquarters—Taliesin West—was constructed in 1932 on the desert in Scottsdale, Arizona, near Phoenix. Built from native materials, it nestled close to the ground. The first section to be completed was the drafting room, which had a white canvas roof to diffuse the light and side flaps for ventilation. The angular shapes of the living room (fig. 160) are reflected in the four large easy chairs. The contrasting straight lines of the built-in benches give the room the feeling of repose so important to Wright.

Fallingwater (1936) in Bear Run, Pennsylvania (fig. 161), was Wright's most important domestic architectural commission after the Robie House. Sited above a waterfall in remote and wooded acreage in the southwestern part of the state, it was the summer house of the Pittsburgh department store owner Edgar Kaufmann, whose son had been a Taliesin fellow. Reinforced concrete was used to construct the cantilevered system of the house, which was actually an extension of the cliff beside a mountain stream. Wright created a "living space over and above the stream upon several terraces upon which a man who loved the place sincerely, one who liked to listen to the waterfall, might well live" (*The Architectural Forum*, January 1938, p. 36). Fallingwater is one of Wright's best examples of a house conforming to and being shaped by its site. The deep overhangs of the house provide the interior with

160 (*left*). Living room, Taliesin West, Scottsdale, Arizona. 1932. (The Frank Lloyd Wright Memorial Foundation)

161 (*below*). Edgar J. Kaufmann House, "Fallingwater," Bear Run, Pennsylvania. 1936.

softened, diffused lighting. Its integral furnishings combine with a variety of rare and beautiful antiques.

The furniture Wright designed for Fallingwater was superbly crafted of walnut by the Gillen Woodworking Company of Milwaukee. In 1937 this firm had revived the recently defunct Matthews Brothers Company, which had made furniture to Wright's designs for some of the Prairie houses. Two of the workmen who made the Fallingwater furniture (Matt Phillippi and Tony Prochaska) had been at the Matthews firm when the furniture for the Martin House had been made.

A fascinating account of the manufacture of the furniture for Fallingwater appeared in the July 18, 1937, *Milwaukee Sentinel* ("Gillen Artisans Create Cabinets for Wright's House on a Waterfall," Collection of Edgar Tafel). This information is further documented by information from Edgar Tafel, the Taliesin apprentice who supervised the construction of the house. North Carolina walnut and walnut veneer, selected for its variety in beautiful graining, were used throughout the house, according to the *Milwaukee Sentinel* article. The entire tree was used, including sapwood as well as heartwood, and Wright requested that the graining of the wood be used horizontally instead of vertically, as would be typical, in order to resist the moisture of the waterfall and to prevent warping. A nine-ply wood was used instead of the usual five-ply. Radiators were camouflaged by seats, tables, or bookshelves. The wardrobes in the bedrooms had concealed lighting above their tops for illumination of the room. Gillen was responsible for making most of the built-in and freestanding furniture at its Milwaukee shop, and the first pieces were shipped to Fallingwater after three weeks of work.

The freestanding furniture, which includes coffee and occasional tables, is parallel in concept and form to the architecture of the house. The tops of the tables and their supports echo the cantilevered forms of the house itself. The refined craftsmanship of the Fallingwater furniture attests to the skills of the Gillen firm. Attention was given to minute details, such as the rounded molding around the edges of the tabletops, the carefully veneered surfaces of all four sides and top, the legs tenoned into the top, and the insertion of wood pegs or wood filler over nails seen from the top. The tables are substantially constructed—supported by rectangular blocks screwed to the top from underneath, with four blocks nailed at each corner.

Although preliminary construction of the S. C. Johnson Administration Building (fig. 162) had begun in the fall of 1936 in Racine, Wisconsin, it was not com-

162. S. C. Johnson Administration Building, Racine, Wisconsin. 1936-1939.

pleted with its special furnishings until the spring of 1939. The spacious interior workroom, 20 x 128 x 228 feet, which is ringed by a balcony (fig. 163) and lighted by skylights, is an incredible and dazzling space. It is broken by a forest of giant-sized piers, which grow like plants from a very small base to large, circular, mushroomlike tops. They serve aesthetic as well as structural purposes, since, although they do not support the roof, they form much of the ceiling. As was the Larkin Building, the Johnson Administration Building was an expression of an ideal working environment by a paternalistic company. Like its predecessor, it also shields the worker from the unpleasant noise and odors of its industrial location. Strips of translucent Pyrex tubing are used as partitions and skylights throughout the building (figs. 164, 165), emphasizing in their circular forms and placement the basic forms of the building. This tubing achieves a rich and unique decorative effect while being integral to the building and is in strong contrast to the geometric art glass of the Prairie houses.

For the Johnson Administration Building, Wright designed special cast-aluminum and magnesite furniture. It was the first metal office furniture to be executed from Wright's designs since the furniture for the Larkin Building (the Dwight Bank furniture of 1905 was of wood). The drawing for the desk and chair in figure 168 was published in the 1938 *Architectural Forum.* It shows a front plus two side elevations, a plan of the desk and chair, and a plan of the armchair alone. The furniture is shown in close juxtaposition, with the chair being overlapped by and the desk overlapping one of the piers, a section of which has been cut away so that the relationship to the desk–chair combination can be seen.

Although both the Larkin and the Johnson chairs were of metal, the aesthetic had changed remarkably. In place of the rigid rectilinear forms of the Larkin furniture (fig. 80), the Johnson furniture was conceived in the curves and circles of the architecture. For example, the circular form of the seat and the back of the chair mirrors the lily-pad-like circular capitals of the columns of the interior, while the half-circles are seen in the desk as well as in the interior walls.

The chair is unusual in the history of furniture. Its gaining support from only three legs not only provided an interesting design opportunity but was functional as well. This design recognized for the first time the support that is given by the legs of a chair's occupant—assuming that one's weight is evenly balanced and both feet are squarely on the floor—thus encouraging good posture (fig. 166). If the sitter chose a different position—for example, with legs crossed—the chair would lose its stability, and the unfortunate individual would be capsized. This evidently has occurred enough times so that today all but a few of the original three-legged chairs have been converted to four legs—a compromise in the design for practicality. The use of the three-legged chair, however, made a striking aesthetic arrangement when considered as a unit with the desk. The chair is still used, as originally intended, throughout the building, both with and without arms.

Although the chair supports would appear to be tubular steel, Wright's response to furniture designs by Marcel Breuer and Mies van der Rohe, they are, in fact, made of cast-aluminum piping that has been soldered together and is quite rigid. Wright wanted the seats and backs reversible so they could be flipped over to even the wear. Although leather was indicated for the upholstery of the seat and back of the armchair, a textured fabric was used when the chairs were executed. A

163 (*below*). Work area, S. C. Johnson Administration Building, Racine, Wisconsin. 1936–1939. 164 (*above, left*). Interior. S. C. Johnson Administration Building. 165 (*above, right*). Interior, S. C. Johnson Administration Building.

few chairs retain this original upholstery material, which has proved very durable; however, the original upholstery has been generally replaced. The chair retains its original paint, a russet color that is used throughout the building, contributing to the overall harmony of the interior. According to Anne Zeller of the Steelcase Co., which made the furniture, Wright specified this color to be the same as the bricks of the building.

The desk and chair frames are one of the early examples of "open office planning" as we know it today, and the multilayer desk was a forerunner of today's work station. Wright specified other models with cutout niches for business machines, which rested on the lower surface at a comfortable working height (fig. 166).

Instead of designing a desk chair and a visitor's chair, Wright designed interchangeable feet. The arms of the officers' chairs repeat the oval shape of the desktop. Variations in the basic design for the secretary's chair were used for the officer's chair (fig. 169). Designed more for comfort than to encourage good posture, these stationary chairs have four rather than three legs and are not thought of as a unit with the desk. Horizontal aluminum piping is used on the sides from the stretcher to the arms, rather than coming around the back below the seats as in the secretary's chairs. Rubber disks or casters can be used at the terminals. These chairs are comfortably proportioned and have an extension of the side arms. Notes in Wright's own handwriting indicate that the weight of the metal and the finish were to be the same as for the other chairs, and the "old Gold" upholstery was to be the same as that used in H. F. Johnson, Jr.'s, house. The drawing is dated April 17, 1939.

The desk in figures 166 and 167 is used throughout the building. The form of the desk, like that of the chair, reflects the interior and exterior architecture, and the three top sections of the desk reflect the overall form of the building itself. The horizontal bars on the sides continue the horizontal lines of the doors and the tubular glass in the partitions. Here the writing surface is daringly cantilevered. A shelf section beneath the writing surface is cantilevered to the right to support the draw-

166 (*below, left*). Desk and chair in use, S. C. Johnson Administration Building, Racine, Wisconsin. 1936–1939. 167 (*below, right*). Desk and chair, S. C. Johnson Administration Building. Painted steel and walnut desk: 33¾" x 84" x 32" (85.7 cm x 173.4 cm x 81.3 cm); painted steel and walnut, upholstered seat and back, chair: 36" x 17¾" x 20" (91.4 cm x 45.1 cm x 50.8 cm). (Lent by Dr. and Mrs. Elias Sedlin, New York)

ers. The wastebasket is supported on the inside horizontal bars, well above floor-mop level. Its half-cylindrical shape matches the drawers, which are hinged at the side and swing out toward the user. These innovations make the desk a more compact and efficient unit under which it is easy to clean. (This efficiency had also been a concern with the Larkin furniture, where swinging chairs had been attached to the desk.) The drawings at Taliesin West for this furniture indicate that a patent was applied for in November 1937.

At the same time the S. C. Johnson Administration Building was being built, Wingspread (fig. 170), the magnificent Herbert F. Johnson House, was being designed for siting in Wind Point, a beautiful and secluded area just north of Racine. Its "living area" (fig. 171) is grouped around an immense chimney that extends through two floors into a clerestory above.

Wright considered Wingspread a late Prairie house that resembled the Coonley House, where various functions were "zoned" in separate units grouped together and connected by a corridor. The plan of Wingspread was oriented so that sunlight would fall in all of the rooms:

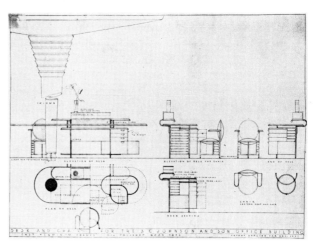

168 (right). Desk and chair (elevations and plans), S. C. Johnson Administration Building, Racine, Wisconsin. 1936-1939. (Architectural Forum, January 1938) 169 (below). Officer's chairs for Herbert F. Johnson office (front and side elevations and plan), S. C. Johnson Administration Building. Pencil on paper, 24" x 24" (60.9 cm x 60.9 cm). (Lent by Steelcase Inc., Grand Rapids, Michigan)

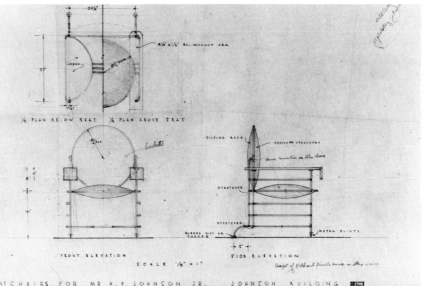

At the center of the four zones the spacious Living Room stands. A tall central chimneystack with five fireplaces divides this vertical space into spaces for the various domestic functions: Entrance Hall, Family Living Room, Library Living Room, and Dining Room. Extending from this lofty central room are four wings—three low and one with mezzanine. The one with mezzanine floor and galleries is for the master, mistress and young daughter. Another wing extends from the central space for their several boys—a playroom at the end, a graduated deep-pool in conjunction—another wing for service and utilities—another for guests and five motor cars. Each wing has independent views on two sides, each has perfect privacy—the whole being united by a complete house telephone system. (*The Architectural Forum*, January 1938, p. 56)

A dynamic tension is set up between the relative stability of the wings, experienced from the inside, and the dramatic upward movement of the central area. The reverse is true of the experience of the exterior, where the central living area is stable, while the wings are cantilevered as if in flight. The hexagonal-shaped furniture designed for the house reflects the stability of the central living area. Coffee tables, end tables, and hassocks were conceived in forms that reflect the shape of the room itself. The end table has a veneered top and supports and a "square-inch" motif is the only ornamentation. "DRWG. F 2/TABLE A" is stamped underneath.

The juxtaposition of oval and hexagonal shapes in the house is reflected in the furniture. The barrel chairs, which were used for the first time in the Darwin D. Martin House (1904; fig. 92), were adapted for use in Wingspread. The inspiration, according to Edgar Tafel, who was the Taliesin superintendent for Wingspread, was a visit by Wright and himself to the Martin House around 1936.

The built-in furniture, the hexagonal-shaped furniture, and the barrel chairs were made to Wright's designs by Gillen Woodwork Corporation of Milwaukee, Wisconsin, who also made the furniture for Fallingwater. Some of the movable chairs were selected from a local furniture store named Porter's. Edgar Tafel explained the procedure for making the Wingspread furniture. Wright made the original drawings, including the details, which he showed to Herbert Johnson at Taliesin. Then Edgar Tafel and other apprentices "expanded the drawings" and sent prints to Gillen, where the shop drawings were produced. The work was done on a "time" basis by Gillen, and according to Tafel:

> All the plywood was made in their shop, with chestnut cores. . . . I selected the flitches and checked progress at their plant, generally Friday afternoons on the way back from Racine to Taliesin, or, Monday's on the return. . . . I had power to make changes and approve, and Mr. Johnson would ask to have certain items included . . . like special drawers. . . . Mr. Wright liked the Gillen outfit, they made everything easy to do—at the time. . . . occasionally we would fall behind in making decisions, and Elmer Gutknecht would come to Taliesin with reams of material for approval. (Letter to the author, June 10, 1977)

■

The Usonian house was developed by Frank Lloyd Wright to provide an inexpensive house for the average middle-income American family. It was the prototype

170 (below). Herbert F. Johnson, Jr., Wingspread House, Wind Point, north of Racine, Wisconsin. 1937. 171 (right). Living area, Herbert F. Johnson, Jr., Wingspread House.

of the ranch house, which was to become the standard modern American home until land costs dictated the development of the multilevel tract home. The word *Usonian* is the term for the United States used by Samuel Butler in his utopian novel *Erewhon* (1917). The first Usonian house was designed in 1936 for another client but was built for Herbert Jacobs in 1937 near Madison, Wisconsin. Various ingenious innovations were developed for the Usonian house in the interest of economy, and yet the client was provided with an individually designed house. In the design of interior spaces, for example, the house was built as a unit on a single concrete slab, which held the gravity heating, thus eliminating radiators; storage areas at the first-floor level replaced the cellar; clerestory windows, which often became perforated wooden light screens, gave wall space for built-in furniture and bookshelves; using only a utility core (often the kitchen, fireplace, and sometimes the bathroom) of masonry, usually brick, the remaining wall sections of dry construction were set up on the site in planning based on a module; the interior wood walls were waxed or varnished rather than plastered or painted; light fixtures became recessed lighting. Built-in and freestanding furniture was designed to be made on the job site and often reflected the module of the house.

The Usonian house designed for Dr. and Mrs. Paul Hanna in 1937 in Palo Alto, California (fig. 172), was an important experimental house for Wright, as it was a preliminary study for prefabrication and the first example of his use of hexagonal design. Its materials—primarily redwood—were native to California. Redwood partitions were erected on a concrete floor, which was cut into hexagonal tiles, hence the name "Honeycomb" for the house (fig. 173). The hexagonal shapes provided the basic modular unit. Wright wrote:

I am convinced that a cross-section of honeycomb has more fertility and flexibility where human movement is concerned than the square. The obtuse angle is more suited to human "to and fro" than the right angle. That flow and movement is, in this design, a characteristic lending itself admirably to life, as life is to be lived in it. The hexagon has been conservatively treated—however, it is allowed to appear in plan only and in the furniture which literally rises from and befits the floor pattern of the concrete slab upon which the whole stands. (*The Architectural Forum*, January 1938, p. 64)

The design of the dining chair in figure 175 can be understood in terms of its basis in the "hexagonal unit or module," which gave the house what Wright called "a livelier domesticity." This chair was one of eighteen dining chairs, some of which are seen in situ around the dining table in figure 174. Designed in 1936, the chairs were not executed until 1957 in a shop in the Hanna House. Although they were integral to the architecture, they were impractical. According to Dr. Hanna, the family

used these chairs for the first few years, but a number of guests tipped forward and lost their balance off the chairs because of the triangular suspension points. Mr. Wright condemned his design vociferously and asked us to destroy them all. . . . Mr. Wright said to us often that he had tried for a lifetime to design

172 (*opposite*). Paul R. Hanna Honeycomb House, Palo Alto, California. 1937. 173 (*right*). Living room, Paul R. Hanna House.

furniture which pleased him, but that he hardly ever succeeded. He said he supposed that the fault was in his attempt to make every piece of furniture a major architectural effort. (Letter from Paul R. Hanna to the author, August 4, 1977)

The cutout design on the base is reminiscent of some of the perforated panels in the other Usonian houses.

■

The Usonian house designed for Mr. and Mrs. Loren Pope in Falls Church, Virginia (fig. 176), was built in 1940. When the house was threatened with destruction

174 (*below*). Dining room, Paul R. Hanna House, Palo Alto, California. 1937. 175 (*left*). Side chair, Paul R. Hanna House. Redwood, upholstered cushion, 34¼" x 22½" x 16" (87 cm x 57.1 cm x 40.6 cm). (Lent by Stanford University, California; Gift of Mr. and Mrs. Paul R. Hanna)

by Interstate Highway 66 in 1964, the house was saved through the efforts of Mrs. Robert A. Leighey, the second owner, who gave it to the National Trust for Historic Preservation. The house was dismantled and moved to the grounds of Woodlawn Plantation, Mount Vernon, Virginia, and is now open to the public.

The Pope–Leighey House has the typical Usonian L-shaped plan, which, despite its small size, provides a spacious living room with eleven-foot-high ceilings. The correspondence between Loren Pope and Frank Lloyd Wright concerning the building of this house was published in a special issue of *Historic Preservation* (April–September 1969) devoted to the Pope–Leighey House. In a letter to Wright dated August 18, 1939, Loren Pope, a young newspaperman with a limited income, asked if the architect would build him a home. He outlined the details of what he wanted and asked if he could personally build the furniture later, "that first cost of the house might not permit." He indicated further that although not a cabinetmaker, he liked working with wood.

Wright wrote about the furnishings for a Usonian house, "Rugs, draperies, and furnishings that are suitable for a Usonian house are those, too, that are organic in character; that is, textures and patterns that sympathize in their own design and construction with the design and construction of the particular house they occupy and embellish" (Frank Lloyd Wright, *The Natural House*, New York: Horizon Press, 1954, p. 167).

The problem of furnishing the Pope–Leighey House was solved by Wright, as most of the furniture was built in. Even the plywood chairs, which are seen in figure

176. Pope-Leighey House, Falls Church, Virginia. 1940. Originally known as the Loren B. Pope House and located in Falls Church, Virginia, this residence was moved to Mount Vernon, Virginia, in 1964 and is now known as the Pope-Leighey House.

177, appear to be built in, although they could be moved from the living area, where they were used as easy chairs, to the dining table. An earlier version of the chair had been designed in 1939 but not made; this simplified version was one of twelve built for the house in 1940. Five were used at the dining table, five as "built-in" benches, and two freestanding in the living room. This simple, forthright chair was designed to be made by the millworkers on the job site rather than by a cabinetmaker, whose time would be expensive. The chair is made up of straight pieces of plywood that are glued and screwed together with L-shaped supports under the seat. The sides of the chair are particularly graceful, as they taper back from 20 to 14⅜ inches. The original upholstery fabric of alternating greens, gold, and coral was chosen by Mrs. Pope. An ottoman was also designed but not built.

At the clerestory level (fig. 177), perforated panels—some hinged for opening, others stationary—provide ventilation and allow varying patterns of light into the interior. The same panel design was used quite ingeniously to produce different patterns. In the living room clerestory, the panel was placed rightside up and upside down in reverse order, and for a floor-to-ceiling grille, the panels were placed horizontally in a vertical stack. In the bedroom, half panels were placed in pairs, vertically facing each other, creating a shutter effect. In situ, the panels are made of glass sandwiched between two pieces of half-inch cypress board (not plywood) and then all screwed together.

■

Before publishing the study of the Pope–Leighey House, the National Trust held an oral history session at the house in May 1969. Included as participants were

177. Living area, Pope–Leighey House, Falls Church, Virginia. 1940. Section of bench, plywood, upholstered cushions, 28½" x 21" x 27½" (72.4 cm x 53.3 cm x 69.8 cm). (Lent by Pope–Leighey House, Mount Vernon, Virginia; A property of the National Trust for Historic Preservation). Perforated panel, plywood, 10¾" x 47½" (27.3 cm x 120.6 cm). (Lent by Mrs. Robert A. Leighey, Mount Vernon, Virginia)

a former Taliesin student, Gordon Chadwick, and a master carpenter, Howard C. Rickert, both of whom supervised the construction of the house. Usonian houses had a common structural system, according to Chadwick, which gave all of them a family resemblance despite their variety. The plans for each house were accompanied by a standard detail sheet, which was applied to all Usonian houses and used over and over. While the pattern for the perforated boards varied from house to house, the furniture was frequently standard for the Usonian houses (fig. 178). A modular chair, like the one used in the Pope–Leighey House, was used in a number of other houses. Wright planned the arrangement of the furniture, which varied with each house. The lumber for the Pope–Leighey House, Tidewater red cypress that was grown and milled in Florida, was ordered from a lumberyard in Baltimore. According to Rickert, much of the carpentry, such as for the perforated boards and the furniture, was done in his workshop at Vienna, Virginia. A radial saw, a joiner, and other equipment were set up at the site so that lumber could be cut there also. The furniture was also made at the Vienna workshop for the Usonian Joseph Euchtman House (1939) in Baltimore, Maryland. What Rickert cut for one, he also did for the

178. Pope-Leighey House (plan and elevation of furniture), Falls Church, Virginia. 1940.

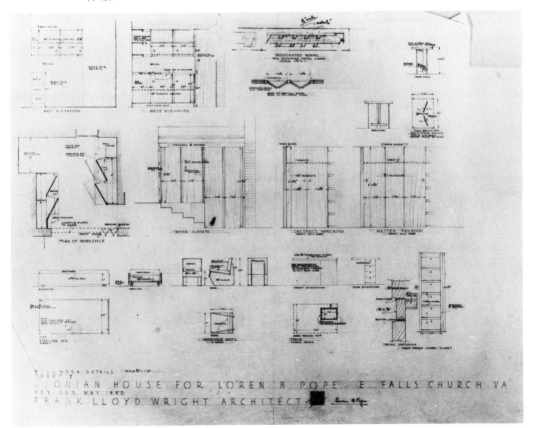

other, so that both houses had approximately the same furniture, though arranged differently.

The perforated panel in figure 179 from the clerestory of the Charles Weltz-heimer House (1948) in Oberlin, Ohio, makes use of a curved design, rather than the rectilinear cutout design typical of the Usonian house that was originally indicated in the working drawings, dated May 10, 1948. A second design for the perforated board, dated July 10, 1948, shows the introduction of curved features in a series of conventionalized floral designs. Further variations were made that changed the conventionalized floral design to a more asymmetrical design in order to allow more light into the house, with the resulting board seen here. The drawings are illustrated

179. Perforated panel, Charles Weltzheimer House, Oberlin, Ohio. 1948–1950. Redwood, 11⅞" x 48" (30.2 cm x 121.9 cm). (Lent by Mr. and Mrs. Wilbert Hasbrouck, Palos Park, Illinois)

180 (below). Usonian Exhibition Room on the site of The Solomon R. Guggenheim Museum, New York. 1953.

in an article by Kenneth W. Severens ("A Perforated Board from the Weltzheimer House in Oberlin," *Museum Studies 8,* The Art Institute of Chicago, Chicago, 1976). Perforated boards are used above the bookshelves of the living area, along the corridor gallery to the four bedrooms, in the master bedroom, and in a small bedroom at the end of the house. An owner who bought the house in 1965 removed the boards from the gallery and inserted glass, which provides more light.

■

The house designed in 1952 for the architect's son, David Wright (figs. 181, 182; pls. 17, 18), was described in a contemporaneous article as "a magnificent coil of concrete block" (*House & Home,* June 1953), as it demonstrates the flexibility and beauty of the standard undecorated concrete block, which could form a circular pattern. Wright was assisted in this experiment by David Wright, who was the area representative for Vibrapac concrete block machines at the time and acted as his own contractor. "The block," according to the *House & Home* article, "far from appearing cheap or crude, proved also to be an exceedingly handsome building material. Since each block is really tangential to the large circles of the plan, the curved walls of straight block have as many different faces as a cut stone" (p. 102). The architect felt that the curved rooms and wide angles would be warmer than straight lines and 90-degree angles. In experiencing the space of the house, one gets an unusual number of surprises from the changes that are effected by the rooms' curvatures. Because of the bending of Wright's basic "in-line" plan, every pie-shaped room has a different view. The ceiling, like the woodwork and the furniture, is of red Philippine mahogany; its curved patterns follow the curves of the rooms, which are lit from recessed ceiling fixtures. Some of the lighting is on the outside roof overhang and shines back into the room, as does the sun. Thus the furniture layout designed for the daytime lighting worked as well for night. The circular plan of the house is reflected in the circular chair seat (pl. 17). A rug designed for the house by the architect in 1956 (fig. 183) also includes these circular forms, as does the circular coffee table.

Unlike so many of Wright's "occasional chairs," the chair shown in situ in the room in plate 17 is light and mobile. It is made of Philippine mahogany, the same material used for the ceilings and woodwork in the house. Its front legs are veneered, but its back legs and broad crest rail are solid. Its angled legs give it a graceful stance. Eight of these chairs were made for the David Wright House by the Kapp Cabinetwork Co. of Phoenix, Arizona. Used for both dining and occasional purposes, they are among the architect's most practical and comfortable chairs.

■

The house that the architect designed in 1953 for his son, Robert Llewellyn Wright (fig. 184), grows out of its site overlooking the steep bank of a valley. Its interior spaces, which offer views in all directions, dictated the external forms.

Although most of the furniture was built in and integral to the architecture, freestanding furniture was also designed by Wright. The hassock in figure 185 is one of six designed for the first-floor living area of the house and was integral to the architecture in several ways. Its boatlike shape is an almost exact reflection of the elevation of the house, and the plan of the hassock duplicates the plan of the house (fig. 186). In addition to the six hassocks, a large "coffee table"—

181 (*below*). David Wright House, Phoenix, Arizona. 1952. 182 (*above, left*). Living area, David Wright House. 183 (*above, right*). Rug, living area, David Wright House.

also boat-shaped—was designed to be used in the living area. The hassocks can be grouped around this table or scattered through the room like miniature toy boats afloat. The Philippine mahogany used in the interior and exterior woodwork was also used for the furniture.

Built-in furniture for the Robert Llewellyn Wright House was detailed and executed by Bob Beharka, the Taliesin Fellow assigned to superintend the project, who is now a practicing architect in California. In Beharka, the Wrights were fortunate to have the skills of an apprentice architect combined with those of a carpenter. The freestanding furniture was executed by a skilled cabinetmaker in the area—S. Brook Moore of Sandy Spring, Maryland—who was also responsible for executing the built-in furniture in the kitchen and the second-floor bedrooms. The construction of the hassocks demonstrates Moore's skills as a cabinetmaker. The structure of the hassocks is strongly supported (more than is practically necessary) by two pieces of plywood placed horizontally across the hassock, one on a lower level, supported by eight triangular-shaped blocks on each curved side. The most amazing feat in the construction was the bending of the plywood around the curved sides. Rather than being bent under pressure, the plywood was scored, slit entirely through, and held together by the veneer on each side. A domed slip seat fits into the grooved top. Although the current upholstery is not original, the earth

184. Robert Llewellyn Wright House, Bethesda, Maryland. 1957.

tone of the replacement is in keeping with the subdued color scheme characteristic of the earlier Prairie interiors.

■

One of the more ambitious of Wright's later houses is the one designed for John L. Rayward (1956–1958) in New Canaan, Connecticut. The side chair in figure 187 was used for dining in this house, and with slight variations, the same design was

185 (below). Living area, Robert Llewellyn Wright House, Bethesda, Maryland. 1957. Hassock, plywood and mahogany veneer, upholstered seat, 12¼" x 28¼" x 16½" (31.1 cm x 71.7 cm x 41.9 cm). (Lent by Mr. and Mrs. Robert Llewellyn Wright, Bethesda, Maryland) 186 (left). Robert Llewellyn Wright House (plan).

used for the Harold Price, Sr., residence in Paradise Valley, Arizona, built a year earlier. Originally designed for Mr. and Mrs. Rayward, the house was brought to completion for H. R. Shepherd. In 1963 the Raywards gave one chair to The Art Institute of Chicago and one to The Museum of Modern Art. The form of the Rayward chair is based on the high-backed chairs used in some of the Prairie houses, such as the Robie (fig. 107) and the Dana dining chairs. The Rayward chair shares with the earlier prototype the vertical slats of the chair's spine, which extend from the bottom of the chair to the crest, and the high back, which gives a feeling of formality and elegance. However, the Rayward chair is very different. It is more strongly sculptural, with emphasis on all the elements of the design of the chair—the wider slats, rails, and crest—giving stronger architectural articulation. As was true of so many of Wright's decorative designs, earlier work served as the inspiration, but the new object was transformed into something unique.

■

The nineteen-story office–apartment building for the H. C. Price Company in Bartlesville, Oklahoma (fig. 188), was based on an earlier unexecuted plan made by Wright for St. Mark's-in-the-Bouwerie in New York in 1929. Wright felt that the skyscraper was unsuitable for an urban area if it increased congestion; therefore it should stand free in an open area, as was planned in Broadacre City. The Johnson

187 (below). Side chair, John Rayward House, New Canaan, Connecticut. 1956-1958. Wood, upholstered cushion, 50¼″ x 20″ x 22¼″ (127.6 cm x 50.8 cm x 56.5 cm). (Lent by The Museum of Modern Art, New York)

188 (right). H. C. Price Company Tower, Bartlesville, Oklahoma. 1953-1956.

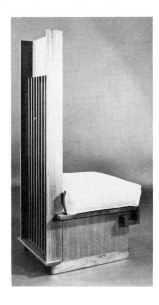

Laboratory and the Price Tower are examples of Wright's executed high-rise build-ings in open areas. Harold C. Price explained (in Frank Lloyd Wright, *The Story of the Tower*, New York: Horizon Press, 1956) how he came to Wright to request him to design a building for his company. Price had intended to build a three-story building for his pipeline-construction and pipe-coating firm, but Wright suggested ten floors. The final result was nineteen stories, which included offices and apart-ments. The lower floors were leased out to other companies.

The Price Tower is a cantilevered steel building, a "treelike mast structure,"

embedded in concrete. All floors and walls are supported solely by four interior wall columns of steel-reinforced concrete. All furnishings were custom-designed for the building, including that for the two-story apartments. Tinted glass and stamped copper plates in a geometric design shield the building and make the control of the climate easier and less expensive. The copper louvers on the outside are placed in a vertical position over the southwest quadrant and horizontally over the other three quadrants. The tightness of plan and the angular rooms and furniture give the feeling of being on shipboard. The design of the tower and its furnishings is based on a diamond modular of 30-degree and 60-degree triangles. This design is seen scored on the floor as a pattern throughout the building. The interior wall supports divide the tower into four separate quadrants. The plans of floors 3 to 15 are basically identical. Originally the Price Tower was the only high-rise in Bartlesville, though today a building by Skidmore, Owings & Merrill is also prominent.

The copper table and the two stools in figure 190 were designed for the dining area on the sixteenth floor of the Price Tower, which also has a buffet, kitchen facilities and open terraces. Wright's idea about continuity and his consideration of the furnishings and the building as one are illustrated in the use of the copper material, which is used on the facing of the building and is folded over the edge of the table and the stools to achieve continuity. The trapezoidal plan of the table is reflected in the sections of the plan of the building, while the ornamental molding around the edge of the table and stools, which echoes the exterior ornament, gives emphasis to the form. Shorter versions of this table and stool were used for the terrace of the H. C. Price, Jr., House in Bartlesville.

Photographs of the apartments and Wright's drawings of the interiors of the apartments are illustrated in *The Story of the Tower* (pp. 126–127). Mr. Price's private office (fig. 189) is in the center of the nineteenth floor (no full-quadrant areas) with an adjoining outside roof garden. A mural by Eugene Masselink is seen to the

189 (*opposite*). Office, H. C. Price Company Tower, Bartlesville, Oklahoma. 1953–1956.   190 (*right*). Table and two stools, H. C. Price Company Tower. Copper, wood frame table: 28½" x 26¾" x 39½" (72.4 cm x 67.9 cm x 100.3 cm); stools: 15½" x 17⅛" x 17⅛" (39.3 cm x 43.8 cm x 43.8 cm). (Lent by H. C. Price Company, Bartlesville, Oklahoma)

left along with the typical cast-aluminum and upholstered office chairs. The sloping arms of the secretaries' chairs, which give one the feeling of repose, were originally used throughout the building. Slight modifications of this basic pattern were used for the casual chair and the executive's chair. All were designed with interchangeable parts that could be reassembled to make three types of chairs—a secretary's chair, a casual chair, or an executive's chair—as is true of the Johnson Administration Building chairs. Instead of the circular back and seats seen in the Johnson chair, Wright used hexagonal forms here, corresponding to the angular plan of the Price Tower. The spines of the chairs reflect the elevation of the Price Tower. With the exception of a few officers' chairs in Mr. Price's office, most of the chairs were abandoned because of the difficulty in moving them.

The most famous of Wright's major work during the 1950s was The Solomon R. Guggenheim Museum in New York City. It was designed in 1943, but construction of the building did not begin until 1957. The building, which is an architectural tour de force whose ornament is truly in the plan of the design, is mentioned here because Wright did not live to attend its dedication. He died on April 9, 1959.

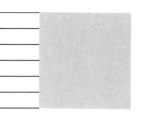

GRAPHIC DESIGNS

A chronological survey of Frank Lloyd Wright's printed works demonstrates stylistic changes comparable to that seen in the furniture, from the tightly contained linear designs seen in *The Eve of St. Agnes* and *The House Beautiful* to the bolder, open, free abstractions of the *Town and Country* cover design.

Printing was one of Wright's favorite hobbies. This lifelong interest was engendered during his boyhood period in Madison, Wisconsin, where he and his friend Robert Lamp shared many hours in this pursuit: "A small printing-press with seven fonts of Devinne type, second-hand, was set up, in the old barn at first and later a quite complete printing office fixed up in the basement of the house. The boys grew to love the smell of printer's ink" (*An Autobiography*, p. 31). Later, when living in Oak Park, Wright was to participate in printing books at the Auvergne Press with his friend and client, William Winslow (see pp. 200–201).

In addition to covers and title pages for books, Wright designed his own letterhead stationery, which changed many times over the years. His early letterhead was in a simple, traditional script, with his name and address; no label or symbol was used. (An example is in the Collection of Mr. and Mrs. Wilbert Hasbrouck, Palos Park, Illinois.) The use of the red square, which was his logo, as the central element of the design of his letterhead began in the 1890s and continued with variations throughout his life. In the design of his announcement for the opening of his Oak Park studio in 1893, Wright used his characteristic red square with a cross within a central circle, the first known instance. The text for the cover was condensed and placed in a rectangular format in the upper left-hand corner of the page. Wright soon abandoned the circle and the cross, using only the red square. The Dwight Bank correspondence (The Burnham Library, The Art Institute of Chicago) contains Wright stationery that uses the red square alone as its logo.

Wright also designed posters, including one for an exhibition of his own work at The Art Institute of Chicago, and programs and covers for Taliesin performances (plays, musicals, concerts). Graphic designs frequently accompanied architectural presentations. For example, in 1949 Wright incorporated the floor plan as a design for the cover of a presentation brochure; the plan of a new theatre for the Wadsworth Atheneum in Hartford, Connecticut, was placed on an acute angle. With the addition of a single line terminating with his red square signature, Wright transformed the floor plan into a handsome abstract graphic design. Most of Wright's graphic designs illustrate his architectural principle of continuity, achieved by overlapping the title page design from the cover to the inside pages of the book; it is also seen in the overlap of the red square signature from the front to the back of his stationery and in his intriguing methods of folding the paper. In the letter-head stationery used in the Dwight Bank correspondence, the letter folds into an envelope.

Wright's typeface also changed, and by the 1920s the early serif type had given way to sans serif. As in his architecture, Wright developed a typeface that was distinctively his own, characterized by proportions in which the top of the letters was unusually high. Wright's own type would have to be drawn by hand, and when lengthier printed material was needed, Wright preferred Futura as the type available commercially.

One of Wright's earliest graphic designs was the title page for *The Eve of St. Agnes* (fig. 191), published in 1896 by the Auvergne Press in River Forest, Illinois. Wright had designed houses for the co-printers of the book, William Winslow (1893) and Chauncey Williams (1896). As the basis of the design for the title page, Wright used the interlocking circle that had been used in the design of the terra-cotta ornament on the Francis Apartments the year before (fig. 19). Here Wright placed a winged Beaux Arts female figure within each section of the overlapped circles. The figures' outstretched hands, linked one to another, stand against a background of Sullivanesque foliage within alternating geometric panels, which extend from their joined hands to the bottom edge of the design. Wright's signature logo of the cross within the circle is located in the far right-hand corner. A similar figure had been illustrated in *Discourses on Architecture* by Viollet-le-Duc, published in an American edition in 1875 (see Donald Hoffmann, "Frank Lloyd Wright and Viollet-le-Duc," *Journal of the Society of Architectural Historians*, October 1969, pp. 173–183). A year after the publication of *The Eve of St. Agnes* Wright used the same design with slight variations in the ornamental terra-cotta frieze of the Isidor Heller House. The commission for executing the frieze was given to Richard Bock, and the changes in design, such as the elimination of the wings of the female figure, were probably due to the nature of the medium (see Donald P. Hallmark, "Richard W. Bock, Sculptor," Part II, *The Prairie School Review*, vol. 8, no. 2, second quarter 1971, p. 9).

One can speculate that Wright's winged female figures represent angels; this figuration was a popular motif in the late nineteenth century and was used, for example, in the lamps for the desk (now in the Philadelphia Museum of Art) designed around 1875 by Frank Furness for his brother's house. Winged female figures were also painted on the facade of Adler and Sullivan's Transportation Building for the 1893 World's Columbian Exposition in Chicago. Later Wright used more abstracted versions of winged female figures for the Larkin Building (see *The Early Work*, p. 103) and as the sculptural reliefs for the interior pier capitals of the Midway Gardens.

The back of the book has the Auvergne Press bookplate with the monogram "W. & W." within a shield in the center and the statement above it:

Printed on a hand press by William H. Winslow & Chauncey L. Williams, for pleasure and their friends, at the Auvergne Press, River Forest, Illinois; and finished the XIX day of December 1896. This Copy is Number WW. of an Edition of sixty five copies, printed on hand-made paper. The title page of this little book is from a design especially made for it by Frank L. Wright.

The inscription on the flyleaf of this book written in ink is:

Dec. 24/96. with Christmas Greetings from/one of the Printers./W. H. Winslow/Mr. Joseph D. Pickett

The introductory essay by Leigh Hunt was selected from his collection of essays *The Seer or, Common-Places Refreshed,* published in 1840.

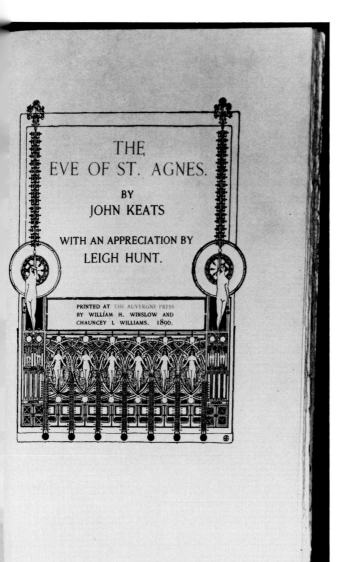

191. Title page for *The Eve of St. Agnes,* published by the Auvergne Press, River Forest, Illinois. 1896. Black and red ink on paper, 8" x 4⅞" (20.3 cm x 12.4 cm) open. (Lent by Newberry Library, Chicago, Illinois; John M. Wing Foundation)

Saint Agnes was a Roman virgin who suffered martyrdom in the reign of Diocletian. A few days after her death, her parents are said to have had a vision of her, surrounded by angels. The date of the Eve of Saint Agnes was January 20, and Keats's opening lines are full of images of winter:

> *St. Agnes' Eve—Ah, bitter chill it was!*
> *The owl, for all his feathers, was a-cold;*
> *The hare limp'd trembling through the frozen grass,*
> *And silent was the flock in woolly fold:*

Wright's design is quite innovative, especially when compared with a more typical Arts and Crafts format, seen in a design for the same poem, that was created and published by Ralph Fletcher Seymour in 1900. In "The Progress of the Title Page," Harrison Garfield Rhodes praised the improvement in bookmaking within

192. Title page for *The House Beautiful*, published by the Auvergne Press, River Forest, Illinois. 1897. Black and red ink on paper, 13½" x 11" (34.3 cm x 27.9 cm) open. (Lent by Chicago Historical Society, Illinois)

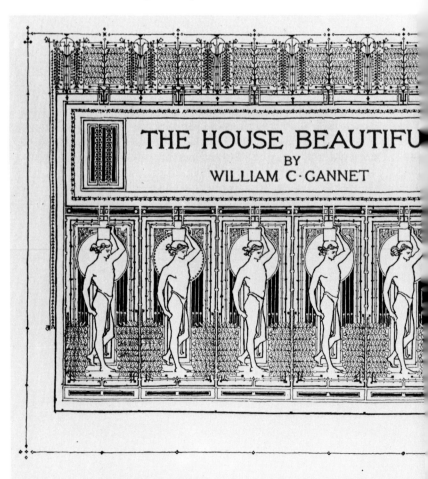

recent years when more emphasis had been placed on bindings. However, he felt the inside of the book was also important, the title pages in particular "should be planned that they will indicate with some accuracy the character of the book they precede (*House Beautiful*, vol. 2, no. 3, August 1897, p. 59).

John Lloyd Wright's recollection of the printing of *The House Beautiful* (fig. 192) confirms that Wright designed the magnificent graphics:

> During the winter nights of eighteen ninety-six and -seven, Dad and Mr. Winslow worked on the magnificent book, *The House Beautiful*. They printed it by hand, on handmade paper, 12 x 14 inches, ninety copies of this matchless book in the basement of Mr. Winslow's River Forest home—then gave them to their friends. Dad designed the setting and drew the intricate pattern freehand with pen and ink. (*My Father Who Is on Earth*, New York: G. P. Putnam's Sons, 1946, p. 42)

Whereas the Keats book (fig. 191) had employed the female figure in a repeating circular motif, Wright here drew, naturalistically, a male figure walking in a styl-

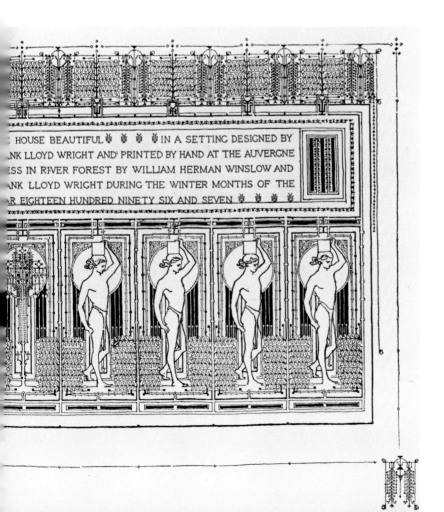

ized landscape and holding a square block on his head. The image is repeated in five rectilinear spaces on the left page and four on the right page, with the first rectangle of the group on the right containing a conventionalized fruit-bearing tree.

■

The House Beautiful is composed of a series of fragile but rich pen-and-ink drawings by Wright of various highly conventionalized plant forms. These designs cover the entire page in a ruglike pattern or serve as frames for the text written by William C. Gannet, a Unitarian minister whom Wright admired. Gannet's uninspired text, which was based on one of his sermons, was a statement of the Arts and Crafts philosophy of the ideal home and was no match for Wright's graphic design.

193 (*below*) and 194 (*opposite*). Graphic designs for *The House Beautiful*, the Auvergne Press, River Forest, Illinois. 1897.

In an article in *The Architectural Review* of June 1900, Robert C. Spencer, Jr., praised the remarkable linear patterns of Wright's designs for this publication, which "sympathize in highly conventional terms with the typographic character of this work." Spencer described the complex scheme, which was "built up and knit together" to create a harmony. One of the most striking aspects of the technique was that the composition of the ornament was "identical with that of musical composition at its best, and in its harmonics it may vary from the simplest and most obvious to the most involved and occult arrangement."

Indeed, Wright's *House Beautiful* can be heard as well as seen. Its opening design (fig. 193) repeatedly returns as a musical theme and ends the work, while new themes are introduced at intervals, seen for example in figure 194. The grandest and last of the five themes works as a climax. Wright's love of

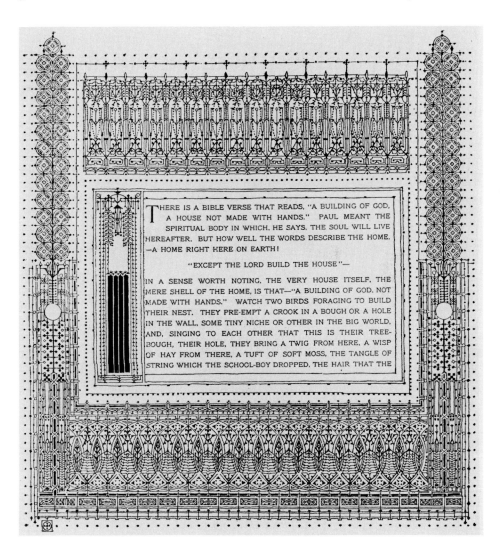

music, especially the works of Bach and Beethoven, is well known, and Wright would design while his wife, Catherine, played the piano. Winslow shared this passion for music; the Wright and Winslow children all were taught to play different instruments, and we can imagine that the two families enjoyed musical evenings together. One can also imagine that Wright drew the designs of *The House Beautiful* while listening to Beethoven.

The repetitive design within a page is reminiscent of the pattern in Oriental rugs, which Wright also admired and collected. The roots of the tree are entwined with stylized branches and leaves that form both a landscape and a connecting pattern through which the figures walk. The young Apollonian figure holding the block, which symbolized integrity, on his head symbolizes the architect; the literary and empathetic metaphor comparing the architect to a growing tree is achieved visually by the repetition of the figure within a rectangle, which is interrupted in one instance by the tree. The figure holding the block was later used in the female sprite figure Wright designed for Midway Gardens (see fig. 122), where the block was held with both hands above the head.

The copy of *The House Beautiful* lent for the exhibition and illustrated here is number 7, and a gift to the Chicago Historical Society from Mrs. George Langhorne in memory of her father, Edward Carson Waller, Wright's client. Pressed leaves from the Oak Park property were found in the copy in the John Lloyd Wright Collection of the Avery Architectural Library, Columbia University, New York.

■

One of Frank Lloyd Wright's most imaginative achievements in graphic designs was the series of cover designs for *Liberty* magazine done in 1926–1927, one of which is illustrated here (fig. 195). Twelve were designed, one for each month of the year, but none was executed by the magazine. Each is abstract but suggests the seasonal aspect of the calendar year. These free abstractions, in Wright's hand, represent a significant departure from the tight linear composition of *The House Beautiful.* Four drawings for the *Liberty* covers are in the Taliesin archives, and some were later adapted for Taliesin program designs. The July *Liberty* magazine cover was adapted in 1937 for a *Town and Country* cover (see pl. 20); the same design was used in 1967 as the cover design for a Taliesin festival of music and dance. The eight drawings included in the exhibition are working drawings owned by Wright's granddaughter.

Frank Lloyd Wright's *Autobiography* was first published by Longmans, Green and Company in 1932. It was divided into five books, each of which was given a title with an accompanying graphic design by Wright. A second edition was published by the same company in the following year. The 1933 edition is slightly longer from bottom to top, giving an extra space below the bottom line of the graphic design. A third edition was published by Duell, Sloan and Pearce in 1943. The graphic designs of the second edition were essentially the same as the first. However, numerous changes were made in the third edition.

Book One of the original edition combined the sections on "Family" and "Fellowship"; in the 1943 edition, each had a separate section, with the addition of another graphic design. The section "Work," which was Book Two in the earlier editions, became Book Three. Similarly "Freedom," which had been Book Three, became Book Four in the 1943 edition. Book Five, "Form," was added to the 1943 edition. The photographs used in the original edition were omitted in the third edition. Visually the graphic designs, which seem to be essentially the same in each edition, do vary considerably, the most striking change being one of color. The vivid white with black lines and bright red square logo were replaced by a more subtle and harmonious color scheme: a reddish brown background was used in place of the white; silver lines appear rather than black; and an orange square logo replaced the red.

Wright's graphic designs for *An Autobiography* marked a move forward toward a simpler, more geometric format. Although still representational, they are as abstracted as the linear designs for *The House Beautiful*. They are bolder, yet retain a delicate quality. The "plowed field," a particularly subtle graphic design that appeared in the original edition of Book Two, "Work," illustrated here (fig. 196), is continued in the graphic design of Book Three, "Freedom." Each has the text "An Autobiography/From Generation to Generation," and the graphic design visually denotes the change in generations. The text is reversed top to bottom in Book Three.

The immediate text for the graphic design of "Work," Book Three, is on pages 119–120, of the third edition, though, of course, the whole section is about this general subject. In his Whitmanesque style, Wright described the plowing of a field of wheat, which was graphically depicted: "The entire field is a linear pattern—a plan

195. Design for cover, "April Showers," one of eight, *Liberty Magazine.* 1926–1927. 14¼" x 24" (36.2 cm x 60.9 cm). (Lent by Mrs. Nora Natof, Lovettsville, Virginia)

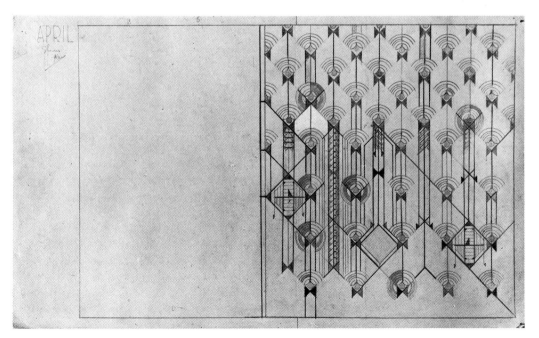

of routine. Work." Wright described the reaper, which sweeps the grain into regular piles: "A certain rhythm in regular and patterned order everywhere established in this work of harvest. Routine fitted to routine." Wright described himself as "the boy, barefoot, bareheaded, running to and fro in the stubble to pick up the bundles by the bands." Pausing to rest and to take a drink from a stone jug, Wright heard a meadowlark:

> Then, to carry on, he goes back a few steps, picks up the bundle on which he had been sitting. From the butt-end of the bundle a snake slips to the ground. A rattler unwittingly bound into the sheaf a few moments before by one of the binders and tossed aside. The rattler smoothly, swiftly coils in the stubble

196. Graphic design for "Book Two: Work," *An Autobiography*, by Frank Lloyd Wright, published by Longmans, Green, and Company. 1932. Ink on paper, 8⅞" x 13¾" (22.5 cm x 34.9 cm) open. (Lent by The Library of Congress, Washington, D.C.)

and—tail upended—rattles, darting a forked tongue—narrow hostile eyes, gleaming.

Wright then picked up a pitchfork

and with a turn and thrust, as swift as the darting tongue, pins the rattler to the ground. . . . He looks around him. His fingers slip again into the stone handle. With the bottom of the stone jug he flattens the evil-spitting head. . . . Work goes on again. The rhythm and routine of the harvest field as before. But with no warning at all something dreadful has suddenly happened to challenge the order of the peaceful harvest field.

Wright's book was enthusiastically reviewed by Lewis Mumford, who wrote in the *Atlantic Monthly* (1932): "No autobiography on this level has appeared since

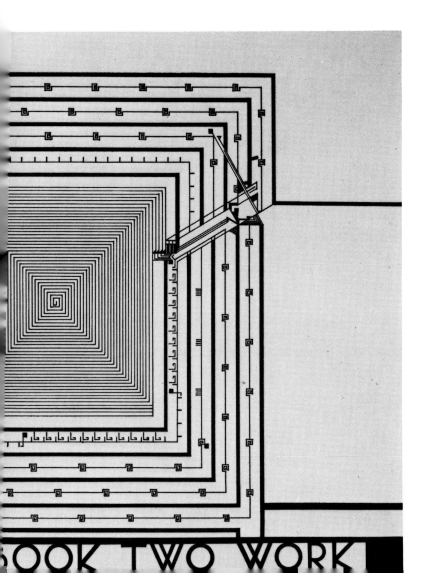

OOK TWO WORK

The Education of Henry Adams . . . Mr. Wright's book is a literary art that compares in brilliance and originality with his buildings, a work with the marks of a novelist, indeed of a poet, on almost every page."

The first promotional brochure for the Taliesin Fellowship, which was organized in 1932, was published in December of 1933. Two striking graphic designs were used for the cover, which was folded twice across the center, the inside of which (fig. 197a) included a slightly stylized rendering of Taliesin at Spring Green on the left page drawn as conceived in plan rather than in actuality. On the right page was a rendering of the Taliesin Playhouse with Wright's own designed lettering done by hand, probably by one of the Taliesin apprentices. The outside cover (pl. 19; fig. 197b) is a variation of the "plowed field" design in *An Autobiography* or of Wright's own square signature. It has the appearance of a musical staff with a large note in the middle. So the words, which he incorporated into the horizontal lines by using the top line of the staff for the tops of the letters, seem to flow along in a musical fashion. Although the design of the cover continues around the fold to the rear, it is seen here as part of the entire design. The sections of the staff with the words also continue into the inside of the brochure. The Taliesin dining room is seen here in elevation and plan. (Wright always regarded the plan of a building

197a and b (*below* and pages 182–183). Graphic designs for brochure, *The Taliesin Fellowship.* 1933. Red and black ink on paper, 8¾" x 17¼" (22.3 cm x 43.8 cm) open. (Lent by Donald Kalec, Oak Park, Illinois)

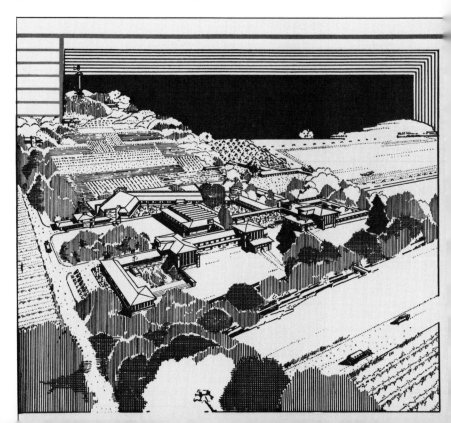

as a beautiful design, and it was used in the Schumacher textiles as well as in this graphic design.)

One of Wright's most exuberant graphic designs executed was the 1937 Fourth of July cover of *Town and Country* (pl. 20), which in the lower left corner states that it was "Designed by Frank Lloyd Wright." Appropriately for this issue, which Wright called "flag," a representation of the American flag was chosen as the theme of his design and red, white, and blue as the basis of the color scheme. As for the Coonley windows, the inspiration may well have been a parade, since the vertical repetition of the American flag, in reverse at the right and conventionally in the center, creates depth in the composition and gives the impression of a street within the large overall design of a flag hanging at an angle. Variations on this theme are used in the three triangular-shaped flags that are placed at an angle to the left in the large flag. The motifs of the flag are seen against a grid pattern of vertical lines, and the effect is one of movement and excitement. Whereas *The House Beautiful* was a symphony, this cover design works as a single measure from a symphony, with contrapuntal variations introduced.

The variations on the red, white, and blue color scheme are subtle, as is the introduction of the vertical and horizontal yellow lines, which give emphasis to the title. Combinations of the primary colors produce hues of pink, purple, and lavender, an effect that is lively, yet harmonious.

The text of the magazine devoted a paragraph to Wright and his architecture, accompanied by a full-page photograph of the architect. Compared with the design of *An Autobiography*, this cover, with its transparent and interweaving

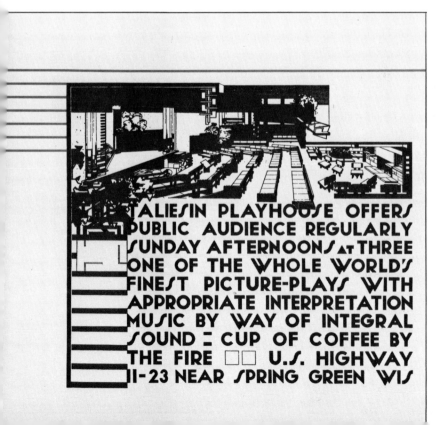

spatial effects, is more lively and complex. In spirit, it more closely resembles the design for the theatre curtain for the Hillside Theater, Spring Green, Wisconsin, 1933 (see Arthur Drexler, *The Drawings of Frank Lloyd Wright*, New York: Bramhall House, 1962, p. 296).

According to Curtis Besinger, who was a Fellow at Taliesin from the early fall of 1939 to the late summer of 1955, Frank Lloyd Wright designed the cover for the 1938 *Architectural Forum* (pl. 21) (letter from Curtis Besinger to the author, July 6, 1977). This is confirmed by the statement from the editors inside the magazine cover, who "worked in close association with Mr. Wright in the development of this issue, which was designed and written by him. . . . Acknowledgement must also be made to the men and women of the Taliesin Fellowship for their untiring and devoted assistance . . . and to the photographers."

The entire issue of the January 1938 *Architectural Forum* is a masterpiece in terms of its totally unified design, which combines the skills of the photographer, the writer, and the graphic designer. The design is a statement of Wright's ideas about architecture expressed in the graphic medium. The bold, simple rectilinear designs characteristic of Wright's furniture are reflected here in the straight lines and right angles that compose the cover. Wright's idea of continuity is expressed in the continuation of the design from the cover to the inside pages and then its repetition at the end. The lettering used on the cover was developed in the 1920s and was also used in *An Autobiography* six years earlier. Five variations on the typeface of the cover were used inside the magazine. Wright's now familiar signature—the red

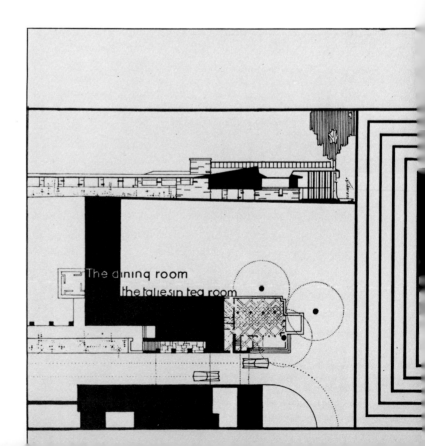

square from the early Oak Park days—appears boldly as the center of the cover's design. The design of this cover is related to the design for the Book Two section on "Work" in *An Autobiography* (see fig. 196). The tiny red square in the earliest design is enlarged here to the entire central area of the field, and the title of the magazine intersects the "plowed field" motif. Appropriately, the issue was dedicated "to my beloved master Louis Henry Sullivan and grand old chief Dankmar Adler."

After Eugene Masselink came to Taliesin in 1933, Wright began to give his talented assistant greater responsibility in the execution of graphic designs. Most of the graphic designs after 1938 can be attributed to Masselink, who continued to work in Wright's style and under his direction.

On page 54 of the 1948 *Architectural Forum*, there is also a statement from the editors in regard to the design of that issue:

> We like to think that the next best thing to building Wright is publishing him and proudly present this issue completely devoted to his new work, on the anniversary of our original Frank Lloyd Wright issue of 1938. Like the first one, this issue was completely designed and written by him; the plans and sketches appear as they were drawn by the 50 young men who now compose the Taliesin Fellowship.

In the instance of the 1948 edition, however, the cover was designed by Eugene Masselink, who was then working on a series of "abstractions," according to Curtis

Besinger. The cover of the 1948 *Architectural Forum* was an adaptation of one of these abstractions, drawn by Masselink. Curtis Besinger, who worked with Masselink on the drawings in the Taliesin studio at that time, states that as an "abstraction" it was in a manner established by Frank Lloyd Wright, a fact that Masselink would acknowledge, if he were still alive.

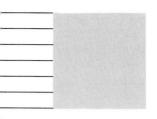

DESIGNED FOR PRODUCTION

Because of the Depression, most of Wright's projects of the 1920s were not executed, and by 1930 he, like other architects, had almost no architectural work. It was at this time that he turned to some nonarchitectural projects, which included an exhibition of his work, which was organized by The Art Institute of Chicago in 1930, and the writing of *An Autobiography*, which was published in 1932. By his choice, Wright's work was not included in the Chicago Century of Progress Exhibition of 1933–1934.

Wright's earliest venture in objects for production was in 1930, when he received a commission from the Dutch Leerdam Glass Company. Until then all of Wright's objects had been specifically designed as part of an architectural whole. In the case of a large structure like the Larkin Administration Building, the metal office furniture, though made on a production-line basis, was custom-designed for that building. With the Leerdam glass commission, Herr P. M. Cochius, the president of the company, met with Wright in the late 1920s at the Waldorf Astoria Hotel in New York City with the proposal that the architect design a line of crystal glassware and dinner service that would be produced commercially in the Netherlands. Wright designed sixteen pieces of crystal for Leerdam, including a full dinner service and a line of glassware. Although sixteen of the Leerdam drawings are in the Taliesin archives, nine are in a private collection in the Netherlands. The glassware includes separate drawings in elevation and plan for wine, cognac, champagne (fig. 198), sherry, and water glasses, and a glass finger bowl and a bread-and-butter plate (fig. 199). The dinner service in the Hemerocallis pattern includes: cup and saucer, dinner plate, platter, vegetable dish and soup tureen, sherbet glass, sugar bowl, and compote. There are two additional designs: for a flower holder and a flower vase. Although these drawings represent fascinating conceptions of Wright's modern style of the 1920s, all the pieces of the service were ceramic forms transformed into glass designs and were thus not amenable to glass production. According to Johan W. M. Ambaum, former curator of the Leerdam Museum, they could not be produced in glass because glassblowing techniques could not be applied to many of these constructions. The decorative lines, however, could be etched or painted with enamel.

A flower vase (fig. 200) was the only piece in the Leerdam series that was actually executed, and since only three examples are known to have been made, it apparently was never put into production. In addition to the vase shown here from the National Museum at Leerdam, a second example is in the collection of the Gemeentemuseum in The Hague, and a third, although damaged, is at Taliesin in Spring Green, Wisconsin. As executed, the vase is quite different from the drawing. It is a beautiful example of clear blown glass—a deep, rich green in a color that the Leerdam Museum calls "mer blau," bubble-formed, and cut in six facets at its base. Although it is unusual for architects to design glassware, the National Glass Museum at Leerdam also includes glass pieces designed by such Dutch architects as Hendrik Berlage and K. P. C. De Bazel and made by the Leerdam Company.

■

Wright's major endeavor in commercial designs, however, did not come until about 1955, when he designed furniture for the Heritage–Henredon Furniture Com-

198 (*below, left*). Champagne glass (elevation and plan), Leerdam Glass Company, Leerdam, Netherlands. 1930. Ink on paper, 11½" x 8⅞" (29.2 cm x 22.6 cm). (The Frank Lloyd Wright Foundation, Taliesin West, Scottsdale, Arizona)

199 (*below, right*). Bread-and-butter plate (elevation and plan), Leerdam Glass Company, Leerdam, Netherlands. 1930. Ink on paper, 11½" x 9½" (29.2 cm x 24.2 cm). (The Frank Lloyd Wright Foundation, Taliesin West, Scottsdale, Arizona)

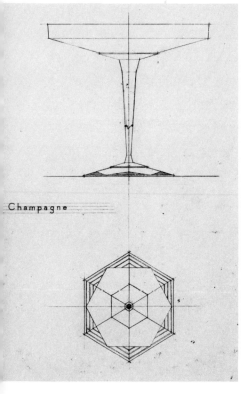

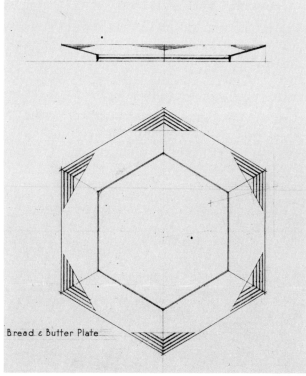

pany (pl. 22; figs. 201–207) and textiles and wallpapers for F. Schumacher and Co. (figs. 208–212). In November 1955, *House Beautiful* announced the "Taliesin Ensemble" ("And now Frank Lloyd Wright designs home furnishings you can buy!" pp. 282–289). By 1955 Wright had been designing furnishings for houses of his clients for sixty years, and although the designs for the Leerdam Glass Company in 1930 attempted to make a line of glassware available commercially, it was not put into production. The Schumacher and Heritage–Henredon lines, therefore, were not only the major effort in the area but also the first to be executed (since the office furniture for the Larkin, Johnson, and Price buildings, although produced in quantity, was still custom-designed for the respective buildings).

The Heritage–Henredon line of furniture offered the average consumer an alternative to what was commercially available at this time. *House Beautiful* for November 1955 contained advertisements for furniture in various revival styles that could rival those of the Victorian period. For example, the Century Furniture Co. in Hickory, North Carolina, advertised "the finest in French Provincial"; the Extensole Corporation in Sparta, Michigan, illustrated an "English Regency style dropleaf extension table"; and the S. R. Hungerford Co. of Memphis, Tennessee, advertised Colonial revival adaptations.

Although some of Wright's contemporaries (Walter Darwin Teague and Ray-

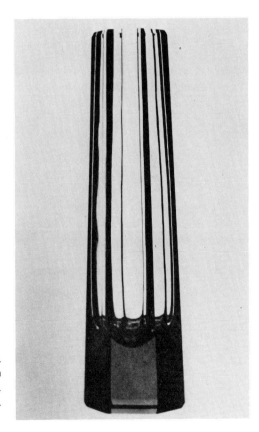

200. Vase, Leerdam Glass Company, Leerdam, Netherlands. 1930. Blown glass, 16⅞" x 3⅛" (42.9 cm x 8 cm). (National Glass Museum, Leerdam, Netherlands)

mond Loewy, among others) specialized in commercial designs, Wright rarely did. His concept of organic architecture required furnishings that would be integral to their spatial environment, and each house was designed specifically to fit the individual personality of the client, his economic requirements, the program of the commission, and the physical location of the setting. The furnishings, therefore, were different for each structure and individual client. As we have also noted, Wright designed each interior detail in his early houses, but in the 1940s and 1950s commercially produced furnishings available in the market were often acceptable and recommended to those clients who commissioned houses. Nevertheless Wright still designed much of the furniture for his later houses.

His designs for a commercial line represent a compromise with his earlier ideal of an organic architectural unity. This commercially produced furniture, however, could offer a part of Wright's genius to a wide public. Whereas only a limited number of people could afford to build a Frank Lloyd Wright–designed house, almost anyone would now have access to his furnishings. The author of the article "Frank Lloyd Wright Designs Home Furnishings" in the November 1955 *House Beautiful* was delighted "to have Frank Lloyd Wright design furnishings for the general homemaker, rather than for special clients," and felt that this was a logical development long overdue. It welcomed "the entry of his great talents and principles into the important commercial field of home furnishings available for all to buy."

201. Hexagonal table and six triangular stools, Heritage–Henredon Furniture Co., Morganton and High Point, North Carolina. 1955. Mahogany stool, 14" x 22" x 11" (35.3 cm x 55.9 cm x 28 cm). (Sectional stool lent by Mr. and Mrs. Harold C. Price, Bartlesville, Oklahoma)

The *House Beautiful* article is important because it was probably written from notes taken in an interview with Wright by the magazine's editor, Elizabeth Gordon. The aesthetic philosophy underlying the Heritage–Henredon designs were based on the same principles held by Wright when he designed his earlier furniture. The furnishings should be sympathetically compatible without being a suite. This unity should create a feeling of integration, harmony, and repose. It should be possible to group and regroup the furniture in many ways in order to meet different situations. The article indicated that Wright's design of the tables, stools, and hassocks in geometric forms of circles, triangles, squares, and hexagons was intended to make them amenable to a variety of arrangements, which was particularly evident when there was "a lack of architectural distinction in the interior setting."

Many of the forms and details of the Heritage–Henredon furniture were based on the furniture vocabulary that Wright had developed in the Prairie years and expanded in the 1930s. The ornamental molding used on most of the Heritage furniture had an earlier precedent in the furniture for the Husser and Bogk Houses. This ornament, which was integral to the furniture rather than added, served both as a decoration and as emphasis for the structural lines of the furniture. Wright's case pieces for the Heritage–Henredon line, which also had the ornamental molding, seemed more "substantial and fully capable" of their function than the furniture with a "floating look" illustrated in the advertisement for Knoll furniture in the same issue. This latter was characteristic of furniture designed by architects of the International School. Resting on sturdy, low cradles, Wright's case pieces also

202. Mahogany hexagonal tables, Heritage-Henredon Furniture Co., Morganton and High Point, North Carolina. 1955.

offered "a sense of security and safety," which was not felt in the Knoll furniture.

Wright designed three separate lines for Heritage–Henredon, which he called "The Four Square" (fig. 205), "The Honeycomb" (fig. 206), and "The Burberry" (fig. 207). Only the first line, "The Four Square," was actually put into production. As designed, its predominantly rectilinear forms contrast with the triangular shapes of "The Honeycomb" and the circular shapes of "The Burberry." Wright's name for the line that was produced was not used; the company called it "The Taliesin Line." As actually produced, its use of rectilinear, triangular, and circular forms combined elements of all these lines. The drawings reveal Wright's intention, which could not be realized in actuality. In the drawings, the furnishings are shown against an architecturally neutral background, whereas in reality, the architectural background usually intruded, breaking up the harmony and repose that were Wright's goal. In each of the Heritage–Henredon drawings, a few lines indicate the background or architectural setting, and the furniture is grouped to form a pleasing composition. In the drawing of "The Four Square" bedroom (fig. 205), the objects on the dressing table are carefully arranged asymmetrically in the Oriental manner, reminiscent of the rendering for the Coonley desk (fig. 104). One of Wright's favorite objects—the copper flower holder (see fig. 58)—which had been designed in the 1890s, is drawn here on the shelf to the right of the dressing table mirror. Since Wright still owned one of these vases as well as his drawing of it, either could have been the inspiration. The extension of the bed at the foot to form a cantilevered bench in both "The Four

Square" and "The Honeycomb" drawings, both of which are in bedroom settings, is an architectural device corresponding to the cantilevered roofs of his houses. This idea was used earlier for the beds he designed for the Francis W. Little House (1913), where benches were integral to the twin beds. The drawing for "The Burberry" line, which is a dining room setting, also includes the copper flower holder on the buffet and a version of the copper urn on the floor. Both "Honeycomb" and "Burberry" are shown in nonarchitectural settings.

The Heritage–Henredon Company chose the quietest and most conservative of the three lines to put into production. This may have been because of convenience of manufacture or because they felt it would have greater sales appeal. In 1955 and 1956 Henredon manufactured about $1 million worth of the furniture. Approximately seventy-five of the different designs were made, forty by Henredon and thirty-five by Heritage. They did not discontinue the line because it was unprofitable (it was marginal); however, as they felt that the buyers of furniture were not familiar with Wright's designs, the repeat orders from the stores were insufficient to justify continuing the line (letter from Donnell VanNoppen to the author, August 11, 1977). According to Bruce Pfeiffer, it was Wright who dissolved the contract with Heritage–Henredon.

The line was promoted in the November 1955 *House Beautiful* after it had been introduced at the Fall Market in the Chicago Furniture Mart in October. A two-page color advertisement also appeared in the issue, which hailed Wright, "the prophet of new ideas in architecture," who had now turned his attention "to designing a group of dining room, bedroom and living room furniture." The new furniture would give "a new adventure in freedom and dignity, a new flexibility of function and design."

203 (*opposite*). Interior, showing Heritage-Henredon furniture and F. Schumacher & Co. fabrics. 1955.   204 (*right*). Interior, showing Heritage-Henredon furniture. 1955.

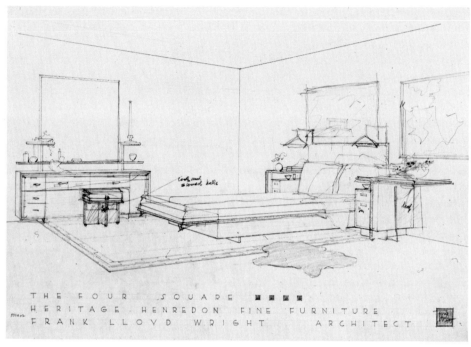

205 (*above*). "The Four Square," Heritage–Henredon furniture (rendering). 1955. Pencil on paper. (Copyright © 1977 The Frank Lloyd Wright Foundation, all rights reserved) 206 (*below*). "The Honeycomb," Heritage–Henredon furniture (rendering). 1955. Pencil on paper. (Copyright © 1977 The Frank Lloyd Wright Foundation, all rights reserved)

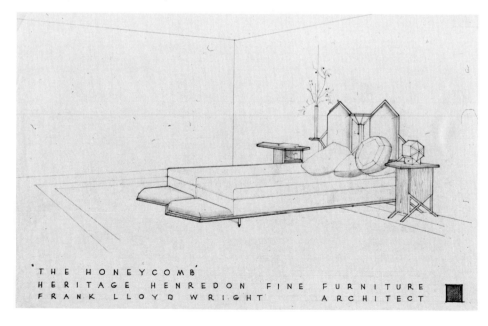

The *Chicago Daily News* of October 18, 1955 ("Frank Lloyd Wright Starts Life Anew at 86"), heralded Wright's new furniture, which was exhibited at the Merchandise Mart showrooms of Heritage–Henredon with some of Wright's Oriental art objects (figs. 203, 204). The article described the various reactions to the new line. Some people were looking for a "style" to describe the furniture, thinking it Oriental in feeling, but that was "because it's scaled low for the comfort of the human being." Others thought it "Western" in style, but that was "because of its natural matte finish on mahogany and carving at the edges." Others even thought it harkened "back to the dark age of furniture design, specifically, the first 25 years of this century," because some of the lines were so strong and perfect in scale. If the *Daily News* article represented anything of the popular reaction to the new line of furniture, then it is clear that Wright's furniture was met with confusion and misunderstanding:

> We're not used to seeing velvet upholstery on modern furniture and Wright has used it on some occasional chairs. It reminds many people of the poorly designed velvet chair grandmother kept in her parlor, the one nobody dared use. You couldn't put Frank Lloyd Wright's furniture in a stark, sterile, "less is more" structure of glass and steel by Ludwig Mies van der Rohe. But you could put this rather sensuous furniture in any of the thousands of "ranch houses," bi-

207. "The Burberry," Heritage-Henredon furniture (rendering). 1955. Pencil on paper.

THE BURBERRY
HERITAGE HENREDON FINE FURNITURE
FRANK LLOYD WRIGHT ARCHITECT

levels and trilevels that have sprouted up since World War II. Wright's furniture would add something special to each.

Wright was probably painfully aware of the reaction of the larger public, who did not understand his architectural principles, and yet, according to John de Koven Hill, in conversation with the author, Wright was pleased with the opportunity to design a commercial line. The *Chicago Sunday Tribune* for November 13, 1955, in an article by Anne Douglas, also described the new line of furniture:

> A group of Furniture that has created the biggest furor in the industry in years has just been put on display in a Chicago store. . . . In settings shown by Heritage–Henredon, the manufacturer, most of the pieces were arranged against the walls or near them, leaving the middle of the room open and uncluttered. Virtually all the pieces are low, so as not to obstruct vision. ("Frank Lloyd Wright Furniture on Display")

In spite of the misunderstanding of some of the critics, the new furniture line was successful in many ways. Certainly the furniture looked especially good in Wright-designed houses. In comparison to most of what was commercially available, Wright's furniture designs were ahead of their time. The Heritage–Henredon furniture seemed to be very successful in its ability to adapt to either contemporary or traditional furnishings. In fact, this adaptability, which was one of its strengths in design, caused confusion in some of the department stores because they could not decide whether to show the furnishings in their contemporary or their traditional sections. Instead of hardware, pulls were recessed slots in the wood, as seen earlier with the Little library table (fig. 116) and therefore were integral to the pieces. Many of the smaller pieces were designed to fit together to form larger ensembles (figs. 201, 202). For example, the sofas, which were upholstered box springs resting on a low cradle and topped with foam rubber pads, had cushions with cutoff corners against which smaller occasional tables could be fitted. Although some of the tables had fin bases (fig. 201), others had square ones on pedestals and could be stacked to make two-tier end tables. The 54-inch round extension dining table could be expanded to an oval. The chests were part of a series of cases made on a unit system, which permitted combining many units along a wall to make one total architectural composition. The line included a sideboard that was fitted with drawers for silver and a removable shelf. A desk was designed that could function as either a dressing table or a desk with its own typewriter table, which could be pulled out of the kneehole or hidden when not in use—a very economical use of space. The typing table could also be used apart from the desk as an end table, either singly or in a group. A bookcase with a movable top was designed so that it could be used on top of a chest of drawers or on top of a low base as a room divider (fig. 204). A line of accessories in exotic woods (with metal liners to hold flowers, branches, or weeds) was designed to go with the furniture. Photographs in the November 1955 *House Beautiful* illustrated these furnishings, showing them in settings that demonstrated their versatility and use. Each piece was stamped with Wright's signature, burned into it in an inconspicuous part.

Although the Heritage–Henredon furniture was available to the average consumer, it was recommended by Wright, and was most appropriate, for the interiors he designed. Such an instance is the Harold Price, Jr., House in Bartlesville, Oklahoma, where the large hexagonal coffee table and six small triangular tables were used. The smaller tables could double as seats when equipped with small cushions, could slide into the table for compactness and efficiency, or could be used at random throughout the room. A variation on this hexagonal table ensemble was a group of hexagonal tables of smaller size (fig. 202) that could be grouped and regrouped in endless combinations, depending on the needs in the room.

■

In 1955 Wright also designed a series of fabrics (figs. 208–212; pl. 24) that were to accompany the furnishings made by F. Schumacher and Co. in New York. Examples of these fabrics are seen in situ with the furniture in figure 203. A number of the printed fabrics in Belgian linen were colorful and provided a lively contrast to the mat earth tones of the furniture. All the printed designs were conceived as two-dimensional surface patterns with no perspective, expressing the flat nature of the material. F. Schumacher and Co. proudly advertised the line in the October 1959 *House Beautiful* (shortly after Wright's death): "The brilliant mind and deft hand of the late Frank Lloyd Wright have left their indelible mark on the panorama of our civilization. For the reproduction of his unique designs in decorative fabrics, Frank Lloyd Wright chose only Schumacher's."

A line of wallpapers that matched some of the fabrics was also produced by Schumacher, also in 1955. Fabrics ranged in price from $3.40 to $13.50 a yard and wallpaper from $5.95 to $7.45 a roll. A sample book for the fabrics and wallpapers, titled *Schumacher's Taliesin Line of Decorative Fabrics and Wallpaper Designed by Frank Lloyd Wright*, is in the department of textiles at the Cooper–Hewitt Museum

208. Fabric design No. 706, F. Schumacher & Co., New York. 1955. Printed duck and cotton. (The Art Institute of Chicago)

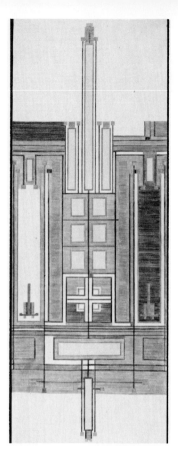

209 (*left*). Fabric design, F. Schumacher & Co., New York. 1955. Pencil and colored pencil on paper. (Archives of American Art, Smithsonian Institution, Washington, D.C.) 210 (*below*). Wallpaper design No. 105, F. Schumacher & Co. 1955. Paper, 30" x 23" (76.2 cm x 58.4 cm). (Lent by Mr. and Mrs. Wilbert R. Hasbrouck, Palos Park, Illinois)

211 (*opposite, left*). Fabric design No. 105, F. Schumacher & Co. 1955. Linen, 21⅝" x 46¾" (54.9 cm x 118.7 cm). (Lent by John J. Celuch, Edwardsville, Illinois)

212 (*opposite, right*). Fabric design No. 106, F. Schumacher & Co. 1955. Cotton and rayon, 25⅜" x 47½" (64.5 cm x 120.6 cm). (Lent by Mr. and Mrs. Jon S. Pohl, Evanston, Illinois)

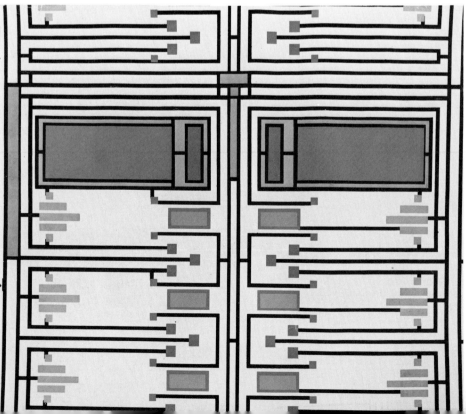

and at The Art Institute of Chicago. This book illustrates Schumacher's "Taliesin Suite," located in the National Republican Club, which had been recently remodeled in one of New York City's historic landmarks. The sample book included fabric samples (fig. 208) and illustrations of rooms with the fabrics and wallpapers in use, as well as photographs of Wright's architecture. Wallpaper identical in design to the fabrics was recommended for use on a single wall in the same room. The fabrics and wallpaper were shown with examples of Heritage–Henredon furniture.

By illustrating examples of his houses and buildings with the fabrics and wallpapers, Wright could demonstrate the close relationship between architecture and decorative design, which created a harmony and unity that was part of his concept of organic architecture. For example, design No. 504—a copper-colored wool fabric—is shown on the same page as a photograph of Florida Southern College. The unusual brickwork in the facade of several of the college buildings was suggested in the design of the fabric. Design No. 102 in printed linen showed five additional color lines in the sample book. Design No. 101, which also had five color choices, was inspired by the facade of the faceted Adelman House, in Phoenix, Arizona, which was illustrated on the opposite page. Design No. 104 (pl. 23) is an elegant printed silk that shows Wright's adeptness with spherical motifs. The fabric was shown in the photographs of the bedroom in Schumacher's "Taliesin Suite," where it was used both for the wall-to-wall draperies and for the quilted bedspread. Shown in "slate" color in the Schumacher sample book, this fabric is a multicolored abstract modular design based on architectural floor plans. Opposite the sample were illustrated the

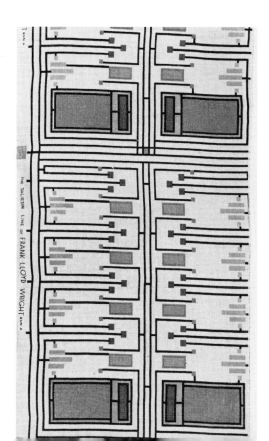

two residences that Wright designed for his sons: Robert Llewellyn Wright (see fig. 184) and David Wright (see fig. 181). The floor plan of each house was incorporated into the design of the fabric. The pattern was developed through overlapping arcs and partial circles. Six color lines were shown, the gold one being the predominant color of the sample here. Illustrated for another design (fig. 208) were the Jorgine Boomer House and the Taliesin North drafting room, with the comment that the angular motif apparent in the sharp lines of the Boomer House and the somewhat similar geometric construction of the drafting room ceiling at Taliesin were integrated into the design, which was based on the triangle.

The drawings for the Schumacher Taliesin Line are now in the Archives of American Art at the Smithsonian Institution. The example illustrated here (fig. 209) is based on one of Wright's earlier designs for a rug for the Avery Coonley House (see fig. 101). Wallpapers identical in design to the fabric were also produced. For example, design No. 105 in wallpaper (fig. 210) is identical to that in the fabric (fig. 211).

To complete the Taliesin Line, Wright chose thirty-six colors for the Martin–Senour Company to custom-mix. Twenty-seven of these colors were to be used for covering large areas, while nine were for accent purposes, chosen to harmonize with the furniture and the fabrics.

Rugs were designed to be made by Karastan of New York, and the company advertised in the November 1955 *House Beautiful:*

> A Collection of Rugs by Frank Lloyd Wright for Karastan. . . . In the firm belief that today's home requires a rug as fresh and provocative as the new trends in building design, we've asked Frank Lloyd Wright to create a series of rugs for Karastan. The Taliesin Collection, to be introduced next Spring, is still on the drawing boards.

Although none of the rugs was marketed, the Karastan Company's archives contain photographs of two that were produced.

Frank Lloyd Wright's ventures into commercial designs were successful in providing well-designed objects that were available to many. As with the Usonian house, the furnishings were directed toward the average middle-income American. Produced in some quantity at the time, Wright's Heritage–Henredon furniture occasionally becomes available and is readily identified by Wright's stamp signature. Because of the delicate nature of the fabrics and the wallpapers, few large samples have survived, and are considered rare today.

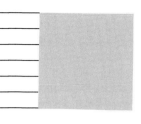

CRAFTSMEN AND MANUFACTURERS

From the 1890s to the 1950s, Frank Lloyd Wright depended on various craftsmen and manufacturers to execute the furnishings that were an integral part of his structures. Changes in design from concept to execution were often the result of technological considerations of the manufacturer. To find competent and sympathetic craftsmen and manufacturers was not an easy task. To understand Wright's ideal of simplicity in the design of furnishings was a difficult lesson for the craftsman to learn.

Concerning Wright's craftsmen "collaborators," Grant Manson wrote:

> In all truth, Wright, despite the power and originality of his ideas about the role of the minor arts in his houses, could not stand alone in executing them. The debt which he owed to clever craftsmen who, to their eternal credit, understood in those unsubtle days of house-furnishing what he was driving toward must be acknowledged. . . . In the sense that what they contributed became physically integrated with the architecture, certain glassmakers, too, were of immense importance to Wright's early success. (p. 118)

Wright's craftsmen, however, as Alan Gowans pointed out, were subordinate to the dominant personality of the architect, and their names are forgotten today. Only occasionally were they given recognition for their important role.

When a craftsman understood Wright's ideals and a good working relationship was established, Wright would return to him again and again, rather than putting his work out for contract bids. Without these "silent partners," Wright's ideal of a total organic architecture could not have been achieved. In many instances, the name of the firm or individual responsible for executing some aspect of the interior is unknown. To gain this knowledge will require years of research, but when it is accomplished, there will be a better understanding of an important dimension in Wright's work.

Since the task of researching all individuals or firms that made objects to Wright's designs would have been too extensive, this catalogue concentrates on the histories of firms known to have made objects that have been included in this exhibition. (A few additional biographies of firms considered important in Wright's career have been added.) Detailed histories were not possible for each entry. The location of many of the later houses, dispersed over a wide geographic area, required Wright to depend on competent local craftsmen and firms, which were too numerous to include.

The entries are listed in alphabetical order, according to the name of the firm or the individual craftsman.

AUVERGNE PRESS
River Forest, Illinois
Organized in 1895

According to an article in the *Chicago Evening Post* (January 23, 1897), Chauncey Williams joined with his neighbor William H. Winslow in 1895 to form the Auvergne Press in River Forest (fig. 213). In February of 1896, they purchased a large-size Washington handpress, which was initially located in the attic of the Williams house, where they worked during the winter and spring. Because of poor ventilation, however, which made work there uncomfortable in the summer, they subsequently moved their press to the basement of Winslow's house. Accounts of the location of the press in Winslow's house vary. The architect's son John Lloyd Wright and Winslow's daughter recall that it was located in the basement; however, the Chicago Architectural Club Catalogue of 1902 mentions that the press was in the Winslow stable. It may have been located in the basement during the winter months and moved to the unheated stable in the summer.

The *Evening Post* article states that their early work was experimental, and their first completed book, published in 1896, was a reprint of John Keats's *The Eve of St. Agnes* with a title page designed by Frank Lloyd Wright (fig. 191). According to the *Post* article, the book was in medium octavo size, and this reprint was done on heavy handmade paper. The *Evening Post* said, "While the typographical perfection of this volume has been much praised, the proprietors of the Auvergne Press modestly declare it to be practically experimental, and have other books in preparation by which they prefer to have their craftsmanship judged."

The Auvergne Press's second volume, *The House Beautiful* (fig. 192), was published in the following year and was described by the *Post* article as the most sumptuous volume ever issued from a strictly private press. Its lavish graphic design by Wright is discussed on pages 173–176. Although the press also intended to publish a collection of prose and poetic tributes paid by contemporary writers to Robert Louis Stevenson at the time of his death, there is no evidence that this volume was actually printed. The press undoubtedly printed some smaller leaflets or broadsides; though if it did, none is known to have survived. William Winslow's interest in the Auvergne Press was as a hobby, but Chauncey Williams was a publisher by vocation.

By the spring of 1895, Williams had joined with Irving Way to form the then well-known publishing firm of Way and Williams. On April 29, 1895, Way visited William Morris at the Kelmscott Press, arranging for the press to print an edition of Rose Hils's *Hand and Soul* for Way and Williams (Joe W. Kraus, "The Publishing Activities of Way & Williams," *Bibliographical Society of America*, vol. 10, no. 70, Spring 1976, pp. 221–260).

Both Chauncey Williams and William H. Winslow lived in River Forest in houses designed by Frank Lloyd Wright. One can imagine the spirit of comradeship and zeal enjoyed by the three men—all creative and successful in their own fields—working together in these publishing ventures.

JOHN W. AYERS CO.
John W. Ayers (1850–1914)
Chicago, Illinois

According to research by Irma Strauss ("John W. Ayers: Chicago Cabinetmaker and Manufacturer of Frank Lloyd Wright's Early Furniture," *Chicago History,* to be published in 1978), John William Ayers was born in Manchester, Massachusetts, the son of Isaac Ayers, a cabinetmaker, and Elizabeth Silver Ayers, on June 27, 1850. Ayers was initially a woodcarver but he established a furniture manufacturing business as early as 1876 in Salem, Massachusetts. He worked there until 1887, the year he moved to Chicago. He was first listed in the Chicago Directory in 1887 as a cabinetmaker with his residence at 853 West Congress. His 1888 listing gave his business address as 197 South Clinton. From 1890 to 1895, Ayers specialized in making mantels, and in 1895 the firm was first listed as the John W. Ayers Co., with Ayers as president. Although his residence changed frequently, his business address at 792 West Madison Street remained the same from 1892 to 1907, when his factory was destroyed by fire. In 1897 Miss Clara Bauerle was listed as secretary for John W. Ayers Co., and in 1910 the firm name was changed to Ayers–Ransom–Bauerle Co., with Albert Ransom, Jr., as secretary, at 726-34 South Seeley. In 1912 the firm name changed to Ayers–Cihlar–Ransom Co., with John Ayers as president, his half-brother Charles B. Ayers as vice-president, and Thomas Cihlar as secretary. John W. Ayers was last listed in the Chicago Directory in 1913 and he died in Chicago on May 9, 1914.

John W. Ayers is documented to have made furniture exhibited by Frank Lloyd Wright in the 1902 Catalogue of Exhibits for the Chicago Architectural Club (The

213. Auvergne Press, River Forest, Illinois.

Burnham Library, The Art Institute of Chicago), which lists the maker for most of the objects exhibited. Items 410 through 475 list the objects as well as drawings exhibited by Wright. Of the six furniture listings, five were followed with the statement "Made by John W. Ayers." This includes the dining chairs, the hall table, and the reception room chairs from Glenlloyd (the B. Harley Bradley House, Kankakee, Illinois, 1900); the dining table and chairs from the Warren Hickox House (Kankakee, 1900); and No. 437, "Other Chairs."

Another group of furniture documented as made by Ayers is the furniture for the Frank L. Smith Bank in Dwight, Illinois (1905). Correspondence between Frank Lloyd Wright, Colonel Frank L. Smith, and John W. Ayers (in The Burnham Library of The Art Institute of Chicago) shows that Ayers made the Wright-designed furniture for this bank.

A letter in the Lang ledger in the University Archives of the State University of New York at Buffalo shows that Ayers was also responsible for making the pergola trim for the Darwin D. Martin House (Buffalo, 1904).

THE F. H. BRESLER COMPANY
Frank H. Bresler
Milwaukee, Wisconsin
Incorporated in 1900

According to the articles of incorporation, The F. H. Bresler Company was incorporated on January 2, 1900, for the purpose of the "producing and reproducing of and the dealing in pictures, and of publishing and marketing the same" (vol. N, *Corporation Record*, Milwaukee County Historical Society), with a capital stock value of $25,000 and five directors. It was signed by William W. Sherman, who was made secretary–treasurer; Frank H. Bresler, who was president; and John H. Gault; their first listing in the Milwaukee City Directory was in 1901. The directory also indicated that the firm succeeded the F. H. Durbin Co., art importers and dealers, at 423 Milwaukee Street. The 1907 Directory indicated that the original purpose of the company had expanded, as they were also including the manufacture of picture frames and original furniture. Edward J. Snyder was listed as vice-president in that year and Carroll Atwood as secretary, with Bresler remaining as president. Entries in the journal of the Niedecken–Walbridge firm indicate that there was a close working relationship between the two firms. On October 12, 1907, Bresler was listed as one of the original holders of capital stock when the Niedecken–Walbridge firm was incorporated. A subsequent entry already cited on pages 44–45 indicates that the Niedecken–Walbridge firm bought furniture from Bresler in 1910. Bresler's venture into special custom furniture, however, did not last, as their listing in the 1908 Directory indicated that their business was only in paintings and the manufacturing of picture frames, though by 1920 they also included antique furniture. The 1937 Directory listed Edward J. Snyder as president–treasurer and Gertrude A. Bresler as vice-president–secretary of the Bresler Gallery. The firm subsequently had additional owners and continues today, specializing only in custom framing.

GIANNINI & HILGART
Orlando Giannini
Chicago, Illinois
Organized in 1899

According to research by Thomas A. Heinz, Orlando Giannini (1861–1928) was born in Cincinnati, Ohio, one of two sons of Joseph and Jeanette Giannini. In 1878, at the age of seventeen, Orlando became a sculptor, following his father's profession. After a five-year apprenticeship as a sculptor, Orlando became manager of the Cincinnati Art Pottery Company. In 1885 he went to New York and was a member of a group of artists called Xentric X (Eccentric Ten). By 1890 Giannini had moved to Chicago, as he was first listed as a designer in the Lakeside Directory in that year. He was employed from 1894 to 1898 by Adams and Westlake, a brass and bronze foundry. Giannini was in partnership with Harry A. Atwood for one year before joining with Hilgart in 1899 to form the firm of Giannini & Hilgart, glass stainers, which was located at 211 Madison (sixth floor).

Fritz Hilgart (1869–1942) was first listed as a glass stainer in 1897. Orlando Giannini's last listing in the Chicago Directory was in 1906 (see *The Glass Worker*, Official Organ of AGWIA, vol. 4, no. 40, December 1906), after which time he eventually appeared in La Jolla, California. He was replaced in the firm by his nephew Joseph R. Giannini, who was born in 1886 in Covington, Kentucky. Joseph Giannini was educated in Norwood, Ohio, and attended the Cincinnati Art School in 1903–1904 before moving to Chicago (*The Book of Chicagoans*, Chicago, 1917). In 1909, when Chicago street numbers changed, the firm's address became 222 West Madison. The firm continues in the art glass business today at 1359 North Noble in Chicago, however under different ownership.

Orlando Giannini did work for Frank Lloyd Wright at an early date. John

214. Jardiniere (rendering), designed by Orlando Giannini. 1897. (*Forms and Fantasies*, July 1898, plate 43a)

Lloyd Wright recalled that " 'Skinny' Giannini from Italy painted American Indians in brilliant colors on the walls of Papa's bedroom" (John Lloyd Wright, *My Father Who Is on Earth*, New York: G. P. Putnam's Sons, 1946, p. 34). Giannini's designs were published in several periodicals. An Indian design for a glass mosaic was published in *Forms & Fantasies* (plate XLII, July 1898). Two jardiniere designs were published in plate XLIII of the same issue, one of which is illustrated here (fig. 214).

One of Giannini's posters of 1895 (illustrated in *Art Nouveau Graphics*, London: Academy Editions, and New York: St. Martin's Press, 1971, p. 84), now in the collection of the Chicago Historical Society, was designed for the Turner Brass Works, a company owned by Chauncey Williams.

The Giannini & Hilgart firm made art glass for numerous Prairie School architects and also designed glass themselves. In a letter to Grant Manson in 1957, Hugh M. G. Garden described the Giannini & Hilgart firm: "Orlando Giannini was the designer while Hilgart managed the shop and cut the glass and did the constructing. Giannini was a real artist with an unfailing eye for color and texture" (Collection of Oak Park Library).

Two Xerox copies of undated catalogues of the Giannini & Hilgart studios are in the collection of Thomas Heinz. The introduction to the first catalogue indicates the specialty of the firm:

> Glass mosaics for wall panels, or mantel facings, etc., are the most beautiful and artistic in richness of their coloring and design; the great variety of opalescent and other glass combined in the metallic effects in gold, silver and bronze coloring of every shade in speckled granite and crackeline surface, showing the color of the rich opal or iridescent glass through the gold or silver covering, giving the beautiful shades of leaves in their fall colors, or antique metals, in their great variety, according to the effect desired in keeping with the architecture and surroundings.

The firm was willing to furnish "special designs in co-operation with the architects and in accordance with their instructions." Such a commission was for the mosaic mantel facing in the Darwin D. Martin House, subsequently destroyed. Giannini's mosaic mantel for the earlier Joseph M. Husser House in Chicago, built in 1899, was presumably destroyed when the house was demolished.

An article in the *Chicago Evening Post* of 1900 or 1901 described the Husser mosaic mantels that had been designed by Blanche Ostertag and made by Giannini:

> Mantel in glass mosaic designed by Blanche Ostertag was greatly admired, and Miss Ostertag was urgent that a goodly share of the credit should go to the glassworker who carried out her design with unsparing pains and artistic sympathy. "But then," she added, "Giannini is himself an artist and has a fellow feeling." This is the same Giannini who some years ago was designing book covers and posters and also executed a mural painting in the residence of Chauncey Williams at River Forest.

It is not known how many of Wright's early houses had art glass by Giannini & Hilgart, but the listing of the makers of objects in the 1902 Chicago Architectural Club Catalogue indicates that they made the glass for three houses: the Joseph M.

Husser House (1899), the Frank Thomas House (1901), built by James C. Rogers, Mrs. Thomas' father; and the Warren McArthur House (1892; remodeled 1902).

Another important commission for the Giannini & Hilgart firm was the Sedgwick S. Brinsmaid House (1902) in Des Moines, Iowa, designed by Arthur Heun. Since glass identical to that in the Brinsmaid House was used in Wright's Charles Ennis House (1923), Giannini may also have been responsible for this later glass commission. Other commissions for the Giannini & Hilgart firm were the A. B. Leach House, South Orange, New Jersey, designed by George Maher; the Moses Wentworth House, Chicago, designed by Howard Van Doren Shaw; and the First Church of Christ Scientist, Marshalltown, Iowa, designed by Hugh Garden (1902–1903).

GILLEN WOODWORK CORPORATION
Milwaukee, Wisconsin
Organized in 1937

When the Matthews Bros. Furniture Company was officially ended with a public auction in 1937, some of the Matthews employees started a new firm, headed by George E. Gillen as president and Ernest Govan as superintendent, both from the predecessor company. The Gillen firm employed fifteen to twenty artisans who had been with Matthews, including Matt Phillippi, the finishing foreman, and Tony Prochaska, who specialized in matching veneers. The firm's first contract was to make the cabinetwork for Fallingwater in Bear Run, Pennsylvania (*Milwaukee Sentinel*, July 18, 1937, collection, Edgar Tafel).

George E. Gillen was born in Oshkosh, Wisconsin, in 1892, the son of George William and Josephine (Pratsch) Gillen. His grandfather, Edward Gillen, was a noted engineer and the founder of the Gillen Marine Engineering Company of Racine, Wisconsin. George Gillen attended public schools in Oshkosh, after which he went to the University of Pennsylvania, where he studied architecture and was graduated in 1917. During World War I, he did special engineering work for the government in Fond du Lac, Wisconsin, and in 1918 he came to Milwaukee to work for the Matthews firm, of which he later became vice-president. He also became vice-president of the Woodwork Scales Company, a subsidiary of Matthews. He married Leone McPartlin in 1916 and had three children (John G. Gregory, *History of Milwaukee*, Indianapolis: S. J. Clarke, 1931). Another important Gillen contract for Wright was for Wingspread, the Herbert F. Johnson, Jr., House in Racine, Wisconsin (1937).

HENREDON FURNITURE INDUSTRIES, INCORPORATED
Morganton, North Carolina
Incorporated in 1945

At the time of incorporation of Henredon Furniture Industries, Inc., the officers were T. Henry Wilson, President; Ralph Edwards, Vice-President and Sales Manager; Donnell VanNoppen, Vice-President; and Sterling R. Collett, Treasurer. (The name Henredon was a combination of *Hen* for Henry; *re*, the initials of Ralph Edwards; and *don* for Donnell VanNoppen.) The factory was built in Morganton, North Carolina, and the first shipments of furniture were made in April 1947. For the first two years, only bedroom furniture was produced; in 1949 dining room pieces were added.

In 1949 Henredon joined with Heritage of High Point, North Carolina, in a merchandising and advertising partnership, although there was no change in the corporate structure of either firm. The merchandising name was Heritage–Henredon, and their lines were nationally advertised as such. Heritage manufactured occasional tables and upholstered sofas and chairs; Henredon manufactured bedroom and dining room pieces. The national advertisements offered furniture for all rooms in the house except the kitchen.

In October of 1956, Heritage Furniture, Inc., was bought by the Drexel Furniture Company. In 1957, in order to continue supplying the occasional tables and upholstered furniture, which had been supplied by Heritage, Henredon acquired the Schoonbeck Company of Grand Rapids, Michigan, and the N. C. Schoonbeck Company of High Point, North Carolina. Henredon then started an occasional table factory in Morganton and began shipments from it in 1958.

Henredon has grown from a single plant to four factories making upholstered furniture and four factories making wood bedroom, dining room, and occasional furniture. The factories making occasional tables and dining room furniture are in Morganton; the bedroom plant is in Spruce Pine, North Carolina; and the upholstery factories are in Grand Rapids, Michigan, and High Point, North Carolina.

THE JUDSON STUDIOS
William Lees Judson (1842–1928)
Los Angeles, California
Organized in 1897

William Lees Judson was born in Manchester, England, and in 1852 at the age of ten moved with his family to Brooklyn, New York. As a child he studied art with his father, eventually becoming successful as a portrait painter. He continued his art studies in New York, London, and Paris. He came to Chicago to work and study at the time of the Chicago Columbian Exposition of 1893, but because of poor health moved to California in that year. Stirred by the beauties of the Arroyo Seco, Judson turned from portraiture to landscape, painting scenes of the Mission days. Judson taught art at the University of Southern California, organized its College of Fine Arts, and became its first dean. In 1901 the college built a new Fine Arts building, studio, and gallery next to his home on the Arroyo at Garranza (*California Design 1910*, exhibition catalogue, Pasadena Center, October 15–December 1, 1974, California Design Publications, 1974).

William Lees Judson organized the Judson Studios in 1897, and it has been in its present location at 200 South Avenue since 1920. His sons, Walter H. and J. Lionel Judson, had organized the Colonial Art Glass Company in 1893 at 7 Mott Alley, Los Angeles. Before starting the Judson Studios, William Lees Judson designed for this firm, which specialized in designing and making art glass and mosaics.

The company's account books include entries for the work done for Wright's house for Aline Barnsdall. (For example, $2,025.00 was paid to the studios on May 25, 1920, which also received a revised set of plans from Wright on January 12, 1921.) The account book also indicates that the Judson Studios supplied the art glass for the Charles Ennis House (letters from Walter W. Judson to the author, fall 1977).

KAPP CABINET SHOP
Phoenix, Arizona
Organized in 1945

The Kapp Cabinet Shop was started by two brothers, Stanley Charles Kapp (born 1910) and Charles Junior Kapp (born 1914), both born in Duran, Michigan. Charles Kapp was graduated from Flushing (Michigan) High School and General Motors Tech in tool and die design; Stanley Kapp was graduated from die school in Flint and later became superintendent of the cabinet shop at Palace Travel Coach in that city. Their father, Charles Arthur Kapp, was a general construction contractor in Flint, and all six sons were trained in woodworking while helping out in their father's company.

The Kapp Cabinet Shop was begun in Phoenix in October of 1945. When Stanley Kapp died in 1951, another brother, Russell Kapp, joined Charles in a partnership. Russell Kapp was graduated from Flushing High School and attended both Michigan State College and Western State Industrial Arts College at Kalamazoo.

The Kapp brothers knew Frank Lloyd Wright and manufactured many of his custom-designed cabinets and furnishings from blueprints furnished by Taliesin West. In addition to furniture made for and installed in the David Wright House, they made the furniture for a number of other Wright-designed houses. Furniture made at the Kapp Cabinet Shop was picked up by Taliesin West and shipped to the various houses.

According to Charles J. Kapp, "Mr. Wright's designs were very unique and also very difficult to make due to so many different angles, curves and cut-outs. . . . All jobs were supervised by Frank Lloyd Wright personally or by one of his students at Taliesin West" (letter to the author, September 9, 1977).

The shop has continued to the present at the same address, 1840 East Madison Street, and specializes in custom woodwork and store fixtures.

WILLY H. LAU
Chicago, Illinois
(Directory 1893–1924)

Willy H. Lau was first listed in the Chicago directories as a designer at 47 South Jefferson. By 1898 he had started his business of designing, manufacturing, and selling gas and light fixtures. In 1902 Willy Lau rented a studio and suite in the Pullman Building at 12 Adams Street, retaining his factory at 89–93 East Indiana Street. From the listing of the objects designed by Frank Lloyd Wright and the names of the manufacturers or makers in the 1902 Catalogue of the Chicago Architectural Club, it is known that Willy Lau made the light fixtures for the B. Harley Bradley House of 1900.

The business was incorporated in 1905 under the name W. H. Lau & Co., with Lau listed as president and Crawford A. Street as secretary. In that same year, the firm advertised in *The Architectural Record*, illustrating a bracket light designed by Willy Lau for the E. J. Mosser House in Chicago, a George Maher commission. In the rectilinear lines of the bracket and the leaded glass lamps, Lau's design was in keeping with the precepts of Prairie School architecture. Correspondence and bills of sale in the Frank L. Smith Collection in The Burnham Library of The Art Institute of Chicago indicate that Lau made exterior lanterns identical to ones flanking the entrance gate of the E. C. Waller estate in River Forest, Illinois, as well as andirons, grates, hanging light fixtures, "lemon" brass wall sconces, and furnished all electrical supplies for the Dwight Bank and Frank L. Smith Insurance office of 1905. He also gave them an estimate for a "lemon" brass umbrella stand, but Colonel Smith decided that the $30 price was too expensive. In the 1906 Catalogue of the Chicago Architectural Club, Willy Lau advertised his company as designers and manufacturers of electroliers, gas and combination fixtures, with its specialties, art glass and architectural wrought-iron work.

In 1909 the firm moved to 26 Lake Street. Lau exhibited "bronze electroliers in L'Art Noveau" in the nineteenth annual exhibition of the Chicago Architectural Club (1906). The company's last listing was in the1923–1924 City Directory.

LINDEN GLASS COMPANY
Frank L. Linden (1859–1934)
Chicago, Illinois

The Book of Chicagoans (1905) states that Frank L. Linden was born and educated in Rockford, Illinois, and that he left school in 1876 to go to New York City, where he worked as an interior decorator until 1881, when he came to Chicago. The following year he entered into partnership with the German émigré Ernest J. Spierling to form the decorating firm of Spierling & Linden. Linden was first listed in the Chicago Lakeside Directory in 1884, the year in which Spierling & Linden was also first listed.

First located at 333 Wabash Avenue, the firm was listed at 1216 Michigan Avenue, beginning in 1890, where it remained until around 1934 (the building still stands today). The first year the Linden Glass Company was listed was 1890. Both firms continued at the same address and in 1900 advertised together in the *Handbook for Architects and Builders* (Chicago): "SPIERLING & LINDEN, / DECORATORS/LINDEN GLASS CO.,/FURNISHERS/STAINED GLASS. MOSAIC./ 1216 Michigan Avenue, Chicago./Tel. South 94." Spierling & Linden advertised extensively in the various architectural and trade periodicals of the period—especially in the Chicago Architectural Club catalogues, where the firm was frequently listed as a sponsor. In 1910 the name of Linden Glass Co. was changed to the Linden Company.

According to Frank Linden, Jr., his father loved to paint, especially roses. One of his first commissions in Chicago was to paint the ceilings of the Potter Palmer House (1350 Lake Shore Drive), which was designed by Henry Ives Cobb in 1882 (the interior was remodeled by J. L. Silsbee in 1884). Linden also painted the ceiling of the ballroom and the library of the Samuel Nickerson House, in its era one of the most important houses in Chicago. All that survives of Frank L. Linden's papers, drawings, etc., are a few of his paintings, including an early still life painting of roses. Frank Linden was active in the Chicago Architectural Club and was closely acquainted with many of Chicago's famous architects. In 1901 he exhibited his own work: a "Scheme for Decoration" (illustrated in the Catalogue of the Fourteenth Annual Exhibition of the Chicago Architectural Club).

Spierling & Linden evidently concentrated on mural and ceiling painting (including the Grand Pacific Hotel and Wilson & Co.'s Palmer House store), while the

Linden Glass Company concentrated on furnishings. *Industrial Chicago*, "The Building Interests," noted in 1891 "that well-known establishment, the Linden Glass Company . . . had done a high-grade trade in stained and decorative glass." Art glass windows were only part of the Linden Glass Company's business, which included all aspects of interior decoration. The firm also designed furniture, textiles, and draperies, and four or five women were employed to sew and embroider. Frank Linden, Jr., recalls the physical layout of the business at 1216 South Michigan. The art glass windows were made by about a dozen craftsmen, almost all foreign-born, in a rear section of the building. In 1892 Ernest J. Wagner was first listed as manager of the Linden Glass Company, and he continued to be listed as an officer of the firm, eventually becoming a partner.

The major Wright commission involving art glass made by Linden was for the Dana House. An advertisement in *The Architectural Record* (1908) documents this:

> Designed For Dana Residence by Frank Lloyd Wright, Arch. Made by the Linden Glass Co. . . .
>
> Linden Glass Company/1216 Michigan Av. Chicago: Designers · Manufacturers/importers: Decorative Leaded Glass · Memorial/ Windows · Glass Mosaic · Lamps · Electric Fixtures · Hand Embroidery · Furniture · Draperies · / Decoration & Everything for Complete Furnishing.

Frank Linden, Jr., remembers his father working with Frank Lloyd Wright and stated that the firm produced most of the art glass for Wright's houses, including the Coonley and Robie Houses and the Midway Gardens. Linden was also responsible for executing the art glass for the Ernest Magerstadt House (Chicago, 1908), designed by George W. Maher. The art glass windows for Frank Lloyd Wright's houses would have represented only a small part of the firm's business.

Frank Linden's business as an interior decorator was quite extensive and, through either Spierling & Linden or the Linden Glass Company, had many important commissions. According to *Inland Architect* of 1888, the Linden Glass Company and Spierling and Linden jointly completed a number of contracts in that year, including the residence of G. M. Pullman on Pullman Island, Alexandria Bay, New York; the Ellis Wainwright House in St. Louis; and the residences of Edwin Partridge and W. S. Jones in Chicago. According to Frank Linden, Jr., the firm also did the interior work for the Pullman Palace Car Company and, in the 1920s, was responsible for designing and executing the interiors of the Mayo Clinic in Rochester, Minnesota, as well as the houses of Drs. Charles and Will Mayo. They did numerous bank interiors in Chicago and the Middle West, including the Chicago National Bank and Louis Sullivan's Owatonna Bank.

MATTHEWS BROS. FURNITURE COMPANY
Milwaukee, Wisconsin
1857–1937

Milwaukee's most celebrated furniture manufacturing firm was founded in 1857 by the brothers Eschines P. (1832–1913) and Alonzo R. Matthews (1835–1901). E. P. Matthews was born in Paynesville, Ohio, and Alonzo R. Matthews in Russell,

Geauga County, Ohio, where the family had moved. Both were educated in schools near Chagrin Falls, Ohio, and in Hiram College in that state before going to Milwaukee in 1856, when young men in their early twenties, to establish a furniture store on East Water Street. Their factory was on River Street. In 1867 Quincy A. Matthews (born 1848), their youngest brother, joined the firm, and eventually became a partner. In 1870 they moved to a new building on Fourth Street, which was described in a contemporary account:

> "Its dimensions are 40 x 100 feet, four stories in height. It is furnished with all the latest and best machinery known for turning out cabinet work, which is driven by a 75-horse power engine. Here they employ seventy hands in the manufacture of chamber sets, book-cases, side-boards, bureaus, etc., for the supply of their immense retail trade, which extends to all parts of the Northwest." (*History of Milwaukee*, Chicago, 1881, p. 1,518)

In 1874, the firm moved to 413 and 417 Broadway, and in 1879 to 407–409 and 411 East Water—which was described in the same account as occupying 40,000 square feet of floor room and employing sixty-three hands:

> The first three floors are occupied as salesrooms, the spacious offices, 30 x 30 feet, being in the rear on the first floor. The fourth floor is occupied as a store room and the fifth by the upholsterers and finishers. The packing and shipping is done in the basement. Connected with the business is a photograph department, where an artist is employed in taking pictures of the various new designs in furniture that they are constantly turning out. They manufacture almost exclusively for their immense retail trade, producing a class of goods superior in quality to that generally furnished to the country jobbing trade.

The Matthews firm (fig. 215) grew to become one of the largest manufacturers of furniture in the Northwest, so that by 1892 the factory plant was valued at $75,000 and the production at $125,000 (*Milwaukee's Great Industries*, Milwaukee: The Association for the Advancement of Milwaukee, 1892). According to an article in *The Evening Wisconsin* (January 13, 1891):

> The extensive and well-known business house of Matthews Bros., interested in the manufacture and wholesale and retail dealers in furniture, is undergoing an important change, as a result of the present magnitude and constantly increasing business done by the house. . . .

> In order to handle both the manufacturing and selling business more perfectly, the firm has organized two distinct companies. The new concern will be known as the Matthews Bros. Manufacturing Company, which will devote its capital and exclusive attention to the manufacturing plant of the old firm which heretofore conducted both branches of the business. The old corporate firm, Matthews Bros. Furniture Company will devote its capital and exclusive attention to sales, wholesale and retail. In this change Mr. Vogel, the well-known contractor and carpenter, becomes a member of the manufacturing company. . . .

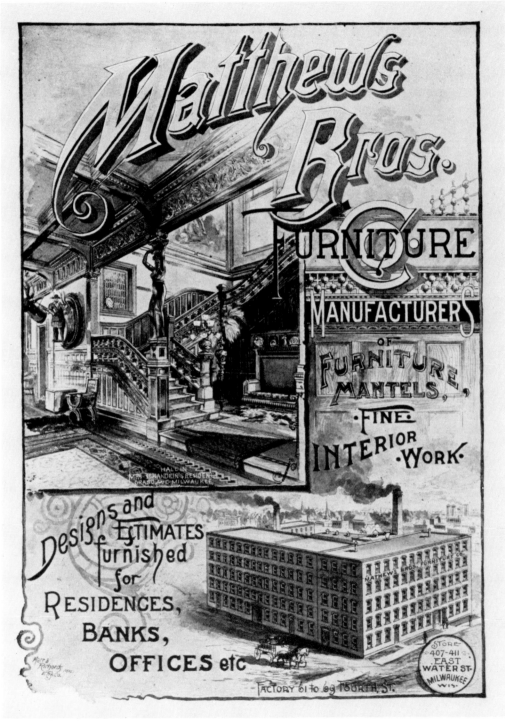

215. Advertisement for Matthews Bros. Furniture Company. 1897.

The company employs over 250 cabinet makers and laborers and its business extends from Maine to Colorado. Especially in the art of interior decoration of houses with fancy wood designs has the company a very large trade all over the country. . . .

Although the factory had been sold by the family following the death of E. P. Matthews in 1913, the company continued to expand into the years of the Depression. Henry E. Judd (born 1880) became president in 1920, and by 1930 the firm had changed its specialization to custom interior woodwork.

According to Judd, 90 percent of the firm's business was done outside of Wisconsin and they had received four or five orders of more than $1 million each ("Big Firms Known Better to Outsiders Than Here," *Milwaukee Journal*, January 3, 1931). In this article, Judd reported that they had no inventory stock, since everything was made to order:

> We do cabinet work, paneling and finishing—and every piece is made to order, nearly all by hand. . . . We cannot have mass production in our kind of work. . . . About all we can do is give these skilled workmen good light, heat and plenty of time. They cannot be pushed. They must take pride in their work. They are artists as well as workmen. . . . Often we get work without competitive bids. We are asked to do it.

Judd described the factory as taking 100,000 square feet of floor space and employing 200–300 men, mostly German cabinetmakers. Some of their important large commissions in Chicago included interior work for the Stevens Hotel, the Palmer House hotel, the Palmolive Building, the Tribune Tower, and the Chicago Board of Trade; there were many others in the United States and abroad.

JAMES A. MILLER AND BROTHER (1889–)
James A. Miller (born 1850)
Chicago, Illinois

James Alexander Miller was born on January 26, 1850, in St. Charles, Illinois, the son of Alexander and Janet (Beith) Miller. He was educated in the public schools of Kane County, and in 1894 married Miss Martha Shorey of Chicago. After leaving school, he went to Chicago and learned the roofing trade. He worked as a journeyman until 1874 when he went into partnership with Abraham and Richard Knisely, who had been established for many years. The firm of Adler and Sullivan designed the Knisely Building at 551–557 West Monroe Street in 1884 (illustrated in pl. 6 of Morrison) and the Knisely Store in 1883 for Richard Knisely. Abraham Knisely was a tinsmith in the 1850s.

Miller is first listed in the 1874 Lakeside Chicago Directory as a tinner, and in the following year as a partner of A. Knisely & Co., which advertised in the Business Directory: "Slate, Tin & Corrugated Iron/Roofers/Manufacturers of/Hayes' Patent Skylights/ELEVATOR BUCKETS/72 and 74 West Monroe St./Chicago, Ill." In 1881 the firm name was changed to Knisely Bros. & Miller, and in 1883 to Knisely & Miller, Abraham Knisely being listed as the surviving Knisely partner. The firm continued as Knisely & Miller (moving to South Clinton Street in 1885) until 1889, when it was listed as James A. Miller and Brother, James A. and Robert B. Miller being the surviving partners of Knisely & Miller.

The firm advertised in the 1896 Catalogue of the Chicago Architectural Club: "James A. Miller and Brother, Roofers in Slate, tin, and iron, and makers of cornices, bays, skylights, etc. in copper and galvanized iron. Special attention given to first class work and large contracts." In the *Handbook for Architects and Builders* (Chicago: Press of William Johnston Printing Company, 1900) James A. Miller and Brother advertised again, this time adding slate roofs, wire glass windows, and metal frames to the above-mentioned list. Miller was a member of the Chicago Architectural Club and frequently advertised in its catalogue (see fig. 216). The skill of his firm in metalwork no doubt explains why Wright turned to Miller to make his copper objects. An advertisement by the W. H. Mullins Co. in *The Architectural Record* (1911) indicates that this sheet metal firm also included sheet metal statuary. The wide stock and manufacturing of James A. Miller and Brother indicated why they could take on the commission of fabricating Wright's objects in copper. An advertisement in the 1905 *Architectural Record* indicates that they took on the manufacture of wire glass windows and sheet metal frames and sash as well as roofing. Wright no doubt was familiar with Knisely and Miller through their work on The Auditorium in Chicago and other projects for Adler and Sullivan. Miller's house, "Shorewood," in Lake Forest, where he had moved from his Washington Avenue house in 1892, was described and illustrated in an article in *House Beautiful* for October 1900.

In his article "In the Cause of Architecture," in the October 1928 issue of *The Architectural Record*, Frank Lloyd Wright wrote about James A. Miller, one of the few instances of Wright's discussing a craftsman:

> Since first meeting, thirty years ago, James A. Miller, a sheet-metal worker of Chicago, who had intelligent pride in his material and a sentiment concerning it (designing a house for himself at one time he demanded a tin-floored balcony outside his bedroom window in order that he might hear the rain patter upon it), I have had respect for his sheet-metal medium.
>
> At that time I designed some sheet copper bowls, slender flower holders and such things, for him, and fell in love with sheet copper as a building material. . . . Miller Brothers in addition to other offices of that factory were then interested in sheet metal window-sash and frames—especially in skylights and metal doors.

S. BROOK MOORE (born 1915)
Sandy Spring, Maryland

S. Brook Moore was born of Quaker parents on a farm in Sandy Spring, Maryland, and it was here that his love of wood and interest in woodworking began. He attended George School, a Friends' school in Newtown, Bucks County, Pennsylvania, from 1930 to 1934, where he received his only formal training as a cabinetmaker. His shop teacher, Robert Brown, was particularly influential and was able to impart to his students his deep feelings for natural materials and a sense of excellence and quality of workmanship. After school, Moore returned to his farm and a small woodworking shop that he had set up. From 1942 to 1946, he worked at Fairchild Aircraft in Hagerstown, Maryland, where his main job was to construct and repair wooden airplanes. In 1947 he again returned to the farm, this time to set up a furniture shop. His skill soon brought more than enough business, so that he never had to advertise.

Gradually Moore became more interested in the Society of Friends and soon became involved in its activities, first locally, then through the state. In 1958 Moore served on the building committee of George School. Rather than expanding the school, Moore recommended building a separate school at Sandy Spring. Although he had no land or money, he was able to found the Sandy Spring Friends' School in that year; it has now grown into a sizable institution. After it was set up and running on its own, he was able to return to woodworking. In December of 1971, he moved his shop to Charlestown, New Hampshire, a rural area, in order to escape the expanding urbanism of Washington, D.C. In 1973 he returned to his Sandy Spring farm, where he continued his woodworking craft, turning now to making musical instruments. All of his work continues to be custom work. Moore has two sons—one of whom now runs a cabinetmaking shop in Sandy Spring, the other being a carpenter in Canada—and a daughter.

About the custom furniture made for the Robert Llewellyn Wright House of 1957 in Bethesda, Maryland, the only Wright-designed house for which he made furniture, Moore writes:

There was a challenge in making the curved kitchen cabinets and other curved pieces. The construction methods took some thought and ingenuity in forming

216. Advertisement, probably designed by Robert Spencer, James A. Miller and Brother. (Chicago Architectural Club Catalogue of the Ninth Annual Exhibition, 1896)

and gluing but nothing too complicated for any good woodworker. In the case of the hassocks, it was a matter of kerfing the back side deep enough to allow the piece to take the bend without rupturing the outer surface. (Letter from S. Brook Moore to the author, August 10, 1977)

NIEDECKEN–WALBRIDGE
George M. Niedecken (1878–1945)
Milwaukee, Wisconsin
Incorporated in 1907

George Niedecken was born in Milwaukee, Wisconsin, the son of Charles Edward Niedecken. Along with Edward Steichen and others, he organized an Art Students League in Milwaukee in 1894, and he first studied at The Wisconsin Art Center, probably under Richard Lorenz, who was teaching there at the time. For the school year 1897–1898, he studied at the school of The Art Institute of Chicago; in the 1897 exhibition of the Chicago Arts and Crafts Society, he exhibited a design for friezes (No. 318 in the catalogue), and in 1898 he received first honors for a medieval book cover. Niedecken's diary (Prairie School Archives, Milwaukee Art Center, Milwaukee, Wisconsin), kept between July 13 and September 16, 1899, documents his travels in Germany and Austria, which included visits to Berlin, Vienna, Innsbruck, Salzburg, Munich, Frankfurt, Weimar, and Leipzig, among other places. A design by Niedecken for a library done in Berlin is illustrated in *Forms and Fantasies* (May 1899, Plate 211). In 1900 he studied at the École des Beaux Arts in Paris and no doubt visited the Universal Exposition in Paris in that year. His diary records his expenses for attending school in that year.

Niedecken's drawings made in Europe indicate that he was learning from nature—he made a number of landscape sketches—as well as from portraits. He undoubtedly saw the work of such avant-garde European designers as J. M. Olbrich and Otto Wagner in Vienna. Like Wright, Niedecken was interested in Japanese prints and collected them in Europe. In 1904 Niedecken was working for Wright in the Oak Park studio (letter of Charles White, Jr., to Walter Willcox, May 20, 1904). It was at this time that Niedecken painted the frieze in the dining room of the Dana House (fig. 71), which is signed "Geo. M. Niedecken," with an additional symbol that appears to be the initials "C.P." above and to the left of his signature. It was at this time that Niedecken became associated with Frank Bresler of the Bresler Gallery in Milwaukee (see p. 202). In 1907 Niedecken joined with John Walbridge to form the Niedecken–Walbridge company, also in Milwaukee. John Walbridge was married to Niedecken's sister Evelyn. According to an advertisement in the *Western Architect*, Niedecken and Walbridge were "Specialists in design and execution of Interior Decorations and Mural Paintings. Makers of Special Furniture—Art Glass—Electric Fixtures." The firm's journal (October 5, 1907–July 31, 1909) indicates that on October 12, 1907, the firm was incorporated with Niedecken and Walbridge each buying twelve shares and F. H. Bresler one share of stock in the company's business. Between 1907 and 1909, Niedecken's furniture was made by the F. H. Bresler Company, as the entry for November 2 indicates a cash payment of $219.38 to the F. H. Bresler Company, for the "October account of furniture and work done." Niedecken's relationship with Wright, which had begun by 1904, continued with major commissions for the Coonley and Robie interiors. The Niedecken–Walbridge firm was also responsible for the execution of the interiors for other Wright houses, including those for F. F. Tomek, Riverside, Illinois (1907); F. C. Bogk, Milwaukee, Wisconsin (1916); and Henry J. Allen, Wichita, Kansas (1917). The firm was also responsible for the interior of the D. M. Amberg House, Grand Rapids, Michigan, and the E. P. Irving House, Decatur, Illinois, both commissions left to H. V. Van Holst and Marion Mahoney by Wright on his departure for Europe in 1909.

217 (below). Cabinet (rendering), designed by George M. Niedecken. 218 (opposite). Desk (rendering), designed by George M. Niedecken, Henry J. Allen House (designed by Frank Lloyd Wright in 1917).

Others included the S. S. Brinsmaid House, Des Moines, Iowa, and the art galleries of the F. H. Bresler Company, Milwaukee, to name a few notable commissions. Niedecken on his own was responsible for executing the interior of Purcell, Feick & Elmslie's Edison Shop on Wabash Avenue in Chicago (1913).

In 1916 or 1917, the Niedecken and Walbridge firm moved from their location at 436 Milwaukee Street to 767 North Jefferson Street—immediately adjacent to their factory building. At the height of its business activity, the firm employed twenty-five artisans. Entries in the journal indicate that most of the firm's work for the Coonley and Robie Houses was delegated to outside craftsmen.

F. SCHUMACHER & COMPANY
Frederick Schumacher (1852–1912)
New York, New York
Founded in 1889

F. Schumacher & Company was founded by Frederick Schumacher, who was born in Paris, was originally connected with Vanoutryve in that city, and later acted as agent for Brown, De Turck & Co. He came to the United States in the early 1880s to sell designs for decorative fabrics, which at that time were made abroad and bought by the distributors in this country. In 1883 he became connected with Passavant &

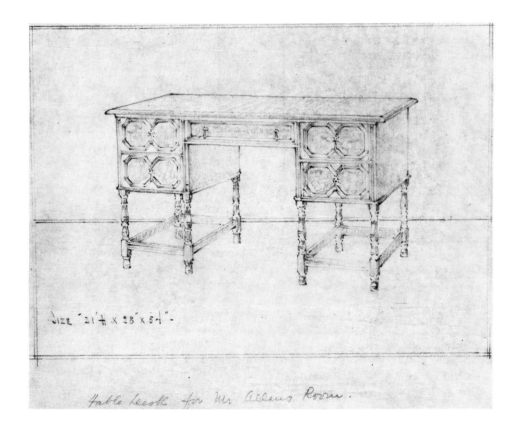

Size 21¼ x 28 x 54"

Table Desk for Mr. Allens Room.

Co., then a well-known New York fabric firm, and opened an upholstery department for them. In 1889 he started his own firm, taking over the Passavant stock and opening an office at 935 Broadway. In 1893 he formed a partnership with Paul Gadebusch, and the business was moved to 222 Fourth Avenue. And in 1901 a move was made to 152 Fifth Avenue. Six years later, the firm was incorporated, with Frederick Schumacher as president. In 1911 the business was moved to 7 West 37th Street and in 1921 to 60 West 40th Street. In 1962 the firm moved to its present location at 56th Street and Third Avenue.

According to an article in the February 1939 issue of *Decorative Finisher,* when Schumacher began his business there were few firms in this country making the fine fabrics required in the decoration of the large houses then being built; they had to be imported from Europe, causing uncertainty and delay in delivery. With Schumacher's expertise in European decorative fabrics, combined with his familiarity with the requirements of the domestic market, he believed he could find a mill in this country to capitalize more readily on this demand for fine fabrics; he also recognized that the company could gain competitive advantage with predictable, prompt deliveries. In 1895 he succeeded in finding in Paterson, New Jersey, a mill and highly skilled weavers who were capable of delivering the same superb quality as foreign producers. Today the company's Paterson mill continues to specialize in weaving premium-priced damasks, satins, brocades, and taffetas to the color and design specifications of its customers. These fabrics can be identified by two narrow stripes that appear in the selvage.

In 1899 Schumacher's nephew, Pierre Pozier, came from France to become his successor in the styling and purchasing of the lines. Pozier had been educated and

219. Couch and tabourette with lamp (rendering), by George M. Niedecken, Edward Bradley House.

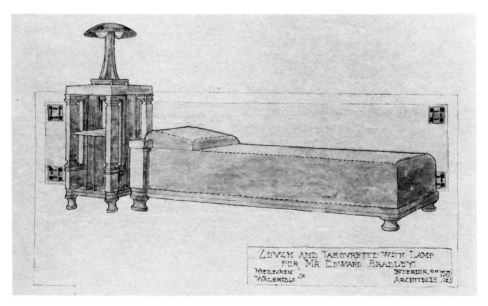

trained in the business in England and Germany, as well as in France. After Schumacher's death in 1912 at his home near Paris, Paul Gadebusch became president of the firm, a position he held until his death in 1943, when Pozier became president. Paul Gadebusch's son, Paul H. Gadebusch, who had been associated with the firm since 1916, succeeded Pozier to the presidency in 1952 and remained president until his death in 1957.

Although imported prints had been part of Schumacher's line, in 1923 it introduced a line of domestic prints, marketed under the trade name of Waverly Fabrics. In 1925 Waverly Fabrics became a division of the firm with separate sales and office staffs concentrating on sales to department stores. As an outgrowth of Waverly Fabrics' piece goods operation, the cut order department, now called Waverly Decorative Fabrics, made fabrics to be sold in cut lengths, to decorators and upholsterers who did not carry piece stock. A carpet department was established in 1930 as a separate division, and in 1939 a wallpaper department was organized.

Schumacher distributes through interior designers, architects, and decorating departments of large stores. Merchandise is sold wholesale only through the main office in New York, its sixteen branches throughout this country and in Paris. Since the middle 1920s a Chicago showroom outlet for Schumacher fabrics has been in existence, located first at 29 East Madison Street and then in the Merchandise Mart since the early 1930s.

Over the years, Schumacher has woven fabrics at the Paterson mill for a number of important commissions, including designs for the Blue Room of the White House during the presidencies of Theodore Roosevelt, Woodrow Wilson, and Calvin Coolidge. Historic restoration fabrics also form an important part of the Schumacher line and include reproductions of fabrics in the collections of Historic Newport and of Colonial Williamsburg, among others.

Schumacher's interest in and support of contemporary design has always been noteworthy. In 1925 the firm imported outstanding modern fabrics from the Paris Exposition of Decorative Arts. The firm has commissioned work by such celebrated American designers as Dorothy Draper, Paul McCobb, James Amster, Vera, William Pahlmann, and Raymond Loewy.

In addition to the 1955 Taliesin Line of Wright-designed fabrics and wallpapers, Schumacher was often the source of fabrics for Wright's earlier houses. For example, the Niedecken journal discloses that payments were made to the Schumacher firm for fabrics for the Frederick Robie House, there is an entry on December 10, 1909, for "Goats Hair Satin" and one on January 11, 1910, for the Robie spreads. On December 22, 1908, 2½ yards of taffeta were ordered from Schumacher for chairs for the Avery Coonley House, and on March 21, 1913, Niedecken ordered 5⅓ yards of plain mohair for Mrs. Coonley.

SHENANGO CHINA COMPANY
New Castle, Pennsylvania
Incorporated in 1901

Located in New Castle, Pennsylvania, near Pittsburgh, the Shenango China Company was incorporated in 1901. It manufactured semivitreous hotelware and home dinnerware. In 1909, after several financial setbacks and reorganizations, the bankrupt firm, which had been chartered in 1905 as the Shenango Pottery Company, was purchased by James M. Smith, Sr. Until 1935 Shenango's entire production was devoted to a type of china suitably durable for hotels, restaurants, and institutions. Custom orders, such as the Midway Gardens china, were common, and the firm's trademark—the Shenango Indian making a pot—was stamped on the bottom of each piece. Shenango's progressiveness is seen not only in its expansion into one of the largest producers of vitrified china in the world but also in its interest in contemporary design in tableware. Castleton China, a subsidiary of Shenango, was formed in 1940, and the company commissioned outstanding designers, such as Eva Zeisel, to do work for them; within a short period of time, Castleton became one of the most prestigious producers of fine china in the United States. Shenango pottery and Castleton china were retailed in Chicago by the Albert Pick Company.

STEELCASE (METAL OFFICE FURNITURE COMPANY)
Grand Rapids, Michigan
Organized in 1912

Peter Wege, Sr. (1870–1947), founder of Steelcase, was born in Toledo, Ohio, and went to New York in 1897. He became the sheet metal superintendent of the J. B. and J. M. Cornell Company in Cold Spring, New York, on the west side of the Hudson River across from West Point. In that year, he developed a method of bending sheet steel to make strong, light document drawers, which were made to order and installed in county courthouses. The U.S. government was beginning to specify fireproof materials, wherever possible, for its buildings and for furnishings as well. Documents formerly stored in wooden boxes were being transferred to steel drawers. Wege became expert in methods of reinforcing sheet metal with L and U channels, producing strength without excessive weight. His expertise and innovativeness enhanced his reputation in the industry.

In 1906 a group of businessmen in Marietta, Ohio, formed the Safe Cabinet Company to manufacture a lightweight insulated steel safe. Up to this time, safes had been made of heavy-duty cast iron. The founders had heard of Wege's work and asked him to join them in this project. The safes proved very successful, and as the demand for sheet metal products grew, Peter Wege decided to launch a company of his own to make a complete line of office furniture. In 1912 Wege persuaded a small group of investors to join him as stockholders in founding the Metal Office Furniture Company, later known as Steelcase. He chose Grand Rapids, Michigan, for the facilities because it had become the "Furniture Capital of the World."

The first product of the Metal Office Furniture Company was a metal wastebasket, followed in a few months by a line of steel safes. In 1914 rolltop steel desks were made. In 1915 the company gained national recognition when it was contracted to supply the steel desks for the Boston Custom House. This commission included a complete line of both flat-top and rolltop desks in various sizes and finishes. In 1919 the firm added steel files to its office line.

In 1933 the firm introduced its "island base" desk at the Inland Steel Company display at Chicago's Century of Progress exhibition. This desk contained two simple, oblong supports under the desk drawers on each side. Conventional desks had four legs on each side, which limited the foot room beneath them, especially under smaller models. The island base gave people more foot room and also simplified maintenance, as it was easier to mop around the island base than around the four legs. When the desk was put into production, the island bases were made thinner (letter from Anne Zeller, Steelcase Inc., to the author, August 22, 1977). It may have been at the 1933 exhibition that Wright first learned of this firm, to which he turned in 1936 for the manufacture of the desks for the S. C. Johnson project. It was the firm's first experience in manufacturing a furniture ensemble that was designed for a specific office interior.

Known for its innovation, the company's production was diverted to work for the U.S. Navy during World War II. In the postwar years, the company continued in the forefront of the industry, introducing their first modular office furniture in 1949 and a line of office furniture in color in 1953. It was not until 1954 that the corporation name was changed to Steelcase Inc.

TEMPLE ART GLASS CO.
Chicago, Illinois
(*Directory 1903–1933*)

The Temple Art Glass Co. was first listed in the 1903 Chicago Directory at 228 Kinzie in Chicago. Henry J. Neithart was president and Joseph J. Vogel was secretary. Vogel, who had been a glass cutter in 1896, had become a foreman for the Flanagan & Biederweg Co. in 1899.

The 1904 Directory indicates that the Temple company manufactured art glass for church, memorial, society, and domestic windows. Neithart was no longer associated with the firm in 1905. The business was moved to 117 Michigan Street, adding art glass shades to its line. In 1910 the firm moved to 140–146 Michigan Street, and William Krewer was listed as president and Joseph J. Vogel as treasurer.

Correspondence between Frank Lloyd Wright and two of his clients indicates that the Temple Art Glass Co. made the windows for the Harvey P. Sutton House in McCook, Nebraska (1907), and the Francis W. Little House, Wayzata, Minnesota (1913). According to Alfonso Iannelli, the art glass for the Midway Gardens was executed by the Temple firm (letter from Alfonso Iannelli to Grant Manson, May 13, 1957); however, this recollection is in opposition to that of Frank L. Linden, Jr. (see p. 209).

THE VAN DORN IRON WORKS COMPANY
Cleveland, Ohio
Organized in 1872

James H. Van Dorn was born and raised on his father's farm in Columbia Station, Ohio. At the age of seventeen, he took a job in an agricultural implement factory and became a specialist in forging plowshares. He moved to Akron, Ohio, married, and built his own house, including an iron fence that surrounded the property. According to family tradition, the new fence was so admired by the neighbors that many of them wanted Van Dorn to make a similar one for them, thus leading to the establishment of his business in 1872. He soon bought the Spring Shoe Forge in Akron to increase his production, and this was the beginning of a pattern of growth that was to lead to one of the larger manufacturing firms in Ohio. In 1878 he moved the business to Cleveland in order to be nearer his supply of raw materials, and the name of the firm became the Cleveland Wrought Iron Fence Works. The main product of the firm continued to be ornamental iron fences, which were sold to large houses, cemeteries, and public buildings. In this same year, Van Dorn went to Milwaukee to bid on an iron cemetery fence; when he heard of the need for a jail, he decided to bid on the job since jails were "fences built indoors." His bid was accepted and he returned to Cleveland with a contract that launched a very successful jail business for the firm. Van Dorn was soon recognized as the largest jail manufacturer in the world.

In 1884 the name of the firm was changed to The Van Dorn Iron Works Company, and all types of ornamental ironwork were added to the line of production, including hardware for stables, hitching posts, iron benches, and weather vanes. In 1891 the firm was incorporated, and in 1892 it began to manufacture small fabricated parts for streetcars. From this experience, the firm soon began to manufacture switchboards and other special parts for the Short Electric Company. In 1895 the company began to supply fabricated steel cases and map drawers of special design for the engineers' office at the Cleveland City Hall. This was to be the Van Dorn Company's first introduction to the metal office furniture business, which made it able to manufacture Wright's custom designs for the Larkin Administration Building furniture. A catalogue titled *Metallic Vault and Office Furniture and Fixtures Manufactured by The Van Dorn Iron Works Company Cleveland Ohio*, published around 1900, is in the collection of the Chicago Historical Society. The firm claimed that it would "manufacture anything in the line of metallic vault and office furniture" and that the advantages of metal furniture were that "the danger from fire, vermin, etc., is lessened, and records, papers and books, which are invaluable, are kept intact at such times where wood furniture would be entirely destroyed." Van Dorn later advertised its metal furniture in *The Architectural Record;* for example, in the July–December 1909 issue, Van Dorn advertised and illustrated á steel and bronze president's chair made for the directors' room of the Pacific Mutual Life Insurance Company in Los Angeles. The company advertised metal furniture for banks, courthouses, libraries, etc., in the January–June 1910 issue. In both advertisements, a metallic furniture department was mentioned.

In 1897 Van Dorn's son T. B. Van Dorn joined the firm. His experience working for two years with the Berlin Bridge Company in Berlin, Connecticut, introduced the Van Dorn Iron Works to the structural steel business. In 1916 the firm began producing six-ton Renault-type tanks for the U.S. Army, and in 1919 the firm entered into the manufacture of special railroad equipment. The Van Dorn firm continued to diversify its manufacturing by purchasing smaller companies with other specialties. The firm continues in business today.

WILLIAM H. WESTON (1878–1968)
Spring Green, Wisconsin

William H. Weston was born near Hillpoint, Wisconsin. Because his mother died when he was quite young, he was raised by foster parents at Richland Center, Wisconsin. After completing the eighth grade there, he began work on a nearby farm; soon thereafter he married Anna Claridge and established his own farm. In 1903 he moved to Spring Green to work for Reely Brothers, a construction firm, where he learned the skills of carpentry. In the summer of 1903 Weston worked a few weeks building the Hillside Home School. Since the construction work was not full-time, Weston had learned many other skills that made him particularly useful when he came to work at Taliesin. Weston's quick mind, natural ability, and great interest in his work brought him to Wright's attention, and the two became close friends. Wright wrote about Weston's heroic efforts in his description of the disastrous fire at Taliesin in 1914:

> He had come to grips with the madman whose strength was superhuman; slipped from his grasps and his blows. Bleeding from the encounter he ran down the hill to the nearest neighbor to give the alarm, made his way back immediately through the cornfields only to find the deadly work finished and the home ablaze. Hardly able to stand, he ran to where the firehose was kept in a niche of the garden wall, past his young son, lying there in the fountain basin, one of the seven dead, got the hose loose, staggered with it to the fire and with the playing hose stood against destruction, himself, until they led him away. (*An Autobiography*, p. 189)

Weston was at Taliesin when it was first built and each time it was rebuilt. By 1913 Weston was put in charge of the construction, maintenance, and farming of Taliesin, and between 1917 and 1919 he lived there with his family, and his wife ran the kitchen. In 1927 he built his own house in Spring Green, adapted from one of the series of houses Wright designed for the American System Ready-Cut houses. He went to Chandler, Arizona, in 1929 when Ocatillo, Wright's temporary residence, was built in 1928. Although he left Taliesin in 1934, he returned in 1938 and worked off and on at Taliesin in the late 1930s and 1940s.

Before the beginning of the Fellowship in 1932, Weston was responsible for making most of the furniture at Taliesin or supervising the local carpenters in its construction. After 1932 the apprentices made furniture for their own rooms and were encouraged to do the work themselves. With the exception of the upholstered pieces, the furniture was made on the site. (Letters from Marcus Weston to the author, July 11, and August 9, 1977.)

WINSLOW BROS. COMPANY (1887–1921)
William Herman Winslow (born 1857)
Chicago, Illinois

"W. H. Winslow of the Winslow Ornamental Iron Works had often been to Adler and Sullivan's office to consult with me about the work of that office. He now appeared to give me my first job" (*An Autobiography*, p. 123).

According to research by Leonard K. Eaton (*The Prairie School Review*, vol. 1, no. 3, third quarter 1964), William Herman Winslow was born of Danish immigrant parents in Brooklyn, New York. He was educated in the public schools in Brooklyn and Chicago. Although he apparently did not go to college, he did study law in New York. In 1881 he joined the Hecla Iron Works of New York as office man and was taken in as a partner in 1883 at the age of twenty-six. According to research by

Margot Gayle, the Hecla firm received the commission to supply the iron for the Rookery Building in Chicago, designed by Burnham and Root in 1886. In 1885 Winslow moved to Chicago and joined E. T. Harris to form the firm of Harris and Winslow, manufacturers of ornamental iron and bronze. After Harris retired, Winslow became associated with his brother Francis in a new concern, Winslow Bros. Company, which was first listed in the Lakeside Chicago Directory in 1887, at 99–109 West Monroe Street, with William as president and Francis as secretary and treasurer. The firm grew and eventually had offices in New York (160 Fifth Avenue), Baltimore, Pittsburgh, New Orleans, Minneapolis, Kansas City, Los Angeles, and San Francisco.

It was undoubtedly through the Winslow Brothers' work on The Auditorium Hotel and Theater commission that Wright was introduced to William Winslow, who became his friend and first independent client. William Winslow was an inventor and was fascinated by mechanical things. He and his brother developed bronze and iron casting processes and also invented the Winslow window, a pioneering variety of movable sash. Winslow Bros. made bronzework and ironwork for architects all over the country and took a deep pride in the high quality of its work. The firm produced such objects as elevator grilles and stair railings for public buildings, including Adler and Sullivan's Carson, Pirie, Scott department store.

The Winslow's work as well as their factory at Carroll Avenue and Fulton and Ada streets was illustrated in a lavish publication *Photographs and Sketches of Ornamental Iron and Bronze Executed by The Winslow Bros. Company* (Chicago, 1901) (no ironwork designed by Frank Lloyd Wright was included). Their work was also illustrated in the publication *Ornamental Iron* (Chicago: The Winslow Bros. Co., August 1893–May 1895). It is not known what of Wright's ironwork was actually made at the Winslow firm, though one assumes that the Wright-designed ironwork made for the Winslow House (fig. 16) was made by the firm. The 1902 Chicago Architectural Club exhibition included an electrolier designed by Wright for the Winslow House that was made by Winslow Bros.

The Winslow firm was represented at numerous international exhibitions. They were awarded eight medals at the World's Columbian Exposition in Chicago in 1893. They won the Grand Prix, two gold medals, and three honorable mentions at the Exposition Universelle in Paris in 1900. A capital they made for the Paris exhibition was illustrated in the October 1900 *Brush and Pencil*.

INDEX

Page numbers in **boldface** indicate illustrations

PHOTOGRAPHIC CREDITS

This list gratefully acknowledges the many photographers and institutions who provided photographs for this book.

Albright-Knox Art Gallery, Buffalo, New York, figs. 90, 92, 93

Art Institute of Chicago, The, figs. 3, 4, 10, 12, 14, 17, 18, 20, 26, 27, 38, 46, 48, 51, 52, 53, 59, 63, 101, 103, 104, 120, 122, 123, 125, 126a, 155, 162, 163, 168, 169, 179, 208, 214, 216

Avery Architectural Library, Columbia University, New York, figs. 25, 70

Morley Baer; Wright Collection, Spencer Library, University of Kansas, Lawrence, figs. 172, 173

Esther Born, fig. 174

Buffalo and Erie County Historical Society, Buffalo, New York, figs. 77, 79, 80, 84

Byron; The Byron Collection, Museum of the City of New York, fig. 45

Chicago Historical Society, figs. 1, 192, 193, 194, 213, 215

Cooper–Hewitt Museum, New York, figs. 141, 142

Martin Curry and Michael Fischer, pls. 1, 16

Department of Municipal Arts, City of Los Angeles, fig. 147

Mrs. Waldron Faulkner, Washington, D.C., fig. 112

Greenville College, Greenville, Illinois, The Richard W. Bock Sculpture Collection, figs. 86, 87

Grey Art Gallery and Study Center, New York University, pl. 8

P. E. Guerrero; Wright Collection, Spencer Library, University of Kansas, Lawrence, fig. 184

Paul Hanna, fig. 175

Wilbert Hasbrouck, fig. 191

Mrs. James E. Haverstock, fig. 115

Hedrich-Blessing; Wright Collection, Spencer Library, University of Kansas, Lawrence, fig. 161

Thomas A. Heinz, pls. 2, 3, 4, 5, 9; figs. 40, 50

Henry-Russell Hitchcock, New York, fig. 74

House Beautiful magazine, Wright Collection, Spencer Library, University of Kansas, Lawrence, figs. 201, 202, 203, 204

S. C. Johnson and Son, Inc., Racine, Wisconsin, figs. 9, 164, 165

Johnson Foundation, Racine, Wisconsin, figs. 170, 171

Donald G. Kalec, Chicago, pls. 15, 16, 17, 19, 20, 21, 22, 23; front matter A; figs. 11, 13, 15, 19, 21, 24, 32, 33, 37, 41, 54, 58, 66, 85, 110, 126c, 197a, 197b

Robert C. Lautman, fig. 185

Library of Congress, The, Washington, D.C., figs. 39, 61, 64, 88, 89, 91, 196

Los Angeles County Museum of Art, fig. 148

Metropolitan Museum of Art, The, New York, figs. 75, 76, 114, 116, 117

Museum of Modern Art, The, New York, figs. 7, 16, 29, 30, 35, 36, 78, 81, 83, 102, 111, 127, 128, 144, 156, 159, 187, 198, 199

National Collection of Fine Arts, Smithsonian Institution, Washington, D.C., pls. 10, 11, 12, 14; figs. 42, 43, 44, 65, 94, 95, 96, 105, 186, 195, 209, 210, 211, 212

National Trust for Historic Preservation, figs. 176, 177, 178

Virginia Robie O'Connor, fig. 109

Maynard L. Parker; Wright Collection, Spencer Library, University of Kansas, Lawrence, pls. 7, 18; figs. 67, 68, 69, 71, 97, 99, 181, 182, 183, 189

David Phillips; Chicago Architectural Photo Company, figs. 28, 60, 98, 100, 106, 107, 118, 119, 121, 124, 135, 136, 140, 158

Prairie Archives, Milwaukee Art Center, Wisconsin, figs. 108, 130, 131, 132, 133, 134, 217, 218, 219

Prairie School Review, fig. 82

H. C. Price Company, Bartlesville, Oklahoma, figs. 188, 190

Marvin, Rand, Los Angeles, fig. 152

Steelcase Inc., figs. 166, 167

Ezra Stoller; Wright Collection, Spencer Library, University of Kansas, Lawrence, figs. 8, 145, 146, 149, 150, 151, 153, 154, 180

Irma Strauss, figs. 2, 5, 6, 22, 23, 31, 47, 49, 62, 129, 200

University Archives, State University of New York at Buffalo, figs. 34, 137, 138

Wright Collection, Spencer Library, University of Kansas, Lawrence, pl. 24; fig. 139

Frank Lloyd Wright Memorial Foundation, The, Taliesin West, Scottsdale, Arizona, pl. 13; front matter B; figs. 55, 56, 57, 72, 73, 113, 126b, 143, 157, 160, 205, 206, 207